Study Guide

for use with

Prepared by PREM LOBO, CA, CBV, CPA

THOMSON
NELSON

Australia Canada Mexico Singapore Spain United Kingdom United States

THOMSON
NELSON

Study Guide for use with Financial Accounting: An Integrated Approach, Sixth Edition

Prepared by Prem Lobo

Associate Vice President, Editorial Director:
Evelyn Veitch

Executive Editor:
Rod Banister

Senior Marketing Manager:
Charmaine Sherlock

Developmental Editor:
Natalie Barrington

Senior Content Production Manager:
Julie van Veen

Proofreader:
Laurel Sparrow

Production Manager:
Cathy Deak

Design Director:
Ken Phipps

Cover Design:
Maria Castelli

Printer:
Webcom

Printed and bound in Canada
1 2 3 4 09 08 07 06

For more information contact Nelson, 1120 Birchmount Road, Toronto, Ontario, M1K 5G4. Or you can visit our Internet site at http://www.nelson.com

Library and Archives Canada Cataloguing in Publication Data

Lobo, Prem, 1978–
Study guide for use with Financial accounting : an integrated approach, sixth edition / prepared by Prem Lobo.

ISBN-13: 978-0-17-610411-5
ISBN-10: 0-17-610411-9

1. Accounting—Problems, exercises, etc. 2. Financial statements-Problems, exercises, etc.
I. Gibbins, Michael, 1942– . Financial accounting. II. Title.

HF5635.G5 2006 Suppl. 1
657'.044 C2006-902744-7

TABLE OF CONTENTS

Preface ... iv
Chapter 1: Introduction: Linking Financial Accounting's Production and Uses ... 1
Chapter 2: Measuring and Evaluating Financial Position ... 13
Chapter 3: Measuring and Evaluating Financial Performance ... 30
Chapter 4: Measuring and Evaluating Cash Flow ... 64
Chapter 5: Standards and Principles Surrounding the Financial Statements ... 97
Chapter 6: Revenue and Expense Recognition ... 116
Chapter 7: Recordkeeping and Control ... 139
Chapter 8: Assets Accounting ... 155
Chapter 9: Liabilities, Equity, and Corporate Groups ... 177
Chapter 10: Financial Accounting Analysis Wrap-Up ... 199

PREFACE

This study guide is intended to accompany *Financial Accounting: An Integrated Approach,* Sixth Edition, by Michael Gibbins, PhD, FCA. It should not be seen as a replacement for the text but rather as an accompaniment. The purpose of this guide is to help you develop your intuition about financial accounting in the manner in which the textbook does. This is not an overnight process. It requires that you begin to understand the difference between accounting and bookkeeping, the nature of users and uses of financial accounting data, and the evolving nature of accounting.

You will find the study guide set up in a complementary way to the textbook showing the objectives of each chapter, a bullet-form summary of key points to which to refer, and a series of questions. The questions have been organized into exercises, problems, integrative problems, and explorative questions. These become progressively more difficult and are not all mechanical in nature. Solutions to all the questions are found at the end of each chapter of this guide.

CHAPTER 1
INTRODUCTION: LINKING FINANCIAL ACCOUNTING'S PRODUCTION AND USES

LEARNING OBJECTIVES

After completing Chapter 1, you should:

- understand what financial accounting is;
- understand what accrual accounting is; and
- understand the users, preparers, and other stakeholders of financial accounting.

CHAPTER SUMMARY

1.1 Book Overview: Financial Accounting's Illumination of the World

1.2 Chapter Introduction: Linking Financial Accounting's Production and Uses

- Accounting is not just number crunching; you need to know what numbers to use and for what purpose.
- Accounting involves making decisions that are based on understanding the potential users of accounting information, concepts, constraints, facts, and techniques involved.

1.3 Financial Accounting

- Financial accounting, the subject of this text, measures the performance and status of an enterprise largely for the use of people external to the enterprise.
- Managerial accounting, on the other hand, helps managers and others within an enterprise better understand and manage the operations of the enterprise.
- Financial statements are the output of financial accounting.

1.4 The Social Setting of Financial Accounting

- As you can appreciate, there are a number of parties who have either a direct or an indirect interest in an enterprise's financial accounting.
- In addition to owners, there are managers, auditors, creditors, governments, competitors, and, if the company is publicly traded, stock market regulators, just to name a few.
- To the enterprise, the significance of this is that, while the enterprise itself is busy initiating and responding to financial events, the enterprise and its financial accounting might also affect the decisions and actions of the broader environment that contains all such interested parties.

1.5 The People Involved in Financial Accounting

- There are three main groups of persons involved in financial accounting—users (decision makers), preparers (decision facilitators), and auditors (credibility enhancers).
- A user makes decisions on the basis of financial statements, using the periodic, credible information provided by a company's accountants. There are many types of users of the information (see pages 16–18 of your text).
- A preparer is responsible for the information contained in the financial statements.

- An auditor stands between the users and the preparers, verifying whether financial information presented is fairly stated, credible, and consistent in all material respects. An auditor is "external" and "independent."

1.6 An Example: Grades

- The "Grades" example in your text provides a discussion of the many factors that need to be considered in measuring performance, whether it be performance in an educational setting or performance in a business.
- Effectively, grades summarize your performance but are not the only measure, or objective, of your education.
- Similarly, the financial performance of a company is only one measure of a company's achievements.

1.7 Financial Accounting's Transactional Filter

1.8 Demonstration Problem: Transactions

- Accounting can be thought of as a filter through which information flows. Observations are selected, collected, and summarized.
- Once data have been collected and summarized, they can be organized to produce usable financial statements and other types of reports. The question is, though, which data should be treated as a transaction and captured by an accounting system, and which data do not constitute a transaction and, hence, should not be recorded?
- To qualify as a transaction, an event (or data) must:
    - involve exchange of something of economic value;
    - be with a party external to the business;
    - produce some evidence of the event; and
    - be measurable in dollars.
- These criteria are important since they:
    - represent the legal basis of contract completion;
    - support the notion of only recording what has happened (historical accounting); and
    - provide the basis for verifiable records during the auditing, which comes later in the process.
- "Adjustments" may also be necessary to adjust the data that have been recorded, or introduce new data, to reflect accounting events that are not handled by routine transactions.
- These other data are important to the measurement of the performance of the entity and are required by accrual accounting (more on this below and in Chapters 3 and 6).
- Section 1.8 of the chapter provides a demonstration problem that requires the use of the transaction criteria identified above.

1.9 Accrual Accounting

- Producing financial statements is a complex task. The many transactions an organization or business encounters can be overwhelming.
- In trying to separate the complex transactions from those that are more simple and routinely dealt with, the concept of accrual accounting has been developed.

- In preparing the financial statements, accrual accounting attempts to:
  - include all the cash receipts and payments;
  - incorporate future cash receipts and payments that should be expected based on present transactions;
  - measure the value of incomplete transactions; and
  - estimate figures when exact amounts are unknown.
- This means that estimates, judgments, and adjustments must be made to make statement interpretation meaningful and to reflect a fair representation of an enterprise's performance and financial position.

1.10 An Accrual Accounting Example: Simone's Jewellery Business

- The chapter provides a detailed example of how accrual accounting works for Simone's Jewellery Business.
- One of the points the example illustrates is that accrual accounting is a more complete measure of business performance than cash accounting.

1.11 Demonstration Problem: Accrual Accounting

- The chapter also provides a simple demonstration problem that illustrates the difference between cash income and accrual income.

1.12 Introductory Examples of Accounting Analysis: Reconciliation and Change Effects

- Reconciliation is the process of explaining differences in two or more separate values.
- These differences arise due to the timing of recording an economic event or due to the availability (or lack thereof) of pertinent information at such a time.
- For example, if you have a chequing account and fail to record each cheque you write and some deposits you make, the bank balance according to your calculations and that according to the bank will be quite different.
- While detailed discussion of change effects analysis is reserved for Chapter 10, this section will serve as an introduction to financial analyses.
- Change effects focuses on changing elements of a company's financial figures in order to understand what "may have been" under different circumstances.
- A simple way to begin this is to focus on the change. If a company were curious how an advertising expense increase of $50,000 would have affected its bottom line, ignoring the effects of any increased revenue brought in from the advertising, a simple way to determine this is:

$$\$50{,}000 \times (1 - \text{Tax rate}) = \text{Effect on net income}$$

- This is known as "net-of-tax" analysis.

EXERCISES

E1. Performance Evaluation Using the comparison of grades and financial accounting, comment briefly on the importance of the concept of performance evaluation.

E2. Bookkeeping vs. Accounting "Accounting is the pulse of a company," your friend Jane says one evening at the local coffee shop. "Nonsense," replies another friend, Steve, "accounting is nothing more than keeping the books." What do you say to your friends?

E3. Financial Statement Uses At a recent business luncheon, a colleague, George, remarks: don't know why financial statements need to be so long. What a waste of paper! All I need to know is the size of my dividend cheque." What is your response to George?

E4. Auditing Another colleague, Mary, seemed to like your answer to George's question and said, "I can certainly see what you mean, but I have always had a question about this auditing business. What purpose does it serve when all we seem to hear about on TV these days is business failure?" Provide an answer for Mary.

E5. Accrual Accounting You have been hired to work for a friend of your father for this summer. The friend has a small business and tells you, "It costs too much to put the accounting system on the accrual basis. Why should I bother?" Realizing that this is a friend of your father, you tactfully respond to his question. What do you say?

E6. Reconciliation As a small business owner, you want to keep careful record of your cash. The last month, however, has been extraordinarily busy and you have not been as diligent in your recordkeeping as you should have been. You received your April bank statement yesterday and it revealed you had a balance of $4,763. Upon glancing at your balance according to your accounting software, you realized that the bank showed $183 less than your records showed. You thought that you should perhaps confirm some numbers. The bank balance showed the following:

April 23	Withdrawal	$200
April 26	Debit adjustment	44
April 30	Flat fee	5
April 30	Monthly fee	15
April 30	Withdrawal	200

You called the bank to learn that the two withdrawals were in error and that these would be corrected immediately; in paying your personal credit card bill from your personal account, the bank had deducted the payments from your company account. The debit adjustment was the bank's charge for some new company cheques you had ordered.

You pulled some receipts off your fridge door at home and noticed the following that you hadn't yet recorded:

April 19	Purchase by cheque	$219
April 29	Bank machine deposit	500

Reconcile the difference in amounts.

E7. Users Identify several parties who may be interested in the financial statements of a company and indicate why they may be interested.

E8. Users Financial statements are intended for a variety of users. What implicit assumption is made about these users?

E9. Change Effect Rimby Leathers recently completed its year with a record profit of $400,000 on sales of $1,200,000. The company's owner, still not content, complained about the 35% tax rate and also wondered how much better performance would have been had he not reluctantly hired his nephew at a salary of $25,000 per year and instead had hired someone more qualified at $40,000 per year.

E10. Transaction Measurement Your company hired a contractor to remove and replace a section of the parking lot surrounding the company's retail building. The contractor received a payment before he began work and was to receive the balance upon completion. After several months, the job was still incomplete. Did an accounting transaction take place?

E11. Transaction Measurement An employee of a company slips and falls on ice on company property and sues the company. If the company loses, it will have to pay $10,000 in damages. Has a transaction taken place? Would a transaction have taken place had it been a customer?

PROBLEMS

P1. Accrual vs. Cash Basis After a tough campaign, you have won the election to be the treasurer of the local Goof and Spoof Club. Upon arriving at the club office, you find that the club's records are in a mess. You can see that the last treasurer kept the books on the cash basis. You realize that the income and cash positions of the club are quite different. Given the following information, what will you tell the membership?

Cash in bank at January 1 (beginning)	$4,150
Owing to club from sale of sweatshirts	4,000
Owing to Harry's Silkscreening for sweatshirts	2,050
Paid to Harry's Silkscreening during year for sweatshirts	2,000
Paid to Campus Copy for photocopying	300

P2. Reconciliation "My accountant must have made a mistake," your friend Margaret groans. "Can you tell me why my cash in the business account does not look even vaguely like the amount the accountant told me I would have to pay income taxes on?" Your friend, Margaret, is an artist who designs and produces stained glass decorations that her customers hang up in windows. You ask to see her records and this is what you find:

Collections in cash from customers	$56,000
Still owing from credit customers	5,000
Paid to suppliers but supplies still on hand	2,000
Owed to suppliers at end of year for supplies already used	1,000
Cost of supplies used during the year	24,000
Amortization on equipment	3,000
Withdrawals for living expenses	12,000

Calculate the cash Margaret should have in the business chequing account and the amount of income that her accountant has calculated. Explain to Margaret the difference between the two numbers.

P3. Reconciliation It's December 31, 2004, at All-Hemp Clothing Ltd. and the following is available:

Cash in the bank, Jan. 1, 2004	$52,000
Collected from customers in 2004	141,210
Paid to suppliers in 2004 for 2004 expenses	48,500
Owing to suppliers at Dec. 31, 2004	5,260
Salaries paid in 2004 for 2004	67,840
Salaries owing at Dec. 31, 2004	6,450
Owed by customers at Dec. 31, 2003 (collected in 2004)	17,590
Owed by customers at Dec. 31, 2004	21,430
Amortization of store equipment	2,760

(a) Calculate the company's accrual and cash income for 2004.

(b) Reconcile its cash and accrual income for 2004.

(c) Determine the company's 2004 year-end cash balance.

INTEGRATIVE PROBLEM

IP1. Bookkeeping vs. Accounting Most people who know little about accounting think that it is a cut-and-dried profession; it's a profession of numbers and is therefore black and white. Yet this is far from being the case. How so?

EXPLORATIVE QUESTIONS

EQ1. Accrual Accounting and Financial Statements The union negotiator was looking over the company's financial statements while preparing himself for labour negotiations the next morning. "I can't believe this company," he thought to himself. "It had unprecedented sales last year, its raw materials costs were way down, it has purchased plush new offices for the bosses, it's never owned more land, buildings, or vehicles, yet it can't give us an extra $2.50 per hour." Does the union negotiator have ground to stand on in the negotiations?

EQ2. Transaction Measurement Is it reasonable to say that all of a company's decisions have a transactional consequence?

SOLUTIONS

EXERCISES

El. A manager needs to know how a performance evaluation will be used to assess performance. When looking at the example involving grades and financial accounting, there are many dimensions to the performance evaluation. You need to know:

- what is being measured/not measured;
- that the evaluation is a summary of events and you must recognize that some of the events may be of greater importance by themselves relative to the final summary; and
- what the evaluation will be used for.

The perceptions of both the evaluator and the person being evaluated need to be understood as well as the motives of both parties. Again, we need to repeat that we are looking for fairness, consistency, and comparability in all of these evaluations. An evaluation will be less credible if these factors are missing. Lastly we need to take into account the possibility of "cheating" or "short-sighted" behaviour that has been seen in some managers. Depending on the evaluation of performance, we may find that a manager can be encouraged to think about what is best for the company in the long run rather than just considering the short run.

E2. "This is a rather typical disagreement," you respond. "Bookkeeping is a part of accounting. The problem in accounting is in trying to decide which numbers are the appropriate ones to use. That is, what is the story that the business wants to tell the users of its financial statements?"

E3. There is no right or wrong response here. You may answer his comment in a number of different ways. The question is designed to have you consider the ways in which financial statements may be presented. After considering these areas, you might include some of the following points:

- George may be interested in only his dividend cheque, but there are many other users of the financial statements;
- The owners of the company, including George, might like to see the details of how the business operates;
- People who are not already owners will want to know if the stock is a good risk;
- Creditors will not lend money unless they are sure that they will get it back;
- Managers use the data for many different reasons, including performance evaluation and bonus decisions;
- The employees of the company want to know if a raise will be possible. Labour unions use the information in contract negotiations;
- Governmental and regulatory authorities, such as taxation, use the statements to find out if the company is following the rules;
- The business's competition wants to know how well the business is doing;
- Market and financial analysts help people decide whether or not to invest;
- Accounting researchers try to understand accounting to help improve it.

E4. The colleague's question is a fairly common one for people (including accounting students) to ask. Remember that the function of an auditor is to see if the statements have been prepared fairly and are consistent with accepted accounting principles. This means that the auditor should be objective and not be influenced by management. The auditor has no vested interest in the results of the audit, good or bad. Even when the auditors do their job properly, it is still possible for a business to fail since that is not part of what the auditor is reporting on.

E5. Accrual accounting helps your business by letting you know how things stand. That is, if there are incomplete transactions, or if there are economic events that are not really represented by a transaction per se (such as amortization), accrual accounting will allow you to account for the value of these so that you can determine what kind of an impact they have on your business.

E6.

Bank balance:	$4,763
Add:	
Withdrawals in error (bank correction)	400
Debit adjustment (recorded by bank, not by you)	44
Flat fee (recorded by bank, not by you)	5
Monthly fee (recorded by bank, not by you)	15
Purchase by cheque (recorded by bank, not by you)	219
Deduct:	
Bank machine deposit cheque (recorded by bank, not by you)	(500)
Your balance	$4,946

E7.

- Managers: Managers act on behalf of the owners, and financial statements often serve as a measure of management's ability to execute its responsibilities successfully.
- Canada Revenue Agency: Taxation authorities are concerned with how income is measured. They are also concerned with asset valuation in the event of capital gains and losses.
- Stock market regulators: Exchanges and securities commissions keep a close watch on publicly traded companies to make sure that their statements and practices provide adequate disclosure for fair trading to be possible.
- Creditors: Lenders are often concerned with the security of their loans and will pay attention to income performance as well as asset and liability growth and cash flow.
- Competitors: In the case of publicly traded companies, competitors can analyze the financial health of their competition. However, this function of statements is limited since statements are only released annually.
- Other users include owners, business analysts, unions, customers, etc.

E8. The assumption is that users of a company's information have a reasonable understand of business and economic activities. The onus, then, is on the reader of the statement to be generally aware of a company's operations, the industry within which it operates, and general economic conditions. This assumption allows preparers to present audited, material information without the worry of being guilty of negligence or fraudulent misrepresentation.

E9.

Salary savings:	$25,000
Alternative salary:	$40,000
Incremental difference:	$15,000
Multiply by tax rate:	1 – 0.35
Effect on profit:	$9,750 less profit

E10. There are four components to an accounting transaction: exchange, externality, evidence, and dollars. In this event, if no contract was signed, there was no evidence. However, since an up-front payment was made, there should have been some receipt or evidence that money was exchanged. So there is, indeed, exchange (cash without a receipt or contract, no evidence). There should have been a signed contract giving rise to an expense and a cash disbursement, and an account payable (for the balance of the contracted price due upon completion). With no contract, only the amount of the cash disbursement is recognized as an expense, not the full price of the job.

If, in fact, no receipt was received at all and cash was paid, there would be no evidence of an accounting transaction.

E11. No transaction is recorded in either the case of an employee or a customer, since the lawsuit has not yet been decided. A prudent company would, however, make a note to accompany its balance sheet to make users aware that there is a potential liability for the amount of the lawsuit (known as a contingent liability).

PROBLEMS

P1. The ending cash balance is $1,850 and, using accrual accounting, the club has income. Without any other information, the club would have reported a cash basis loss since no cash was apparently received, yet cash was spent. For the members of the Spoof Club, this information may be worthwhile if, for example, the club is being evaluated for a grant. It would be better for them to reflect the whole story such as accrual accounting does.

P2. Margaret is in the uncomfortable spot of not understanding the difference between cash and accrual income. In order to assist her, you calculate the cash in her business banking account as follows:

Cash collections		$ 56,000
Cash payments from account		
Supplies	$(24,000)	
Withdrawals	(12,000)	(36,000)
Cash in bank		$ 20,000

The net income for her business is calculated as follows:

Cash collections	$ 56,000
Owing from customers	5,000
Supplies on hand	2,000
Owed to suppliers	(1,000)
Paid for used supplies	(24,000)
Amortization	(3,000)
Net income	$ 35,000

The problem is that she is working with accrual accounting in the calculation of her net income while she is looking at the cash in her bank account. Accrual accounting attempts to make the appropriate adjustments for her business. For example, she has taken $12,000 from her business. Her business earned that $12,000 as a result of the work she did. It is, therefore, part of the business's earnings, even though she has already spent it. What she is trying to do is come up with a reasonable figure to measure the performance of her business and she is using cash, not income, to do this. While this is one measure of performance, it is not the sole measure.

P3. (a)

Cash Income:	
Cash collected from customers	$141,210
Cash paid for supplies	(48,500)
Cash paid for salaries	(67,840)
Cash income	$ 24,870
Accrual Income:	
Revenues ($141,210 – $17,590 + $21,430)	$145,050
Expenses:	
Supplies ($48,500 + $5,260)	$ 53,760
Salaries ($67,840 + $6,450)	74,290
Amortization	2,760
Accrual Income	$130,810
	$ 14,240

(b) Reconciliation

Cash Income (from above)	$ 24,870
Non-cash items:	
Owing from customers, net ($21,430 – $17,590)	$ 3,840
Owing to suppliers	(5,260)
Owing to employees	(6,450)
Amortization	(2,760)
Total non-cash items	$(10,630)
Accrual income	$ 14,240

(c) Cash in the bank:

Cash in the bank, Jan. 1, 2004		$ 52,000
Collected from customers in 2004		141,210
Payments to suppliers	$48,500	
Payments to employees for salary	67,840	(116,300)
Cash in the bank, Dec. 31, 2004		$ 76,910

INTEGRATIVE PROBLEM

IP1. Most people feel that numbers tell the whole story and that accounting means adding and subtracting numbers to get to a bottom line. For example, if $100 cash was taken in and $65 was paid to make the products you sold, then you must have made $35. This is necessarily so. Accrual accounting is practised. This means that estimates are made if exact figures are not known, and that incomplete transactions are still noted. In other words, accounting is more than just keeping track of how much cash comes into and goes out of the company; that would be the cash basis of accounting. Cash basis accounting, however, is not accepted practice because there are a variety of economically important things that would be missed, such as a substantial lawsuit that you might lose. Accrual accounting would record—or at least make note of (called note disclosure)—such an event that has not yet happened.

EXPLORATIVE QUESTIONS

EQ1. The question is debatable; it depends on what those statements have to say. First off, just because a company has unprecedented sales does not mean that it has cash available. Accounting permits us to record revenues even if cash is not collected, so the company may not have a whole lot of cash to put toward wage demands. Second, while what the company owns may be at an all-time high, how were those things purchased? Was debt or cash used to finance purchases? If debt was used, it is probably because the company is trying to preserve the cash it has to meet its bills. If cash was used, then there is probably little excess lying around beyond that needed to meet operating needs. Third, while the raw materials costs may be down, it does not mean that the company does not have other expenses that it must consider. For example, the assets that it has are depreciating; this does not involve cash but is an expense nonetheless and reduces the company's income. The negotiator should concern himself with income of the company, not sales. Fourth, can the negotiator rely on those statements? He should be concerned as to their fairness and whether they have been competently prepared in accordance with accepted accounting principles; that is, they should have been audited.

What the negotiator must recognize is that there is often more to statements than the bottom line. Wages must be paid in cash. Therefore, the company will look at its cash flow in deciding whether or not it can meet a wage demand. It does not matter how successful a company may be or how much it owns in assets. The fact of the matter is that it must pay its bills in cash. Some bills may be postponed for one, two, or three months (known as trade credit), but others, such as wages, are due in fairly short order after employees have performed work for the company. Imagine being paid in three months for work you did today. Employees cannot live by these terms since they typically have only one source of cash, their jobs. But companies have many sources of cash (different customers paying at different points in time). So the company will try to ensure foremost that there is adequate cash to meet payroll.

EQ2. No, but generally speaking, a company's decisions are likely to have a direct or an indirect financial consequence. Clearly, all financial decisions such as purchases, sales, payments, expenses, etc., have a direct transactional consequence. But there are numerous other strategic decisions that do not have a direct impact on the books. Marketing, strategic policy, human resource management, or operations decisions are such examples. A marketing decision to enter a new market, in itself, is not an accounting event giving rise to a transaction. However, the sub-decisions thus arising—such as paying for market survey data or promotional brochures—obviously cause transactions to be recorded. So, while a decision itself may not cause a transaction, its execution may ultimately do so.

On the other hand, many decisions are never obviously reflected in a company's books. A policy decision to avoid doing business in a particular country will never give rise to any kind of transaction. However, you can argue that such a decision would affect a company's bottom line. This is an evaluation of the company's position/performance but the books have not been affected, per se.

CHAPTER 2
MEASURING AND EVALUATING FINANCIAL POSITION

LEARNING OBJECTIVES

After completing Chapter 2, you should:

- have a better understanding of double-entry accounting;
- understand the basics of balance sheet preparation; and
- comprehend basic balance sheet interpretation.

CHAPTER SUMMARY

2.1 Chapter Introduction: Measuring and Evaluating Financial Position

- The chapter examines one of the four types of financial statement reports: the balance sheet. The others—the income statement, the statement of retained earnings, and the cash flow statement—are the subject of later chapters.
- The balance sheet provides summary information about everything that financial accounting has recorded about a company—such as what it owns (resources), what it owes (obligations), and what's left over for the owners (owners' interests) at a point in time.
- The balance sheet is a cumulative record of an entity's financial activities. This is a static picture and we see the change from year to year when we compare the balance sheets.

2.2 A Brief History of Early Accounting

- Developments in business and society over time produced a demand for information that has resulted in the development of financial accounting methods. Accounting did not spring forth fully formed at the beginning of the commercial world.
- Mesopotamia to Rome: 4500 B.C. to 400 A.D.—With flourishing civilizations and commerce, administrative recordkeeping was needed. The earliest administrative records were found in Mesopotamia. Throughout the centuries that followed, the medium may have changed but the objective has been much the same: that is, to keep records of what was owned or owed.
- The Dark Ages to the Renaissance: 400 A.D. to 1500 A.D.—This time period saw the fall of the Roman Empire and the rise of "merchant banks." More exacting recordkeeping became important and refinements were made. During this time, Friar Pacioli published his treatise on double-entry bookkeeping.
- The development of commercial activity contributed to the early development of double-entry accounting and the balance sheet. However, growing commercialism required more evaluative tools, resulting in the income statement as a stand-alone measure of performance.
- The twentieth century brought enormous pressures to bear on the accounting profession to set standards and respond to growing world trade and the introduction of income tax.
- The results of financial accounting are relied on today by business, social, and political interests alike.

2.3 Introduction to The Balance Sheet

- The balance sheet is part of a full set of financial statements of an organization. It is a snapshot of the organization at a point in time.
- The balance sheet is also known as the statement of financial position because it describes the financial status (resources and sources) of an organization at a particular point in time.
- It is called a balance sheet because the statement has two sides, one showing the resources of the organization and the other showing their sources. The two sides must be equal to each other.

Resources = Assets
Sources = Liabilities + Owners' equity
Resources = Sources

- The resources (or assets) are things that the company needs in order to conduct business (e.g., merchandise to sell, cash to pay bills, etc.); assets generate future cash flows.
- The sources (or liabilities and owners' equity) are how those assets have been financed. Liabilities are debts to creditors such as banks. Owners' equity is what the owners have contributed to the business or the earnings of the business that have accumulated. Earning income means that there will be more assets and/or fewer liabilities.
- From the balance sheet we can look for information to assist in our decision making, such as: the amount of risk involved due to financing; whether or not a dividend should be declared; whether we have sufficient cash to pay some of our debts; and so on.
- The balance sheet relies on the practice of "double-entry accounting" (discussed in Section 2.4), which requires that a financial transaction recorded by a company have at least a debit (which normally appears on the left-hand side of a balance sheet) and a matching credit (which normally appears on the right-hand side of the balance sheet). In this manner, debits always equal credits and the balance sheet will always balance.
- The dual nature of the balance sheet leads us to the equality of the balance sheet equation.

Assets = Liabilities + Owners' Equity
Debits = Credits

- Using the information from the How's Your Understanding box on page 74 of your text, we can assemble a balance sheet for Northern Inc..

Assets		Liabilities	
Current		*Current*	
Cash	$ 500	Owing to suppliers	$2,100
Due from customers	1,100		
Unsold products	1,700	Total liabilities	$2,100
Non-Current			
Equipment	2,000	Owners' Equity	
		Share capital	$1,000
		Retained earnings	2,200
		Total owners' equity	$3,200
Total assets	$5,300	Total liabilities and owners' equity	$5,300

- What does this balance sheet tell us about the company? The following are just a few ideas:
  - Northern owes $2,100 to suppliers. The problem is that Northern only has $500 in cash. Even if Northern collects the money that the customers owe, there will not be enough cash to pay off the debt.
  - The retained earnings are large enough to pay a dividend to the owners. Again, we have the problem of insufficient cash.
  - The company is financed 40% by creditors and 60% by the owners. Northern does not have huge debts in relation to the equity.
  - It seems that the inventory of unsold products may be on the high side. It amounts to about 32% of the total assets.

2.4 Recording Transactions: Double-Entry Bookkeeping

- Double-entry bookkeeping means that each transaction is recorded twice: once to record the resource involved, and once to recognize the source or effect of that resource change.
- Resources are said to be "debited" if they are increased and "credited" if they are decreased. Sources are credited if they are increased and debited if they are decreased.
- Each transaction shows what has happened to the resources of an entity *and* what the sources of those resources were. As an example, suppose a company bought a new factory building. That is an increase to the resources of the entity. How it was acquired (via a bank loan or mortgage or paid for with cash) is the source of the resource (the factory building).
- The dollar value of debits in a transaction must equal the dollar value of credits in order to maintain the equality of the balance sheet equation (Assets = Liabilities + Owners' equity).
- There may be many debits and many credits to various accounts in a transaction, but total debits must always equal total credits.

- One entity's debit will be another entity's credit. For example, if you deposit your paycheque into a savings account at a bank, you debit the cash account in your own records. The bank, however, credits its account for your cash. This is because your deposit is a liability to the bank; it owes you that money at any time.
- Transactions are recorded in a general journal, which is simply a convenient place to store all transactions.
- A journal entry, then, is the recording of a transaction showing which accounts have been affected by the transaction.

2.5 More About Accounts

- An account is an accounting record that classifies and accumulates the effects of financial transactions into particular assets, liabilities, equities, revenues, or expenses.
- A separate account is used for each asset, liability, equity, type of revenue, and type of expense.
- The difference between total debits and total credits to an account is the account balance.
- A general ledger is a "book" of all the various accounts showing the history of transactions to each account and its current account balance.
- The following accounts normally maintain a debit account balance:
    - assets
    - expenses
- The following accounts normally maintain a credit account balance:
    - liabilities
    - revenues
    - equity
- Keep in mind that accounts are summaries of the transactions that have been recorded. A T-account is a crude but effective means of analyzing the transactions that affect various accounts.
- You can use T-accounts with debits on the left and credits on the right as a crude means of keeping score of the effects of transactions on the various accounts.

2.6 How Debits and Credits Make the Accounting System Work

- Using the debit/credit methodology, each accounting transaction is recorded in, and accumulated by, an account via an entry to a general journal.
- That entry may debit an account or credit an account, to use these terms as verbs.
- An account is simply a place to store the effects of transactions on various resources and sources.
- Remembering that debits are normally on the left-hand side of a balance sheet and credits normally on the right-hand side, asset accounts have debit balances, liability accounts have credit balances, and equity accounts have credit balances.
- So, to increase assets, we debit those accounts; to decrease them, we credit those accounts.
- To increase liabilities and owners' equity, we credit those accounts; to decrease them, we debit those accounts.
- Double-entry accounting reflects the dual nature of each transaction.

- Every transaction affects two or more items in the balance sheet equation.
- If one item within the equation changes, then another item must also change in order for the equation to continue to balance.
- For example, an increase in an asset must be accompanied by a decrease in another asset, or an increase in a liability or equity account.
- Here's an example of the double-entry process:

Jiffy Express Ltd. has the following account balances in its ledger of accounts as of January 31, 2007:

Account Balances

	Debit	**Credit**
Cash	$ 2,000	
Inventories	15,000	
Owed by customers	3,000	
Building	87,000	
Accumulated amortization on building		$ 12,000
Owed to suppliers		2,500
Owed to Canada Revenue Agency (CRA)		4,000
Six-month bank loan	15,000	
Mortgage on building	35,000	
Share capital		30,000
Retained earnings		8,500
	$107,000	$107,000

- The above is known as a trial balance. A balance sheet using the above accounts follows.

Jiffy Express Ltd.
Balance Sheet
As at January 31, 2007

ASSETS		LIABILITIES	
Current:		Current:	
Cash	$ 2,000	Six-month bank loan	$15,000
Owed by customers	3,000	Owing to suppliers	2,500
Inventories	15,000	Owing to CRA	4,000
	$ 20,000		$21,500
Non-Current:		Non-Current:	
Building	$ 87,000	Mortgage on building	35,000
Accumulated amortization	(12,000)	Total liabilities	$56,500
	$ 75,000		
		EQUITY	
		Share capital	$30,000
		Retained earnings	8,500
		Total equity	$38,500
Total assets	$95,000	Total liabilities and equity	$95,000

- The following transactions happened in February 2007:
  (1) Jiffy paid one of its suppliers $400 that it owed.
  (2) Jiffy collected $1,200 owed by one of its customers.
  (3) An additional owner was found who contributed $2,000 cash in exchange for part ownership in Jiffy.
  (4) Jiffy bought $500 of inventory with cash.
- To record the above transactions (as entries in a general journal) using the double-entry system, you must first determine whether an account normally has a debit or a credit balance (see list of accounts above), and then whether that account is being increased or decreased:

Entries:

(1)	Debit: Owed to suppliers *(being decreased)*	400	
	Credit: Cash *(being decreased)*		400
(2)	Debit: Cash *(being increased)*	1,200	
	Credit: Owed by customers *(being decreased)*		1,200
(3)	Debit: Cash *(being increased)*	2,000	
	Credit: Share capital *(being increased)*		2,000
(4)	Debit: Inventories *(being increased)*	500	
	Credit: Cash *(being decreased)*		500

- After recording these entries, the accounting system requires you to "post" them from the accounting journal to the appropriate accounts in the ledger of accounts. To "post" simply means to transfer the value of each transaction to the accounts. In other words, posting updates the account balances to reflect the effects of the new transactions. After posting, the trial balance, as at the end of February, would appear as follows:

Account Balances

	Debit	**Credit**
Cash	$ 4,300	
Inventories	15,500	
Owed by customers	1,800	
Building	87,000	
Accumulated amortization on building		$ 12,000
Owed to suppliers		2,100
Owed to Canada Revenue Agency		4,000
Six-month bank loan		15,000
Mortgage on building	35,000	
Share capital		32,000
Retained earnings		8,500
	$108,600	$108,600

- The above trial balance proves that debits did equal credits for each of the transactions.

- A new balance sheet as of the end of February would appear as follows:

Jiffy Express Ltd.
Balance Sheet
As at February 28, 2007

ASSETS		LIABILITIES	
Current:		Current:	
Cash	$ 4,300	Six-month bank loan	$15,000
Owed by customers	1,800	Owing to suppliers	2,100
Inventories	15,500	Owing to CRA	4,000
	$ 21,600		$21,100
Non-Current:		Non-Current:	
Building	$ 87,000	Mortgage on building	$35,000
Accumulated amortization	(12,000)	Total liabilities	$56,100
	$ 75,000		
		EQUITY	
		Share capital	$32,000
		Retained earnings	8,500
		Total equity	$40,500
Total assets	$96,600	Total liabilities and equity	$96,600

- So, to summarize, a transaction results in:
  - – a journal entry;
  - – a posting to the accounts in the ledger from the journal entry;
  - – a trial balance, prepared from the account balances in the ledger; and
  - – a balance sheet, prepared from the trial balance.

2.7 Arranging Accounts on the Balance Sheet

- The balance sheet presented earlier in the Jiffy Express Ltd. example illustrates what is known as a "classified" balance sheet, which breaks assets and liabilities into two sub-categories: current and non-current.
- Despite having a credit balance, an account such as accumulated amortization appears on the left-hand side of the balance sheet as a means of showing that it offsets the value of some non-current assets such as a building.

2.8 Demonstration Problem: Journal Entries and Accounts

- The chapter provides a demonstration of creating and recording journal entries using the balance sheet of Petro-Canada.

2.9 Proprietorships, Partnerships, Corporations, and Financing

- A proprietorship is owned by one person, but this does not imply that only that person runs the business; the business may have employees.
- A partnership is owned by two or more people.

- Proprietorships and partnerships are unincorporated, meaning that the business affairs of the owners are not separate from their personal affairs; that is, a business of one of these types is not a separate legal entity.
- A corporation *is* a separate legal entity from its owners, being incorporated under either federal or provincial legislation.
- The corporation is afforded all the rights and privileges of an individual, such as the right to own property or assume debts.
- Corporate groups are related companies under one "umbrella."
- General Motors is a corporate group of companies comprising Chevrolet, Pontiac, Buick, and General Motors Acceptance Corporation, among others, all of which are separate legal entities (incorporated) by themselves.
- Accounting for corporate groups attempts to consolidate (or amalgamate) the financial statements of each of the separate, but related, companies.

2.10 A Closer Look at Balance Sheet Content

- A balance sheet indicates the financial resources (assets) available to carry out economic activities as well as the claims against those resources (sources).
- Assets are those items that an enterprise owns and may be tangible, such as buildings or vehicles, or intangible (characterized by legal right), such as accounts receivable (what customers owe the enterprise) or patents.
- Liabilities are the claims against the business by creditors (e.g., employees to whom the enterprise owes wages, suppliers, banks, or government agencies).
- Equity, or owners' equity, represents the residual interests of the owners; residual meaning what is left over of assets after accounting for what is owed as liabilities.
- Equity includes the amounts the owners have contributed (share capital) as well as the earnings that have accumulated over the years (retained earnings).
- Most balance sheets show the current year's information *and* the preceding year's information for the sake of comparison.

EXERCISES

E1. Debit and Credit Classification Decide whether the following accounts of Christine Wright's Glassblowing should have debit or credit balances (place check marks in the appropriate column):

		Dr.	Cr.
Cash	200	✓	
J. Mowry, capital	1,420		
Owed by customers	75	✓	
Payable to suppliers	400		✓
Inventory	450	✓	
Bank overdraft	60		✓
Wages owed to employee	300		✓
Shelves and furniture	600	✓	
Business licence fees owed	45		✓
Equipment	1,200	✓	
Accumulated amortization, equipment	100		✓

E2. Accounting Records "Wait a minute now," said a young manager. "All this talk about journals and ledgers and posting ... aren't journals and ledgers the same thing?" Are they? Explain.

PROBLEMS

P1. Balance Sheet Values Ben's Delicatessen is a famous Montreal landmark that opened in 1908. The restaurant sits in downtown Montreal surrounded by skyscrapers. Estimates place the property value to developers at $3 million to $9 million. What value should Ben's accountants show on the balance sheet for the company?

P2. Balance Sheet Analysis Refer to the balance sheet of Canadian Pacific Railway Ltd. on page 104 of the text.
- (a) What sorts of things does the balance sheet tell you?
- (b) Did its working capital improve or worsen from 2003 to 2004?

P3. Journal Entries The balance sheet equation for Jennie Jones Handcrafts is shown below for the first 10 business days of May. For Jennie, the 10 days are consecutive due to the craft show at which she is exhibiting. Assume that only one transaction takes place on each day. Prepare the likely journal entries that might have occurred for May 2 to May 10.

	Assets				**= Liabilities + Equity**	
	Cash	**Accounts Receivable**	**Inventory**	**Supplies**	**Accounts Payable**	**Owner's Equity**
May 1	5,000	3,000	8,000	1,000	5,000	12,000
May 2	6,000	3,000	7,500	1,000	5,000	12,500
May 3	6,000	3,000	7,500	1,500	5,500	12,500
May 4	6,000	5,000	6,000	1,500	5,500	13,000
May 5	5,500	5,000	6,000	1,500	5,000	13,000
May 6	5,500	5,000	7,000	1,500	6,000	13,000
May 7	7,500	3,000	7,000	1,500	6,000	13,000
May 8	5,000	3,000	7,000	1,500	3,500	13,000
May 9	5,000	3,000	7,000	1,000	3,500	12,500
May 10	4,000	3,000	7,000	1,000	3,500	11,500

P4. Business Organization, Journal Entries The following information relates to Donray Auto Repair.
- (a) By looking at the account names below, decide if this business is incorporated or unincorporated.

Accounts Payable	Income Taxes Payable
Accounts Receivable	Land
Accumulated Amortization, Equipment	Mortgage Payable
Accumulated Amortization, Furniture	Property Taxes Payable
Buildings	Wages Payable
Cash	Share Capital
Equipment	Retained Earnings
	Furniture

(b) Prepare journal entries for the transactions below, which occurred on March 31, 2007.
   (1) Unpaid wages amounting to $12,000 were paid.
   (2) New office equipment was purchased for $750 on credit from a supplier.
   (3) One of the buildings was sold for $55,000 plus $68,000 for the land on which it sat.
   (4) A customer paid an overdue invoice for $225.
   (5) Half of the property taxes owing were paid, leaving $8,000 left to pay by June 1.
   (6) One of the owners contributed his home computer to the business. Its value was $2,000.
   (7) A mortgage payment of $1,100 was made.
   (8) New furniture was acquired for $2,400. Of this, $2,000 was paid in cash and the balance put on credit with the vendor.

P5. Account Classification State whether or not, and why, each of the following is likely to be an asset, a liability, or an equity item (or perhaps more than one item) of the company indicated:

Company	**Item**
Burago Ltd.	Patents held on the model cars it produces
Syncrude Canada Ltd.	The buffalo herd put on its property to demonstrate safe reclamation of land
Beaver Foods Ltd.	Seasonal contract workers
Echo Bay Mines Ltd.	Funds collected from an increase in shares issued
BHP Billiton	Equipment leased for the underground mine at the Ekati diamond claim in the Northwest Territories

INTEGRATIVE PROBLEM

IP1. Journal Entries, Balance Sheet Preparation Shane Gallagher, a dog enthusiast and dog owner for many years, decided to supplement his income by opening a dog training school that he would operate in the evenings and on weekends. By the time he was ready to open his doors on June 1, 2007, the following transactions had taken place for his new business, Burnt Paw Dog Training, Ltd.

(1) On May 9, 2007, he took $15,000 out of his personal savings account to use as "seed" money to get his school going. He deposited this money in a bank chequing account opened under the company's name.

• (2) On May 10, he rented a stand-alone warehouse in an industrial area far away from neighbouring businesses (for obvious reasons!). He paid $1,000 for June's rent in advance and could move in on June 1.

(3) On May 12, he purchased rubber floor mats (for traction) to put in the warehouse in the dog-training area. These mats cost $6,000, for which he wrote a cheque.

(4) On May 12, he also bought a used office computer for $900 cash to keep track of clients (and their pets).

(5) On May 17, he borrowed $3,000 from his brother to buy training equipment such as ramps, hoops, hurdles, steps, tubes, and Morris (a stuffed life-size dummy to be used to train drug-sniffing dogs). The loan was to be paid back in six months.

(6) On May 23, he contacted a local leather artisan who agreed to make three dozen leashes that Shane could sell from his dog school. On May 30, these were received by mail along with an invoice for $360.

(7) On May 25, he ordered a variety of items that he would sell (such as dog food, collars, play toys, and muzzles) from an eastern Canadian pet supplier. The goods arrived on May 27 along with a bill for $4,200.

(8) On May 30, he purchased liability insurance, in the event of an unfortunate canine accident, paying a $100 premium for June in advance.

(9) On May 31, a painted sign arrived, which he had contracted to have made on May 18. When the sign arrived, he wrote a cheque for $2,200.

(10) On May 31, he picked up various stationery items he had ordered, such as letterhead and business cards shaped like dog bones. He wrote a cheque for $350.

(11) On May 31, while walking his own dog to the training school to prepare for opening day demonstrations, his dog broke free from the leash and bit the adjacent tenant who was just coming out of his store. Within hours, Shane was served with a $250,000 lawsuit by a well-clad "ambulance-chaser" (lawyer).

(a) Prepare journal entries to record the above and then prepare a balance sheet as of May 31, 2007, the eve of Shane's opening day.

(b) Calculate working capital, the working capital ratio, and the debt–equity ratio on May 31, 2007.

EXPLORATIVE QUESTION

EQ1. Balance Sheet Analysis "The balance sheet shows what a company is worth at a particular point in time." Discuss the validity of this statement.

SOLUTIONS

EXERCISES

E1. Christine Wright's Glassblowing:

		Dr.	Cr.
Cash	200	√	
J. Mowry, capital	1,420		√
Owed by customers	75	√	
Payable to suppliers	400		√
Inventory	450	√	
Bank overdraft	60		√
Wages owed to employee	300		√
Shelves and furniture	600	√	
Business licence fees owed	45		√
Equipment	1,200	√	
Accumulated amortization, equipment	100		√

E2. A general journal and a general ledger are not the same thing. A general journal is a book of entry to record transactions. A general ledger holds the individual accounts used by the company, and each account is debited or credited by any transactions affecting it. The general journal is used to post transactions to the general ledger. It is the general ledger that gives you account balances that would be used in preparing trial balances and financial statements.

PROBLEMS

P1. Regardless of the value of the property that the restaurant sits on, the value on the balance sheet should be what was paid for that property whenever it was purchased. In cases where there has been an extreme appreciation of property value, the company may make a note to accompany the balance sheet to indicate that the property is, in fact, worth more than the balance sheet would suggest. Such extra information should be backed by a real estate appraisal confirming the current value of the property. But, again, appraised value and the price that would be received if the property were sold could be two very different figures.

P2. (a)

- Cash and short-term investments increased either due to operations or due to the sale of non-current assets.
- Accounts receivable decreased, meaning less extension of credit or tighter collections or more prompt payments by customers.
- Materials and supplies decreased, meaning less cash tied up in these assets.
- Non-current assets increased, meaning that assets such as properties must have been purchased.
- Current liabilities increased marginally, due to more trade credit (accounts payable).
- Longer-term liabilities increased, likely due to the purchase of properties. Considering that cash increased, these purchases were more than likely financed.
- Notice also that the company's share capital decreased. This is usually the result of the company's repurchasing its stock from shareholders.

(b) Working capital improved from a current ratio of 0.70 to 1.02. Effectively, the company's liquidity improved considerably, due mostly to more cash and short-term investments.

P3.

Date	Account	Debit	Credit
May 2	Cash	1,000	
	Cost of Goods Sold*	500 (deduced)	
	Inventory		500
	Revenue*		1,000 (deduced)
	To record the sale of inventory for cash.		
	** A sale affects an account called Revenues and an account called Cost of Goods Sold Expense. Both of these accounts directly affect owners' equity (discussed in Chapter 3).*		
May 3	Supplies	500	
	Accounts Payable		500
	To record purchase of supplies.		
May 4	Accounts Receivable	2,000	
	Cost of Goods Sold	1,500 (deduced)	
	Inventory		1,500
	Revenue		2,000 (deduced)
	To record sale of inventory on account.		
May 5	Accounts Payable	500	
	Cash		500
	To record payment on account.		
May 6	Inventory	1,000	
	Accounts Payable		$1,000
	To record purchase of inventory on account.		
May 7	Cash	2,000	
	Accounts Receivable		2,000
	To record collection of accounts receivable.		
May 8	Accounts Payable	2,500	
	Cash		2,500
	To record payment on account.		
May 9	Supplies Expense	500 (deduced)	
	Supplies		500
	To record supplies usage.		
May 10	Jennie Jones, Withdrawals	1,000 (deduced)	
	Cash		1,000
	To record owner's withdrawal.		

P4. (a) This business is incorporated, given that the equity accounts distinguish between that which was contributed by owners (share capital) and that which was earned and held by the business (retained earnings). Therefore, the legal name of the business would end with Ltd., Inc., Corp., or Corporation, although the operating name need not be so identified.

(b) Journal entries:

(1)	Dr	Wages Payable	12,000	
	Cr	Cash		12,000
(2)	Dr	Equipment	750	
	Cr	Accounts Payable		750
(3)	Dr	Cash	55,000	
	Cr	Buildings		55,000
	Dr	Cash	68,000	
	Cr	Land		68,000
(4)	Dr	Cash	225	
	Cr	Accounts Receivable		225
(5)	Dr	Property Taxes Payable	8,000	
	Cr	Cash		8,000
(6)	Dr	Equipment	2,000	
	Cr	Share Capital		2,000
(7)	Dr	Mortgage Payable	1,100	
	Cr	Cash		1,100
(8)	Dr	Furniture	2,400	
	Cr	Cash		2,000
	Cr	Accounts Payable		400

P5.

Company	Item	Classification
Burago Ltd.	Patents held on the model cars it produces	Asset. Patents are resources that have future value.
Syncrude Canada Ltd.	The buffalo herd put on its property to demonstrate safe reclamation of land	Asset, if Syncrude has purchased the buffalo. If Syncrude is merely leasing the land to the owners of the buffalo, then the buffalo are not an asset of Syncrude.
Beaver Foods Ltd.	Seasonal contract workers	Neither. People, themselves, are neither assets nor liabilities.
Echo Bay Mines Ltd.	Funds collected from an increase in shares issued	Asset. The funds are cash, strictly speaking.
		Equity. The shares issued represent share capital.
BHP Billiton	Equipment leased for the underground mine at the Ekati diamond claim in the Northwest Territories	Neither. The leased equipment is not the property of BHP Billiton but that of the leasing company.

INTEGRATIVE PROBLEM

IP1. (a) Journal entries:

(1)	Dr	Cash	15,000	
	Cr	Share Capital		15,000
(2)	Dr	Prepaid Rent	1,000	
	Cr	Cash		1,000

(Note: Prepaid Rent is an asset since it represents future economic benefit as of May 30, benefit that will be used up during June.)

(3)	Dr	Equipment	6,000	
	Cr	Cash		6,000
(4)	Dr	Computer Equipment	900	
	Cr	Cash		900
(5)	Dr	Cash	3,000	
	Cr	Loan Payable		3,000
	Dr	Equipment	3,000	
	Cr	Cash		3,000
(6)	Dr	Inventories	360	
	Cr	Accounts Payable		360

(7)	Dr	Inventories	4,200	
	Cr	Accounts Payable		4,200
(8)	Dr	Prepaid Insurance	100	
	Cr	Cash		100

(Note: Prepaid insurance is an asset since it represents the future economic benefit of coverage as of May 30, a benefit that will expire during June.)

(9)	Dr	Equipment	2,200	
	Cr	Cash		2,200
(10)	Dr	Stationery Supplies	350	
	Cr	Cash		350

(11) No journal entry. There has not been any exchange, nor is the amount measurable since the lawsuit has not been settled.

Burnt Paw Dog Training, Ltd.
Balance Sheet
As at May 31, 2007

Assets		Liabilities	
Cash	$ 4,450	Accounts Payable	$ 4,560
Inventories	4,560	Loan Payable	3,000
Stationery Supplies	350		
Prepaid Rent	1,000		
Prepaid Insurance	100	Equity	
Equipment	11,200		
Computer Equip.	900	Share Capital	15,000
		Retained Earnings	0
Total Assets	$22,560	Total Liabilities & Equity	$22,560

(b)	Working capital ($10,460 – $4,560):	$5,900
	Working capital ratio ($10,460/$4,560):	2.29
	Debt/equity ($7,560/$15,000)	0.504

EXPLORATIVE QUESTION

EQ1. The balance sheet can be somewhat misleading. The reason is that the balance sheet values assets and liabilities at historical costs; that is, at the costs or values at the time assets were purchased or at the time liabilities arose. Why put today's date, then, on yesterday's numbers? One reasonable answer lies in being conservative and fair. We could value our assets at what we *think* they could be sold for today. But would we get those asking prices? Even more importantly, would they be our assets to value today if we sold them? In using historical cost, we are being as fair as possible and being as conservative as possible by using verifiable information.

Accrual accounting does allow us to make estimates and adjustments. But it is accepted practice to err on the side of conservatism rather than on the side of idealism.

CHAPTER 3
MEASURING AND EVALUATING FINANCIAL PERFORMANCE

LEARNING OBJECTIVES

After completing Chapter 3, you should:

- understand the necessity of looking at financial performance over time;
- comprehend the concept of income;
- be able to carry out basic income statement preparation;
- understand and be able to prepare basic statements of retained earnings; and
- understand the connection between the income statement and the balance sheet.

CHAPTER SUMMARY

3.1 Chapter Introduction: Measuring and Evaluating Financial Performance

- The chapter examines two of the financial reports that are integral to determining a company's financial position and performance: the income statement, and the statement of retained earnings.
- The income statement measures financial performance over a period of time.
- The retained earnings statement connects the income statement to the balance sheet.

3.2 Financial Performance and the Development of Stock Markets

- The importance of financial accounting for the purpose of evaluating financial performance evolved over time. *Stewardship* was seen as important by governments, nobles, and monarchs, who relied on reporting systems to assess whether their interests and investments were being adequately managed by their subjects.
- With the creation of stock markets in the 1800s in Britain and elsewhere, legislation was passed which required companies to report on their financial performance to their investors. The balance sheet by itself was insufficient to assess financial performance as it presented a static picture rather than a dynamic picture of how a company performed.

3.3 Introduction to the Income and Retained Earnings Statements

- In order to measure how a company performs over a period of time, an income statement is prepared.
- This statement is simply an accounting of revenues a company earns and the expenses it incurs in the process of earning those revenues. The resulting difference is a net income (if revenues exceed expenses) or a net loss (if expenses exceed revenues).

Net income (loss) for the period = Revenues – Expenses

- Revenues are increases in the wealth of a company resulting from the provision of goods or services to the customer, while expenses are decreases in the wealth of the company that are incurred in order to earn revenues.
- Expenses do not include any payments made as returns to owners of the business, such as withdrawals or dividends. These are considered to be distributions of net income rather than expenses leading to net income.

- The statement of retained earnings adds this net income figure to all the prior net incomes (less all dividends previously declared) to come up with the earnings that remain within the business.
- Retained earnings are derived as follows:

Retained earnings at end of period	=	Retained earnings at the beginning of the period + Net income for the period – Dividends declared during the period

- The ending retained earnings figure appears in the equity section of the balance sheet.
- The statement of retained earnings pulls together the income statement and the balance sheet, since net income finds its way to the balance sheet via the retained earnings figure.
- For proprietorships and partnerships, the statement of retained earnings is called the statement of owner's (or owners') equity.
- The income statement is used to record the revenues and expenses for *one* period, whereas the balance sheet is a *cumulative* measure, at a particular date, of various assets, liabilities, and equity items over time.

3.4 A Closer Look at Income and Retained Earnings Statements' Content

- The Canadian Pacific Railway Ltd. example on page 151 of your text shows you that an income statement is for a period of time ("... year ended December 31") and, like the balance sheet, often tends to show previous years' data for the sake of comparison.
- Some income statements can be quite detailed (itemized), and others less so, depending on how much owners care to reveal above and beyond what is required for tax or other regulatory purposes (such as that required by securities commissions).
- Note the organization of the income statement, moving down from operating to non-operating items. It is usual to show ordinary (or operating) revenues and expenses first, followed by non-operating—and perhaps unusual—revenues and expenses.
- Interest revenues or expenses are an example of non-operating items, since these relate to the financing and investing structure of the business.
- Income taxes, too, are shown separately since they arise as a consequence of operations, not in the course of operations.
- Items that may appear on the statement of retained earnings include corrections of errors affecting prior years' incomes, or items associated with transactions with shareholders such as the costs resulting from a share issue.

3.5 Format of Income and Retained Earnings Statements

- This section elaborates on some common income statement and retained earnings statement formats and discusses common line items that are found in these statements.
- Income statements frequently include the following line items: operating revenue and expenses; non-operating revenues and expenses; continuing income before income tax; current and future income tax expense; income from continuing operations; discontinued operations and extraordinary items; and net income.

- Retained earnings statements frequently include the following line items: adjustments to retained earnings; reported net income for the year (from the income statement); transactions with shareholders; and ending retained earnings.
- Read this section carefully to understand why these particular line items are reported on the income statement and the retained earnings statement.

3.6 Debits and Credits, Revenues and Expenses

- The example of Jiffy Express Ltd. in Chapter 2 of this guide will be expanded to include transactions affecting the income statement. Refer back to the trial balance as at the end of February 2007.
- Suppose the following events took place in March 2007:
  - (1) Cash sales amounted to $12,300 and credit sales came to $3,200.
  - (2) A physical inventory count revealed that inventories amounted to $9,400.
  - (3) Amortization on buildings amounted to $1,000.
  - (4) Income taxes for the month came to $1,960.
  - (5) General expenses of $2,800 were paid in cash and another $700 was incurred on credit.
  - (6) $1,500 of the credit sales were collected.
  - (7) Suppliers were paid $1,100.
  - (8) The Canada Revenue Agency (CRA) was paid $2,000.
  - (9) The company's board of directors declared and paid a $500 dividend. (Note: it is not usual practice to declare or pay monthly dividends.)

The ensuing entries to record these events are:

(1)	Dr	Cash	12,300	
	Dr	Owed by Customers (formally Accounts Receivable)	3,200	
	Cr	Revenues		15,500
(2)	Dr	Cost of Goods	6,100	
	Cr	Inventories*		6,100
		*Inventories: $15,500 – $9,400		
(3)	Dr	Amortization Expense, Buildings	1,000	
	Cr	Accumulated Amortization, Buildings		1,000
(4)	Dr	Income Tax Expense	1,960	
	Cr	Owed to Canada Revenue Agency (formally Income Taxes Payable)		1,960
(5)	Dr	General Expenses	3,500	
	Cr	Cash		2,800
	Cr	Owed to Supplier (formally Accounts Payable)		700

(6)	Dr	Cash	1,500	
	Cr	Accounts Receivable		1,500
(7)	Dr	Accounts Payable	1,100	
	Cr	Cash		1,100
(8)	Dr	Income Taxes Payable	2,000	
	Cr	Cash		2,000
(9)	Dr	Retained Earnings	500	
	Cr	Cash		500

- Once posted, these transactions result in the following trial balance at the end of March 2007, with the new accounts needed (account names in italics):

	Balance, Feb. 28, 2007 Dr ($)	Cr ($)	Debits During March ($)	Credits During March ($)	Balance, Mar. 31, 2007 Dr ($)	Cr ($)
Cash	4,300		12,300 +1,500	2,800 +1,100 +2,000 +500	11,700	
Inventories	15,500			6,100	9,400	
Accts. Receivable		1,800		3,200	1,500	3,500
Building	87,000				87,000	
Accum. Amort., Bldg.		12,000		1,000		13,000
Accounts Payable		2,100	1,100	700		1,700
Income Taxes Payable		4,000	2,000	1,960		3,960
Six-Month Bank Loan		15,000				15,000
Mortgage on Bldg.		35,000				35,000
Share Capital		32,000				32,000
Retained Earnings		8,500	500			8,000
Revenues		0		15,500		15,500
Cost of Goods Sold	0		6,100		6,100	
Amortization Expense	0		1,000		1,000	
Income Tax Expense	0		1,960		1,960	
General Expense	0		3,500		3,500	
TOTAL	$108,600	$108,600	$33,160	$33,160	$124,160	$124,160

- Thus, the trial balance is still in balance.
- The income statement for March can be prepared from this trial balance:

Jiffy Express Ltd.
Income Statement
For Month Ending March 31, 2007

Revenues			$15,500
Expenses:			
	Cost of Goods Sold	$6,100	
	General Expenses	3,500	
	Amortization Expense	1,000	10,600
Income Before Tax			$ 4,900
Income Tax Expense			1,960
Net Income			$ 2,940

- To close the revenue and expense accounts and bring their balances to zero before the next period begins, the following journal entries are made:

Dr	Revenues	15,500	
Cr	Retained Earnings		15,500
Dr	Retained Earnings	12,560	
Cr	Cost of Goods Sold		6,100
Cr	General Expenses		3,500
Cr	Amortization Expense		1,000
Cr	Income Tax Expense		1,960

- When these two closing entries are posted to the accounts, all revenue and expense accounts end up with a zero balance.
- The "post-closing" trial balance for March is given below. The posted closing entries and resulting account balance are in bold face:

	Balance, Feb. 28, 2007 Dr ($)	Cr ($)	Debits During March ($)	Credits During March ($)	Balance, Mar. 31,2007 Dr ($)	Cr ($)
Cash	4,300		12,300 +1,500	2,800 +1,100 +2,000 +500	11,700	
Inventories	15,500			6,100	9,400	
Accts. Receivable		1,800		3,200	1,500	3,500
Building	87,000				87,000	
Accum. Amort., Bldg.		12,000		1,000		13,000
Accounts Payable		2,100	1,100	700	1,700	
Income Taxes Payable		4,000	2,000		1,960	3,960
Six-Month Bank Loan		15,000				15,000
Mortgage on Bldg.		35,000				35,000
Share Capital		32,000				32,000
Retained Earnings		8,500	**12,560** +500	**15,500**	**10,940**	
Revenues		0	**15,500**	15,500		**0**
Cost of Goods Sold	0		6,100	**6,100**	**0**	
Amortization Expense	0		1,000	**1,000**	**0**	
Income Tax Expense	0		1,960	**1,960**	**0**	
General Expenses	0	3,500	**3,500**		**0**	
TOTAL	$108,600	$108,600	$61,220	$61,220	$111,600	$111,600

- From this post-closing trial balance, the statement of retained earnings and the balance sheet can be prepared:

Jiffy Express Ltd.
Statement of Retained Earnings
For the Month Ending March 31, 2007

Retained Earnings, Beginning of Month	$ 8,500
Add: Net Income for March	2,940
Deduct: Dividends Declared and Paid	(500)
Retained Earnings, End of Month	$10,940

- This ending retained earnings figure is as per the trial balance:

Jiffy Express Ltd.
Balance Sheet
As at March 31, 2007

ASSETS		LIABILITIES	
Current:		Current:	
Cash	$ 11,700	Six-Month Bank Loan	$15,000
Accounts Receivable	3,500	Accounts Payable	1,700
Inventories	9,400	Income Taxes Payable	3,960
	24,600		20,660
Non-Current:		Non-Current:	
Building	87,000	Mortgage on Building	35,000
Accumulated Amortization	(13,000)	Total Liabilities	55,660
	74,000		
		EQUITY	
		Share Capital	32,000
		Retained Earnings	10,940
		Total Equity	42,940
Total Assets	$ 98,600	Total Liabilities & Equity	$98,600

Another Preparation Illustration

- Consider the following balance sheet:

Christine Stationeries Ltd.
Balance Sheet
As at December 31, 2006

ASSETS		LIABILITIES	
Cash	$ 3,200	Accounts Payable	$ 3,400
Accounts Receivable	1,600	Income Tax Payable	400
Inventories	7,200	Rent Payable	400
Fixtures & Equipment	9,400	Wages Payable	1,600
Accum. Amortization, Fix. & Equip.	(1,410)	EQUITY	
		Share Capital	3,500
		Retained Earnings	10,690
TOTAL	$19,990	TOTAL	$19,990

- During fiscal 2007, the following events transpired:
  - Credit sales, $40,000;
  - Purchases of inventory for re-sale, on credit, $9,000;
  - Cash sales, $16,000;
  - Rent charged by building owner, $7,200;
  - Cost of goods sold, $11,200;
  - Income tax owing from 2006 earnings, $2,200
  - Rent paid to building owner, $7,400;
  - Payments received from credit customers, $38,400;
  - Payments made to suppliers, $6,800;

- Tax payments made, $2,300;
- Wages incurred, $24,500;
- Wages paid, $26,100; and
- Amortization incurred, $470.

- If necessary, use T-accounts to verify that these events result in the following account balances:

Cash (3,200 + 16,000 + 38,400 – 7,400 – 6,800 – 2,300 – 26,100)	$15,000	
Accounts Receivable (1,600 + 40,000 – 38,400)	3,200	
Inventories (7,200 + 9,000 – 11,200)		$ 5,000
Fixture & Equipment	9,400	
Accumulated Amortization, Fixtures & Equipment (1,410 + 470)		1,880
Accounts Payable (3,400 + 9,000 – 6,800)		5,600
Income Taxes Payable (400 + 2,200 – 2,300)		300
Rent Payable (400 + 7,200 – 7,400)		200
Wages Payable (1,600 + 24,500 – 26,100)		0
Share Capital		3,500
Retained Earnings		10,690
Revenues (40,000 + 16,000)		56,000
Rent Expense	7,200	
Cost of Goods Sold	11,200	
Income Tax Expense	2,200	
Wages Expense	24,500	
Amortization Expense	470	
TOTALS	$78,170	$78,170

- From this trial balance, you should be able to prepare the following income statement:

Christine Stationeries Ltd.
Income Statement
For Year Ending December 31, 2007

Revenues		$56,000
Expenses:		
Cost of Goods Sold	$11,200	
Rent Expense	7,200	
Wages Expense	24,500	
Amortization Expense	470	43,370
Income Before Tax		12,630
Income Tax Expense		2,200
Net Income		$10,430

- The statement of retained earnings can now be prepared:

Christine Stationeries Ltd.
Statement of Retained Earnings
For Year Ending December 31, 2007

Beginning Retained Earnings	$10,690
Add: Net Income for period	10,430
Ending Retained Earnings	$21,120

- In order to make sure that the Retained Earnings account is up to date, it is necessary to close the revenue and expense accounts to Retained Earnings. Simply preparing the above statement does not do this:

Dr	Revenues	56,000	
Cr	Retained Earnings		56,000
Dr	Retained Earnings	45,570	
Cr	Rent Expense		7,200
Cr	Cost of Goods Sold		11,200
Cr	Wages Expense		24,500
Cr	Amortization Expense		470
Cr	Income Tax Expense		2,200

- Upon completing these two closing entries, confirm that the following post-closing trial balance would result:

Cash	$15,000	
Accounts Receivable	3,200	
Inventories	5,000	
Fixture & Equipment	9,400	
Accumulated Amortization, Fixtures & Equipment		$ 1,880
Accounts Payable		5,600
Income Taxes Payable		300
Rent Payable		200
Wages Payable		0
Share Capital		3,500
Retained Earnings		21,120
Revenues (40 000 + 16 000)	0	
Rent Expense	0	
Cost of Goods Sold	0	
Income Tax Expense	0	
Wages Expense	0	
Amortization Expense	0	
TOTALS	$32,600	$32,600

- Finally, you can now prepare the balance sheet. As you should see, when income is earned (or lost), the balance sheet will change:

Christine Stationeries Ltd.
Balance Sheets
As at December 31, 2006 and 2007

ASSETS	2006	2007	LIABILITIES	2006	2007
Cash	$ 3,200	$15,000	Accounts Payable	$ 3,400	$ 5,600
Accounts Receivable	1,600	3,200	Income Tax Payable	400	300
Inventories	7,200	5,000	Rent Payable	400	200
Fixtures & Equipment	9,400	9,400	Wages Payable	1,600	0
Accum. Amortization, Fix. & Equip.	(1,410)	(1,880)	EQUITY		
			Share Capital	3,500	3,500
			Retained Earnings	10,690	21,120
TOTAL	$19,990	$30,720	TOTAL	$19,990	$30,720

3.7 Demonstration Problem: Entries, Closing, and Statement Preparation

- The chapter presents the demonstration problem of Flashy Fashions Inc. in order to show the preparation of an income statement and a statement of retained earnings.

3.8 Accrual Accounting Adjustments

- In order to capture the true nature and intent of economic events, it is often necessary to adjust the accounting records. This is usually done prior to preparing financial statements.
- An economic event may occur and already have been recorded, such as the purchase of an asset, but there is an associated economic event that occurs after the purchase that should be considered; that is amortization. Thus, amortization expense needs to be recognized.
- If this asset was purchased on credit, the accumulating interest is also an economic event that would be recognized under accrual accounting even though such interest may not be paid by the end of a reporting period.
- As a result, such accrual "adjusting entries" must be made to augment any previously recorded cash transactions.
- It is important to appreciate that accrual accounting relies upon professional judgments, but it also attempts to portray a company's complete economic position.

3.9 Demonstration Problem: Accrual Accounting Adjustments

- The Pelforth Retail Inc. example (page 183 of your text) highlights the difference between an unadjusted trial balance and an adjusted trial balance.
- The unadjusted trial balance is simply a trial balance prepared before any adjusting entries or closing entries.
- It is generally based on ledger account balances resulting from the transactional base without yet having been adjusted for accrual events.
- The adjusted trial balance can be prepared after posting these accrual adjustments. From this, the financial statements can be prepared.

EXERCISES

E1. Balance Sheet Preparation The following list was handed to you by Alice, the high school intern who just started working for your dad's business, Handy Dandy. Thinking that the books should be kept as neatly as a filing system, Alice alphabetized the list:

Accounts payable	$ 2,000 Cr.
Accounts receivable	3,000 Dr.
Accumulated amortization—equipment	3,000 Cr.
Amortization expense—equipment	1,500 Dr.
Cash	44,200 Dr.
Dan D. Handy, capital, Jan. 1, 2007	5,000 Cr.
Dan D. Handy, withdrawals	32,000 Dr.
Equipment	15,000 Dr.
Insurance expense	600 Dr.
Prepaid rent	2,000 Dr.
Rent expense	6,000 Dr.
Revenue	80,000 Cr.
Salaries expense	3,000 Dr.
Salaries payable	1,000 Cr.
Supplies	500 Dr.
Supplies expense	2,000 Dr.
Utilities expense	1,200 Dr.
	$ 0

This showed Alice that it balanced, so she assumed everything was fine.

Prepare a balance sheet for Handy Dandy as of December 31, 2007. (Note: For this problem, you will need to deduce the figure for Dan D. Handy, capital, December 31, 2007, since you have not yet prepared the income and retained earnings statements.)

E2. Statement Articulation Refer to E1 above. Now that you have prepared the appropriate balance sheet at the year-end, your father has asked you to prepare an income statement and a statement of retained earnings for the year ended December 31, 2007. What do you notice about the retained earnings balance calculated here versus what you deduced in E1 above?

E3. Statement Articulation Why do we say that income is part of the equity component of the balance sheet equation?

E4. Income Disclosure Why is there resistance to increased income statement disclosure requirements?

E5. Expense Recognition An owner of a company pays himself a $500 dividend, thus reducing the company's wealth. Is this considered to be an expense? Why or why not?

E6. Retained Earnings Calculation If Myriam Company earns revenues of $16,600, has general expenses of $9,400, pays income tax at a rate of 25% of income before tax, declares a dividend of $1,200 and pays $700 of that, what is its new retained earnings? (Assume its original retained earnings are $4,300.)

E7. Accrual Accounting What are accrual accounting adjustments?

E8. Adjusting Entries Prepare adjusting journal entries at fiscal year-end for each of the following events that have occurred during the year at Waverly Company:

(a) Waverly assumed a bank loan for the amount of $15,000 bearing interest at 6.5% per annum payable monthly in blended payments (combined principal and interest). Last month's payment was met.

(b) The insurance company notified Waverly that last quarter's insurance premium had not been paid and, as a result, requested not only last quarter's payment, but payment in advance for the next year. Fortunately, the annual premium of $1,500 had not risen. Waverly's office manager intended to pay promptly.

(c) The purchase of an office chair, desktop calculator, and electric three-hole punch for $700 had been charged to supplies expense. These, however, were considered assets.

(d) Waverly special ordered merchandise for customers, provided the customer paid for the entire value of the order in advance. Of the $1,400 in special orders this past year, $400 had not yet been delivered to customers.

(e) Waverly pays income taxes monthly so as to ease the year-end tax burden. At year-end, it appears that $3,300 in income taxes were overpaid.

(f) Waverly leases store space in a shopping mall and must pay the landlord 0.5% of its yearly revenues no later than three months after year-end. At year-end, revenues amounted to $240,700.

PROBLEMS

P1. Retained Earnings Effect If a company declares a dividend at the end of this year, but does not pay it until early next year, are retained earnings affected this year? How is the balance sheet affected?

P2. Income Disclosure Public companies (i.e., those that have offered shares for sale publicly) often report quarterly earnings information. In one quarter, General Motors may report unusually low income and in another, unusually high income by comparison. Whatever the results, the information usually receives considerable attention in the business press. Why not just wait until the end of the fiscal year to report income? Why is income information so critical to the business world?

P3. Expense Recognition Is amortization or depreciation really an "expense"? If you pay your annual insurance premium in January, are there insurance expenses for the rest of the year?

P4. Income Calculation and Balance Sheet Preparation

(a) From the list of accounts below (not a trial balance) given as at March 31, 2007, decide which accounts are income statement accounts.

Dividends Declared	$ 4,200	Cash Sales	$73,500
Cash	21,500	Supplies Expense	1,850
Building	185,000	Insurance Expense	2,400
Mortgage	127,000	Property Tax Expense	11,250
Cost of Goods Sold	26,700	Prepaid Insurance	4,800
Utilities Expense	3,600	Wages Payable	4,400
Share Capital	55,000	Income Tax Payable	6,200
Wages Expense	64,500	Accumulated Amortization	32,000
Retained Earnings (03/31/06)	70,275	Income Tax Expense	12,475
Accounts Receivable	44,650	Advertising Expense	16,000
Equipment	47,450	Office Furniture	22,400
Credit Sales	102,700	Dividends Payable	4,200
Amortization Expense	6,500		

(b) Prepare a balance sheet as at March 31, 2007, the company's year-end.

P5. Statement Articulation Fill in the blanks in the following schedule of financial accounting numbers for Berstock Enterprises Inc. Start with 2007 and work forward.

	2007	2008	2009
Revenue for the year	?	32,000	34,000
Expenses for the year (except income tax)	19,000	?	26,000
Income before income tax for the year	?	?	8,000
Income tax expense for the year	1,500	2,000	?
Net income for the year	3,000	5,000	?
Retained earnings, beginning of the year	?	?	16,500
Dividends declared during the year	2,000	2,500	2,000
Retained earnings, end of year	14,000	?	20,000
Other equity, end of year	21,000	?	43,000
Liabilities, end of year	70,000	63,000	?
Assets, end of year	?	122,000	125,000

P6. Statement Preparation A self-declared accounting technician, working for a small manufacturing shop, recently prepared the following financial statements. What needs correcting and how so?

Pickyford Manufacturing Ltd.
Balance Sheet
As at July 31, 2007

ASSETS		LIABILITIES AND EQUITY	
Current assets:		Current liabilities:	
Cash	$ 62,400	Bank loan	$ 42,000
		Inventories	139,200
		Accumulated amortization	283,200
Operating expenses	274,800	Income tax expense	49,200
Share capital	180,000	Current portion of mortgage	26,400
Current assets	$656,400	Amortization expense	88,800
Non-current assets:		Current liabilities	$489,600
Warehouse	$734,400	Non-current liabilities:	
Land	120,000	Other non-current liabilities	$ 19,200
Mortgage (minus current)	(290,400)		
Net non-current assets	$564,000	Shareholders' equity:	
		Retained earnings	608,400
		Total equity	$ 608,400
TOTAL	$1,220,400	TOTAL	$1,117,200

Pickyford Manufacturing Ltd.
Statement of Income and Retained Earnings
For the Year Ended July 31, 2007

Revenues:		
Revenue	$1,138,800	
Add accounts receivable	140,400	$1,279,200
Expenses:		
Cost of goods sold	$ 645,600	
Accounts payable	117,600	
Prepaid expenses	25,200	
Dividend declared	24,000	812,400
Income before income tax		$ 466,800
Income taxes payable		32,400
Net income for the year		$ 434,400
Retained earnings—beginning of year		174,000
Retained earnings—end of year		$ 608,400

P7. Journal Entries, Adjusting Entries

(a) Prepare journal entries to record the following events in July 2008 for SeaWest Products Inc.:

(1) The company sold 11 power boats at $22,000 each, along with marine supplies of $6,300, water safety products of $3,900, and water recreation apparel of $2,800. The company sells strictly on a cash or bank credit card basis (bank credit card sales are equivalent to cash).

(2) Wages and salaries for the month amounted to $68,000 and were paid in full by month-end.

(3) The company rents retail space for $12,000 per month. July's rent will be paid in the first week of August.

(4) Utilities for the month amounted to $1,300 and were fully paid by month-end.

(5) The physical inventory count at month-end showed inventories at $221,000. Inventories at the end of last month were valued at $280,000. New inventory arrived during July amounting to $90,000. The additional inventory was bought on credit.

(6) Based on a preliminary analysis, the company will pay $7,840 in income tax for July, which is due at year-end.

(7) Trade suppliers were paid $42,000 during the month.

(8) An additional investor put $5,000 into the business in exchange for 3% ownership.

(9) Amortization on store fixtures was $800 for the month.

(10) The company paid $1,500 for advertising on four Saturdays in the month.

(b) Prepare an income statement for July.

(c) Prepare the closing entries for July.

(d) By how much have retained earnings changed from June 30, 2008?

P8. Transaction Recognition, Journal Entries The following events took place for JBJ Construction Ltd. during the week of July 6, 2007. For each event, decide if a journal entry is necessary and, if so, prepare that entry.

(1) The company purchased auto insurance on July 7, paying $2,400 for a one-year policy.

(2) The company signed a sales agreement on July 8 with a customer for the construction of a building. Construction is scheduled to begin on August 1 for a total sale price of $48,000.

(3) Activities in the month of June had drained the company of cash so, on July 8, a shareholder lent the company $5,000 from her personal savings. She was given the option of converting her loan to shares effective September 1.

(4) On July 10, the company received a credit card statement showing that $1,000 of interest had accrued in June on the company's outstanding credit card balances.

(5) On July 11, the company was served notice that a lawsuit had been filed against it. The claim was for damages of $23,000. The company intends to settle this out of court.

P9. Journal Entries Prepare a journal entry for the following account changes. Include a description to identify what you believe to be the transaction giving rise to the account changes.

(1) Cash up $10,000, Share Capital up $10,000.
(2) All expenses down $12,500 (to zero), Retained Earnings down $12,500.
(3) Unearned Revenues up $5,000, Cash up $5,000.
(4) Pension Expense up $12,000, Pension Payable up $10,000, Cash down $2,000.
(5) Accounts Payable up $5,000, Utility Expense up $3,000, Prepaid Insurance Expense up $2,000.
(6) Accounts Receivable down $1,000, Cash up $1,000.
(7) Demand loan up $500, Shareholder Loan down $500.
(8) Dividends Payable up $2,000, Cash down $1,000, Retained Earnings down $3,000

P10. Adjusting Entries Prepare adjusting entries for the following items pertinent to Geo-Systems Research (GSR) Incorporated's year-end, March 31.

(1) GSR pays its employees every second Friday. Bi-weekly payroll amounts to $4,000. March 31 falls on the Friday before the next payday.
(2) GSR had issued a note payable to one of its suppliers. The note was dated March 1 for a term of six months with a $12,500 principal balance bearing interest at 12% per annum. Principal and interest are due at the end of the term.
(3) GSR's opening parts inventory for the current fiscal year was $11,500. During the fiscal year, GSR purchased $7,200 in parts and closed March 31 with a balance of $9,750.
(4) GSR's board of directors decided on March 27 to pay a dividend to company shareholders of $17,000. Dividend cheques would be issued April 3.
(5) The company has been invoiced for a print ad that it will run in April in *Oil Patch* magazine. The invoice is for $700 and is yet unpaid.
(6)) Office equipment was purchased in December and expensed as office supplies. The equipment was purchased for $4,200.

P11. Adjusting Entries Following are the unadjusted and adjusted trial balances of Thermo Cups Company. Prepare the adjusting entries that would explain the differences in the two trial balances.

Thermo Cups Company
Trial Balance ($)
June 30, 2008

	Unadjusted Dr	Unadjusted Cr	Adjusted Dr	Adjusted Cr
Cash	1,800		1,800	
Accounts Receivable	21,400		21,750	
Allowance for Doubtful Accounts		3,300		3,445
Supplies	2,025		1,790	
Prepaid Insurance	4,200		3,400	
Office Furniture	39,500		39,500	
Accumulated Amortization, Office Furniture		12,400		13,100
Accounts Payable		12,700		12,700
Salary Payable				1,050
Interest Payable				310
Note Payable		15,000		15,000
Unearned Revenue		1,600		1,200
Share Capital		12,500		12,500
Revenue		31,800		32,550
Amortization Expense			700	
Bad Debts Expense			145	
Salary Expense	5,400		6,450	
Supplies Expense			235	
Utilities Expense	2,250		2,250	
Rent Expense	12,000		12,000	
Insurance Expense			800	
Interest Expense	725		1,035	
	89,300	89,300	91,855	91,855

P12. Adjusting Entries Prepare adjusting entries for Burlington Electrical Limited's December 31 year-end, given the following items.

(a) All cash collections have been recorded as revenues. It appears that there is still $3,305 to be collected from customers.

(b) The company started the year with a $92,000 merchandise inventory. During the course of the year, it replenished its inventory with two $44,000 purchases. By year-end, it had $47,400 left in inventory.

(c) The company held a one-year investment bond maturing June 30 of the following year. The principal of the bond was $5,000 bearing 9% per annum.

(d) The company had replaced all the electrical wiring in its building and had charged the $900 in parts to Maintenance Expense. It was now felt that the rewiring should instead have been capitalized.

(e) The company's vehicles were depreciated by 20% of their original cost of $90,000 collectively.

INTEGRATIVE PROBLEMS

IP1. Dividend Policy A company reports a working capital ratio of 0.67 at year-end with a strong net income of $232,400. Fixed assets have grown during the year and the company has reduced its long-term liabilities. Should the company pay a dividend?

IP2. Statement Preparation

(a) The following list was prepared from the books of the Medford Company for the year ended December 31, 2007.

Owing from customers	$ 500
Supplies on hand	100
Goods available for sale	1,600
Rent paid in advance	800
Owed to supplier	400
Owed to telephone company	60
Bank loan	350
Share capital	5,000
Retained earnings, Jan. 1, 2007	1,500
Cash	1,110
Office equipment	8,000
Accumulated amortization	1,000
Revenue	20,000
Cost of goods sold	12,000
Rent expense	2,400
Utilities & telephone expense	550
Amortization expense	250
Dividends declared and paid	1,000

Prepare a classified balance sheet, an income statement, and a statement of retained earnings for Medford Company.

(b) Referring to the above question and the first two chapters of the text, what do these financial statements tell you about Medford Company?

IP3. Statement Preparation Verbatim Developments Inc., a software engineering company, ended 2007 with the following account balances:

Cash	$ 12,400	Office Supplies	$ 1,600
Computer Equipment	415,400	Accum. Amortization	89,150
Accounts Receivable	174,600	Accounts Payable	24,300
Short-Term Bank Loan	94,500	Wages Payable	33,100
Taxes Payable	12,400	Share Capital	175,000
Retained Earnings	173,300	Utilities Payable	2,250

During 2008, the following events transpired:

(1) Clients paid $321,400 of what was owed.
(2) Suppliers were paid $21,200.
(3) Amortization of $30,350 was incurred on computer equipment.
(4) Clients were billed $386,350 for services rendered.
(5) The company's board declared a dividend of $10,000.
(6) Utilities usage amounted to $2,400.
(7) Wages amounted to $210,000, of which $195,000 were paid.
(8) Income taxes were expected to be 40% of income before tax and $40,000 was paid toward this.
(9) Office supplies were purchased for $400 on credit.
(10) Office supplies used during the year amounted to $800.
(11) The short-term loan was reduced by $5,250.
(12) $4,000 was paid toward utilities.

(a) Prepare an income statement for 2008.
(b) Prepare a statement of retained earnings for 2008.
(c) Prepare comparative balance sheets as at December 31, 2007 and 2008.

IP4. Deduce Income Dorion Plumbing, Inc. opened its doors in January 2007. As a commercial and residential contractor, its first month was surprisingly busy. As a result, the company's owner kept the company's books on a cash basis since it seemed only logical. Income for July was $54,000, far better than the owner had expected. At a small business seminar, the owner learned that he needed to keep his books on an accrual basis if he ever hoped to borrow money from a bank in the future. What follows are balance sheet figures for June and July:

	June ($)	July ($)
Cash Basis:		
Current Assets	4,000	6,000
Fixed Assets	0	0
Current Liabilities	2,500	3,500
Non-Current Liabilities	0	0
Accrual Basis:		
Current Assets	9,000	8,500
Fixed Assets	65,000	62,000
Current Liabilities	5,000	10,500
Non-Current Liabilities	0	6,000

Calculate the accrual basis income for July.

EXPLORATIVE QUESTIONS

EQ1. Income Analysis "As long as my income statement is positive, I'll know I'm doing all right with my business," your friend Les says. What is your response to Les?

EQ2. Income Measurement Since one cannot really know how well a company has performed unless the business is closed down and sold off to see whether there is any money left over for the owners, why do we bother trying to measure performance in the first place?

SOLUTIONS

EXERCISES

E1.

Handy Dandy
Balance Sheet
As at December 31, 2007

Assets		Liabilities	
Cash	$44,200	Accounts Payable	$ 2,000
Accounts Receivable	3,000	Salaries Payable	1,000
Supplies	500		
Prepaid Rent	2,000		
		Owner's Equity	
Equipment	15,000		
Accum. Amortization — Equipment	(3,000)	Dan D. Handy, Capital	58,700
Total Assets	$61,700	Total Liabilities & Equity	$61,700

E2.

Handy Dandy
Income Statement
For the Year Ended December 31, 2007

Revenue		$80,000
Expenses:		
Amortization	$1,500	
Rent	6,000	
Salaries	3,000	
Supplies	2,000	
Utilities	1,200	
Insurance	600	14,300
Net Income		$65,700

Handy Dandy
Statement of Owner's Equity
For the Year Ended December 31, 2007

Dan D. Handy, Capital, January 1, 2007	$ 25,000
Net Income	65,700
Dan D. Handy, Withdrawals	(32,000)
Dan D. Handy, Capital, December 31, 2007	$58,700

The ending Capital balance is exactly equal to the deduced figure used in Exercise E1. This demonstrates how the retained earnings statement (or statement of owner's equity) articulates the income statement to the balance sheet.

E3. Income is part of the equity component of the balance sheet equation because income is a temporary account that is calculated and transferred to the statement of retained earnings. The new retained earnings figure then shows up on the balance sheet as part of the equity section.

E4. There is resistance by companies to providing detailed information on how revenues and expenses are calculated because such information can be used by competitors to a company's disadvantage. Sales figures, for example, tell a competitor how much market share another competitor has. Expense information tells a competitor where another competitor is better at controlling costs or where a competitor spends more money (such as advertising) in the hope of generating more sales.

E5. This is not an expense. While expenses do decrease a company's wealth, they do so in order to earn revenues. Paying a dividend is not done to earn revenue; it is done to keep owners content. Dividends are a means of distributing income, not earning it.

E6. \$16,600 – \$9,400 = \$7,200 (before-tax income)
\$7,200 – (0.25)(\$7,200) = \$5,400 (net income)

Beginning Retained Earnings	$4,300
Add: Net Income	5,400
Deduct: Dividends Declared	1,200
Ending Retained Earnings	$8,500

E7. Accrual accounting adjustments are additions and corrections to transaction-based recordkeeping. The additions are intended to augment the accounts and recognize and record economic flows that do not necessarily involve a transaction (e.g., amortization). The corrections are intended to amend previously recorded transactions to reflect proper recognition and recording (e.g., correcting a previously recorded expense that should have been an addition to an asset).

E8. Note that explanations have been excluded below although they are normally required for adjusting entries:

	Account	Debit	Credit
(a)	Interest Expense	81.25	
	Interest Payable		81.25
(b)	Insurance Expense	375	
	Prepaid Insurance	1,500	
	Accounts Payable		1,875
(c)	Office Equipment	700	
	Supplies Expense		700
(d)	Deposits Liability (or Unearned Revenues)	1,000	
	Revenues		1,000
(e)	Income Tax Receivable	3,300	
	Income Tax Expense		3,300
(f)	Lease Expense	1,203.50	
	Accounts Payable		1,203.50

PROBLEMS

P1. It does not matter when a company pays a dividend. When a dividend is declared, retained earnings are reduced since dividends are like an expense. The balance sheet is affected twice: firstly, when the dividend is declared and becomes payable (a liability is created), and secondly, when the dividend is paid (cash is reduced and the payable is reduced).

P2. Income information is usually demanded by shareholders and creditors on a periodic basis. Generally, one year is too long a period for investors or creditors to wait to evaluate whether or not they should invest in/lend to a company. The information that is released is picked up by the financial markets and acted upon. The company's share prices will likely respond in some manner to the income information. For a company such as General Motors, quarterly income information has important ramifications to the auto industry and its related industries such as steel, rubber, and glass. If, for example, GM reported record losses for a given quarter, thousands of suppliers would be affected.

P3. An expense is a decrease in the wealth of a company as a result of trying to earn revenues. In the case of amortization, amortization expense represents the consumption of an asset, consumption that is necessary in the regular course of earning revenues.

In the case of insurance, if you pay your annual insurance in January, for the rest of the year you create a prepaid expense or prepaid asset. In other words, you've paid in advance for something you will use in the future. So when that prepaid asset is, in fact, used, you will have to show the consumption of it. When you initially pay your annual premium, you are simply exchanging one asset (cash) for another (prepaid insurance). Then, as the year progresses, that asset becomes worth less and less. That decline in asset value is shown as an expense as each month of the insurance policy expires.

P4. (a) Income statement items are identified with an asterisk below:

Dividends Declared	$ 4,200	*Cash Sales	$73,500
Cash	21,500	*Supplies Expense	1,850
Building	185,000	*Insurance Expense	2,400
Mortgage	127,000	*Property Tax Expense	11,250
*Cost of Goods Sold	26,700	Prepaid Insurance	4,800
*Utilities Expense	3,600	Wages Payable	4,400
Share Capital	55,000	Income Tax Payable	6,200
*Wages Expense	64,500	Accumulated Amortization	32,000
Retained Earnings (03/31/06)	70,275	*Income Tax Expense	12,475
Accounts Receivable	44,650	*Advertising Expense	16,000
Equipment	47,450	Office Furniture	22,400
*Credit Sales	102,700	Dividends Payable	4,200
*Amortization Expense	6,500		

(b) Before the balance sheet can be prepared, it is first necessary to calculate income for the prior fiscal year. This is so because the retained earnings balance given is for the end of fiscal 2006 (beginning of fiscal 2007). Net income is as follows (not intended to be a proper form income statement):

Sales: (102,700 + 73,500)	$176,200
Expenses:	
Cost of Goods Sold	26,700
Utilities	3,600
Wages	64,500
Amortization	6,500
Supplies	1,850
Insurance	2,400
Property Tax	11,250
Advertising	16,000
Tax	12,475
Net Income	$ 30,925

Ending retained earnings are thus:
$70,275 + $30,925 – $4,200 (dividends) = $97,000.

Balance Sheet
As at March 31, 2007

Assets:		Liabilities:	
Cash	$ 21,500	Wages Payable	$ 4,400
Accounts Receivable	44,650	Dividends Payable	4,200
Prepaid Insurance	4,800	Income Tax Payable	6,200
Office Furniture	22,400	Mortgage	127,000
Equipment	47,450		
Building	185,000	Equity:	
Accum. Amort.	(32,000)	Share Capital	55,000
		Retained earnings	97,000
Total Assets	$293,800	Total Liab. & Equity	$293,800

P5. Numbers in bold are the values that have been solved.

	2007	2008	2009
Revenue for the year	**23,500**	32,000	34,000
Expenses for the year (except income tax)	19,000	**25,000**	26,000
Income before income tax for the year	**4,500**	**7,000**	8,000
Income tax expense for the year	1,500	2,000	**2,500**
Net income for the year	3,000	5,000	**5,500**
Retained earnings, beginning of the year	**13,000**	**14,000**	16,500
Dividends declared during the year	2,000	2,500	2,000
Retained earnings, end of year	14,000	**16,500**	20,000
Other equity, end of year	21,000	**42,500**	43,000
Liabilities, end of year	70,000	63,000	**62,000**
Assets, end of year	**105,000**	122,000	125,000

P6. The balance sheet is not in balance because various accounts have been placed in the wrong statements, in the wrong section of a statement, or, in the case of ending retained earnings, simply improperly calculated (see below).

Pickyford Manufacturing Ltd.
Balance Sheet
As at July 31, 2007

ASSETS		LIABILITIES AND EQUITY	
Current assets:		Current liabilities:	
Cash	$ 62,400	Bank loan	$ 42,000
Accounts receivable	140,400	Accounts payable	117,600
Inventories	139,200	Income taxes payable	32,400
Prepaid expenses	25,200	Current portion of mortgage	26,400
Current assets	$367,200	Current liabilities	$218,400
Non-current assets:		Non-current liabilities:	
Land	$120,000	Long-term mortgage	$290,400
Warehouse	734,400	Other non-current liabilities	19,200
Acc. amort.—warehouse	(283,200)	Non-current liabilities	$309,600
Net non-current assets	$571,200	Total liabilities	$528,000
		Shareholders' equity:	
		Share capital	$180,000
		Retained earnings	230,400
		Total equity	$410,400
TOTAL	$938,400	TOTAL	$938,400

Pickyford Manufacturing Ltd.
Statement of Income
For the Year Ended July 31, 2007

Revenues:		
Revenue		$1,138,800
Expenses:		
Cost of goods sold	$645,600	
Operating expenses	274,800	
Amortization expense	88,800	1,009,200
Income before income tax		$ 129,600
Income tax expense		49,200
Net income for the year		$ 80,400

Pickyford Manufacturing Ltd.
Statement of Retained Earnings
For the Year Ended July 31, 2007

Retained earnings—beginning of year	$174,000
Net income	80,400
Dividend declared	(24,000)
Retained earnings—end of year	$230,400

			Dr	Cr
P7. (a) (1)	Dr	Cash	255,000	
	Cr	Revenues		255,000
(2)	Dr	Wages Expense	68,000	
	Cr	Cash		68,000
(3)	Dr	Rent Expense	12,000	
	Cr	Accounts Payable		12,000
(4)	Dr	Utilities Expense	1,300	
	Cr	Cash		1,300
(5)	Dr	Inventory	90,000	
	Cr	Accounts Payable		90,000
	Dr	Cost of Goods Sold	149,000	
	Cr	Inventory		149,000
(6)	Dr	Income Tax Expense	7,840	
	Cr	Taxes Payable		7,840
(7)	Dr	Accounts Payable	42,000	
	Cr	Cash		42,000
(8)	Dr	Cash	5,000	
	Cr	Share Capital		5,000
(9)	Dr	Amortization Expense	800	
	Cr	Accumulated Amortization		800
(10)	Dr	Advertising Expense	1,500	
	Cr	Cash		1,500

(b)

SeaWest Products Inc.
Income Statement
for July 2008

Sales		$255,000
Expenses:		
Cost of Goods Sold	$149,000	
Wages and Salaries	68,000	
Rent	12,000	
Utilities		1,300
Amortization	800	
Advertising	1,500	232,600
Income Before Tax		22,400
Income Tax Expense		7,840
Net Income		$ 14,560

(c)

Retained Earnings	240,440	
Wages Expense		68,000
Rent Expense		12,000
Utilities Expense		1,300
Cost of Goods Sold		149,000
Income Tax Expense		7,840
Amortization Expense		800
Advertising Expense		1,500
Revenues	255,000	
Retained Earnings		255,000

(d) Since there were no dividends declared, retained earnings increases by $14,560.

P8. (a)

Prepaid Insurance	2,400	
Cash		2,400

Purchased vehicle insurance.

(b) No transaction yet.

(c)

Cash	5,000	
Shareholder Loan		5,000

Operating loan from shareholder.

(d)

Interest Expense	1,000	
Credit Card Payable		1,000

Interest accrued on credit card.

(e) No transaction yet.

		Account	Debit	Credit
P9.	(a)	Cash	10,000	
		Share Capital		10,000
		Issue of new shares.		
	(b)	Retained Earnings	12,500	
		Various Expenses (these would be itemized if known)		12,500
		Closing entry		
	(c)	Cash	5,000	
		Unearned Revenue		5,000
		Received customer deposit.		
	(d)	Pension Expense	12,000	
		Pension Payable		10,000
		Cash		2,000
		Accrual and payment of pensions.		
	(e)	Utilities Expense	3,000	
		Prepaid Insurance Expense	2,000	
		Accounts Payable		5,000
		Utility and insurance invoices received.		
	(f)	Cash	1,000	
		Accounts Receivable		1,000
		Collected receivables.		
	(g)	Shareholder Loan	5,000	
		Bank Loan		5,000
		Paid shareholder with bank loan proceeds.		
	(h)	Retained Earnings	3,000	
		Dividends Payable		2,000
		Cash		1,000
		Declared and paid dividends.		
P10.	(a)	Salaries Expense	2,000	
		Salaries Payable		2,000
		To record one week's accrued salaries.		
	(b)	Interest Expense	127.40	
		Interest Payable		127.40
		To record one month's accrued interest (calculated daily).		
	(c)	Parts/Materials Expense	8,950	
		Parts/Materials		8,950
		To record parts usage.		

			Debit	Credit
	(d)	Dividends	17,000	
		Dividends Payable		17,000
		To record dividend declaration.		
	(e)	Prepaid Advertising	700	
		Accounts Payable		700
		To record advertising that will run in April.		
	(f)	Office Equipment	4,200	
		Office Supplies Expense		4,200
		To correct a previous error.		
P11.	(1)	Accounts Receivable	350	
		Revenue		350
		To record sales made on account.		
	(2)	Bad Debts Expense	145	
		Allowance for Doubtful Accounts		145
		To recognize doubtful accounts.		
	(3)	Supplies Expense	235	
		Supplies		235
		To record supplies usage.		
	(4)	Insurance Expense	800	
		Prepaid Insurance		800
		To record consumption of insurance paid in advance.		
	(5)	Amortization Expense	700	
		Accumulated Amortization		700
		To record amortization of office equipment.		
	(6)	Salaries Expense	1,050	
		Salaries Payable		1,050
		To record accrued salaries.		
	(7)	Interest Expense	310	
		Interest Payable		310
		To record accrued interest.		
	(8)	Unearned Revenue	400	
		Revenue		400
		To record previously unrealized revenues.		

			Debit	Credit
P12.	(a)	Accounts Receivable	3,305	
		Revenue		3,305
		To record sales on account.		
	(b)	Cost of Goods Sold	132,600	
		Inventory		132,600
		To record sale of merchandise inventory.		
	(c)	Interest Receivable	225	
		Interest Revenue		225
		To record accrued interest.		
	(d)	Building	900	
		Maintenance Expense		900
		To record capitalization of an expense.		
	(e)	Amortization Expense	18,000	
		Accumulated Amortization		18,000
		To record amortization on vehicles.		

INTEGRATIVE PROBLEMS

IP1. A current ratio of less than 1 indicates that the company has fewer current assets than current liabilities. This means that its ability to pay short-term debt is jeopardized since it has only $0.67 for every $1.00 owed to creditors. Further, not all of this $0.67 is cash since other current assets include receivables and inventories. The company may have had strong earnings for the year, but dividends are not paid out of net income although they do reduce the net income that is added to retained earnings. Dividends are paid out of cash. With such a low current ratio, the company is not in a position to pay a dividend. It could declare a dividend and create another current liability (Dividends Payable), but that would only worsen its current ratio. Its creditors (and shareholders would become creditors, in effect, if they are owed a dividend) would start to worry, if they have not already done so, about the company's ability to pay its short-term debts. If the company has been buying assets and has reduced its long-term debt, and the current ratio is as weak as it is, it is likely to have minimal cash and is not likely in a position to pay a dividend.

IP2. (a)

Medford Company
Income Statement
For the Year Ending 12/31/2007

Revenue		$20,000
Cost of Goods Sold		12,000
Gross Profit		$ 8,000
Expenses:		
Amortization	$ 250	
Rent	2,400	
Utilities	550	3,200
Net Income		$ 4,800

Medford Company
Statement of Retained Earnings
For the Year Ended 12/31/2007

Beginning Retained Earnings	$1,500
Add: Net Income	4,800
Deduct: Dividends	1,000
Ending Retained Earnings	$5,300

Medford Company
Balance Sheet
As at 12/31/2007

ASSETS			LIABILITIES	
Current:			Current:	
Cash		$ 1,100	Accounts Payable	$ 460
Accounts Receivable		500	Bank Loan Payable	350
Supplies		100	Total	$ 810
Inventory		1,600		
Prepaid Rent		800	OWNERS' EQUITY	
Total		$ 4,110		
			Common Shares	5,000
Non-Current:			Retained Earnings	5,300
Equipment	$ 8,000		Total	10,300
Accum. Amort.	(1,000)			
Total		7,000		
Total Assets		$11,110	Total Liabilities & Equity	$11,110

(b) After examining the statements above, it appears that Medford has had a reasonably successful year, if income is any measure. The company earned a net profit of $0.24 on every dollar of sales, which is quite healthy. The company's working capital is at $3,300 and all of the short-term debt could be paid in cash if required. So the company has done well to reassure its creditors about its ability to repay its debts. The company's investors saw a cash return on their investments in the form of a dividend, yet another sign of a healthy company. The company has very little debt in its structure and the company's management should be commended for increasing the wealth of the shareholders. A large proportion of the company's assets are non-current, and this should serve it well should it decide to borrow money as non-current debt since its equipment could be used as security for the debt. All in all, without doing a detailed analysis of the numbers and without knowing how the company fared one or more years prior, the company seems to be in a healthy financial position

IP3. (a)

Verbatim Developments Inc.
Income Statement
For Fiscal Year 2008

Revenues		$386,350	
Expenses			
Wages	$210,000		
Supplies	800		
Utilities	2,400		
Amortization	30,350	243,550	
Income Before Tax			$142,800
Income Tax Expense (40%)			57,120
Net Income		$ 85,680	

(b)

Verbatim Developments Inc.
Statement of Retained Earnings
For Fiscal Year 2008

Beginning Retained Earnings	$173,300
Add: Net Income	85,680
Deduct: Dividends Declared	10,000
Ending Retained Earnings	$248,980

(c)

Verbatim Developments Inc.
Balance Sheets
As at December 31, 2007 and 2008

ASSETS	2007	2008	LIABILITIES	2007	2008
Cash	$ 12,400	$ 68,350	Bank Loan	$ 94,500	$ 89,250
Accounts Receivable	174,600	239,550	Accounts Payable	24,300	3,500
Office Supplies	1,600	1,200	Wages Payable	33,100	48,100
Equipment	415,400	415,400	Utilities Payable	2,250	650
Accum. Amortization,			Taxes Payable	12,400	29,520
Equipment	(89,150)	(119,500)	Dividends Payable	0	10,000
			EQUITY		
			Share Capital	175,000	175,000
			Retained Earnings	173,300	248,980
TOTAL	$514,850	$605,000	TOTAL	$514,850	$605,000

IP4. Note the following abbreviations: CA—current assets; NCA—non-current assets; CL—current liabilities; NCL—non-current liabilities.

July cash income:	$54,000
June current asset difference:[1]	(5,000)
July current asset difference:[2]	2,500
July change in NCA:[3]	(3,000)
June current liability difference:[4]	2,500
July current liability difference:[5]	(7,000)
July change in NCL:[6]	(6,000)
Accrual Income	$38,000

1	CA, June, cash basis:	$4,000
	CA, June, accrual basis:	9,000
		$5,000

Since June's accrual basis current assets were greater than the cash basis current assets, this means that $5,000 of June's revenues were not collected in June. When the $5,000 was collected in July (presumed), the revenue was recognized. With accrual accounting, however, that $5,000 is really June's revenue, not July's, and should be treated as Accounts Receivable. So, $5,000 is deducted from the $54,000 cash basis income.

2	CA, July, cash basis:	$6,000
	CA, July, accrual basis:	8,500
		$2,500

If current assets are greater under the accrual basis, it is likely due to accruing credit sales as Accounts Receivable. Hence, revenue is recognized and the $2,500 is added to the cash basis income. The only other current assets that might have increased are inventories and marketable securities. Neither of these affect revenue. If these were paid for in cash, there would not have been a net change in current assets. But if these were paid for on account, cash basis accounting would not have recognized the current asset increase and current liability increase, since no cash was exchanged. Only the accrual basis would have recognized such an increase in current assets and current liabilities. An increase in current liabilities, in this case, would not have meant an expense incurrence and would not, therefore, have affected income.

3	NCA, June, accrual basis:	$65,000
	NCA, July, accrual basis:	– 62,000
		$ 3,000

A decrease in non-current assets under accrual accounting is most likely due to amortization. As a non-cash expense, this is deducted from the cash basis income. If the reduction in non-current assets was due to a sale of assets, then income would be unaffected except as for a gain or loss on such sales. However, with cash basis accounting, such gains or losses are not cash gains or losses and would not have been included in the cash basis income figure anyway.

4	CL, June, cash basis:	$2,500
	CL, June, accrual basis:	5,000
		$2,500

If the accrual basis current liabilities are greater than the cash basis current liabilities, this means that there were $2,500 more in expenses incurred, on account, in June. If these bills were paid in July (presumed), July's cash basis income would be understated. So, the $2,500 is added back.

5	CL, July, cash basis:	$3,500
	CL, July, accrual basis:	10,500
		$ 7,000

If the current liabilities are greater under the accrual basis than the cash basis, there is another $7,000 that should be expensed against July's revenues. So, $7,000 is deducted from July's cash basis income. It is possible that the current liabilities recognized under accrual accounting were due to increases in current assets. If such were the case, no expense would be incurred and there would be no effect on income. But, as explained in note 2 above, the current asset increase would not have been recognized under that cash basis since no cash was exchanged. Since accrual accounting does recognize such a current asset increase, it would have been added to the cash basis income in note 2 above and deducted here, yielding a net zero effect on income.

6	NCL, July, cash basis:	$ 0
	NCL, July, accrual basis:	6,000
		$6,000

If non-current liabilities increased under accrual accounting, it was likely due to recognition of an expense that would be payable in the distant future (such as pensions). Hence, the $6,000 is deducted from the cash basis income to reflect this additional expense. If, however, the increase in non-current liabilities was not the result of an expense, but rather a non-current asset acquisition, for example, the non-current asset increase would have been added back in note 3 above and the increase in non-current liabilities deducted here, yielding a net zero effect on income since no expense was incurred.

EXPLORATIVE QUESTIONS

EQ1. An income statement is only one measure of performance. As will be seen in Chapter 4, cash flow is another measure. Just because the income statement is positive does not mean the company is doing well. If the company is not generating sufficient cash to pay its bills, or if the company has inordinately high debt relative to owners' interest, the company may not be as healthy as the income statement might otherwise lead you to believe. Les should also be concerned about what his balance sheet reveals. The balance sheet tells creditors or potential investors whether the company is in a stable financial position, or whether there is adequate security (collateral), or if other creditors may shut the business down tomorrow.

EQ2. A business is viewed as a going concern. We cannot, therefore, close the business down to see how much cash the owners could take out of it. As a going concern, the business must be periodically evaluated. This is done to tell the owners, and other interested parties such as creditors, how well or how poorly the company is faring. This evaluation takes the form of the balance sheet, income statement, and statement of retained earnings. These statements keep score, if you will, of the results of decisions made by management and owners who direct management. The score is kept to determine whether the decisions being made are indeed good for the company and whether other decisions need to be made to take advantage of opportunities (such as investing in other companies) or to solve problems (such as cash shortages due to credit customers who do not pay on time).

The business exists to increase the wealth of the owners. This wealth does not come in the form of cash, necessarily, but rather in the form of ownership interest. If owners' interest is increased, they have more of a stake in the company. In other words, they have more of a claim on the company's assets. Owners should not be interested solely in what cash they can take out of the company, but also in what financial interest they have in the company. Financial statements are prepared to show owners (and others) whether their interest has been increased or diminished. If they are fortunate, they may receive cash from dividends to the company, but this should not be their sole objective.

CHAPTER 4
MEASURING AND EVALUATING CASH FLOW

LEARNING OBJECTIVES

After completing Chapter 4, you should:

- understand the various components of a cash flow statement;
- intuitively understand the derivation of the cash flow statement;
- appreciate the interdependence of the cash flow statement and the other three financial statements discussed so far;
- recognize the importance of cash flow and how it differs from income;
- be able to prepare a simple cash flow statement; and
- understand the purpose of cash flow information in financial analysis.

CHAPTER SUMMARY

4.1 Chapter Introduction: Measuring and Evaluating Cash Flow

- It is not sufficient in financial analysis to focus on the three statements you have seen so far. It is also necessary to evaluate a company's cash management.
- The cash flow statement is derived from the balance sheet, income statement, and statement of retained earnings.

4.2 The Purpose of Cash Flow Analysis

- Remembering that there is a difference between cash basis income and accrual income, it should be apparent that an important aspect of company health is the ability to generate cash.
- Accrual basis income does not include certain cash inflows (such as bank loans) and outflows (such as asset purchases). Cash income does not include these examples of cash flows either, since they are neither revenues nor expenses, and also excludes non-cash revenues (such as credit sales) and non-cash expenses (such as amortization).
- Cash, and not income, is critical to survival. As some put it: "Cash is king."
- The purpose of the cash flow statement is to show how a company has come up with and used cash.

4.3 The Cash Flow Statement

- Typically, in proper format, the cash flow statement is arranged according to those changes that are a result of **operating** activities, those that are a result of **financing** activities, and those that are a result of **investing** activities.
- The finished cash flow statement shows where cash and cash equivalents (CCE) came from and where they were used. The "bottom line" of the cash flow statement shows whether there was a net increase or a net decrease in CCE from the balance sheet at the beginning of a year to the balance sheet at the end of a year.

4.4 Cash Flow Analysis Using Receipts and Payments

- The simplest, most direct method of preparing the cash flow statement is to look at the Cash account.
- Cash flows into and out of the account will reveal the change in the account over a period of time.

4.5 Cash Flow Analysis Using Adjusted Accrual Income and Balance Sheet Changes

- In order to keep the balance sheet in balance, any transaction that affects cash must also affect some other account on the balance sheet.
- Since that is the case, we can examine the changes in these other *non-cash* accounts to determine how *cash* has been affected.
- The cash flow statement prepared in this manner lists all the changes to non-cash balance sheet accounts.
- Since we are trying to determine how balance sheet account changes have affected cash flow, we exclude all cash accounts, including those defined as CCE, in the preparation.
- In effect, by doing so, the bottom line of the cash flow statement shows us the net change in cash (CCE) caused by changes to the non-cash accounts on the balance sheet.
- To determine the effect of a change in cash, remember the following two assumptions:
    - increasing assets costs cash; and
    - increasing debt and contributed capital increases cash.
- To help you to intuitively understand the effect of balance sheet changes, ask yourself whether a change would increase or save cash, or whether it would decrease or tie up cash.
- Bear in mind that the cash flow statement is prepared from more than just the balance sheets of a company.
- We also use information from the income statement since we know that some of our accrual income is also cash income.
- We also use the statement of retained earnings since dividends, which appear on the cash flow statement, are ultimately paid out in cash to shareholders
- Do not expect to be able to re-create a company's cash flow statement. Although you may be given a cash flow statement and comparative balance sheets for two years, the cash flow statement you prepare may not be the same as that already prepared by the company, although the bottom line should be the same. The reason for this is that the balance sheet is a summary of many accounts. Working with a summary, then, will yield imprecision. The accountant for the company, on the other hand, is working with detailed information.
- As will be introduced in Chapter 8, sometimes assets are sold. If an asset is sold for more than its net book value (cost less accumulated amortization), there is a "gain on sale." If it is sold for less than book value, there is a "loss on sale." Gains on sales are added to earnings on the income statement, whereas losses are subtracted.

- For example, if a vehicle cost $15,000 and had depreciated by $6,000 after two years, its net book value would be $9,000. If it were sold at this point for $10,500, there would be a gain on sale of $1,500 ($10,500 – $9,000). The $1,500 is an additional earning added to the income statement.
- So, net income would include an extra $1,500 from this sale. Yet, it is not additional cash flow. The additional cash flow was $10,500. These proceeds are shown on the cash flow statement in the Investing section as an increase in cash on the disposal of assets. The $1,500 is a book gain, not a cash gain. As a result, it is subtracted on the cash flow statement in the Operations section to adjust accrual income to a cash basis.
- By similar reasoning, losses on sales are added back on the cash flow statement.
- As another nuance, sometimes liabilities are created that do not affect cash. Increases in such liabilities, then, do not increase cash and vice versa. For example, a pension liability would be created by a pension expense, but cash may not actually be paid for some time.
- In this case, an expense is recognized, thus having reduced income, but no cash is paid out. Thus, such non-current accrued liability additions are added back on the cash flow statement because these effectively reduced income but did not reduce cash.
- If non-current accrued liabilities are decreased, then it is treated as if a payment has been made and thus the decrease is subtracted on the cash flow statement.
- To summarize, we prepare the cash flow statement by starting with net income, adjusting it for any revenues or expenses that were not cash based, then adjusting it for any non-cash balance sheet account changes.

4.6 Demonstration Problem: Doing the Cash Flow Statement from Balance Sheet Changes

- This section in the chapter provides a demonstration of how to use balance sheet changes and net income adjustments to analyze cash flow for Simplistic Enterprises Ltd. using the indirect method.

4.7 Interpreting A Company's Cash Flow Statement

- Using the cash flow statement to explain a company's performance is best done by carefully scrutinizing the cash flow statement line by line.
- It is necessary to attempt to link cash flow statement results to other statements and certainly to other information the company may provide you.
- To explain an observation on the cash flow statement, try to establish some cause. For example, if, in the Financing section, the cash flow statement shows several asset disposals, thus bringing in cash, could it be that the company is liquidating old assets in order to acquire new ones in the near future? Or could it be that the company has divested a subsidiary? Other information is needed to answer these questions.
- Also, compare the major sources of cash versus the major uses of cash. For example, was the major source of cash financing and a major use of cash investing? This might suggest that the company has borrowed to purchase new assets.

- It is impossible to generalize conclusions about the cash flow statement. The best advice at this point to explain observations is to establish relations with other cash flow statement items or other information the company may have provided.

4.8 Cash Flow and The Manager

- Earning income is not the only responsibility of management.
- Of prime importance is the ability of the company to meet its obligations when they come due. Bills are paid in cash, not income. Therefore, cash management is vital.

4.9 Revisiting Cash Basis Versus Accrual Basis Accounting

- In preparing an accrual basis income statement, not all revenue and expenses necessarily involve cash.
- For example, a company can make a credit sale, thus recording revenue, but not receive cash immediately.
- Similarly, a company can incur an expense such as amortization but not have to disburse any cash for that expense.
- As a result, accrual income captures transactions *not* involving cash as well as those that do.
- In preparing the cash flow statement using the indirect method, the objective is to adjust accrual income to a true measure of actual cash flow.
- The following example is identical in principle, but different in illustration, to that on page 254 of your text:

Cash in bank, beginning of this month		$ 1,400
Cash Receipts:		
Collections on last month's revenue	$ 800	
Collections on this month's revenue	37,600	
Deposits received (to be earned next month)	500	
Additional long-term debt	3,000	
Proceeds on sale of office computer	250	42,150
		43,550
Cash Disbursements:		
Payment for last month's expenses	$ 450	
Payment for this month's expenses	30,650	
Prepayment of next month's expenses	750	
Payments on long-term debt	1,500	
Purchase of new office computer	7,200	40,550
Cash in bank, end of this month		$ 3,000

Other Information:

Amortization on the computer this month	$300
Sales from this month yet be collected	$1,150
Expenses from this month yet to be paid	$950
Book value of the computer at the time of sale	$400

The **cash basis income** for the month would be:

Operating receipts: ($800 + $37,600 + $500)	$ 38,900
Operating expenditures: ($450 + $30,650 + $750)	(31,850)
Cash income for the month	$ 7,050

Note that the opening cash balance ($1,400) plus the cash income ($7,050) does not equal the ending cash balance ($3,000). This is because there are non-operating receipts and non-operating expenditures involving cash.

Remember, the income statement measures only income arising from operating revenues and expenses. The cash flow statement accounts for non-operating cash receipts and disbursements (investing and financing activities) in addition to cash flow from operations.

So, to account for the total increase in cash (from $1,400 to $3,000):

Cash income for the month	$ 7,050
Non-operating cash receipts ($3,000 + $250)	3,250
Non-operating cash expenditures ($1,500 + $7,200)	(8,700)
Net cash increase	$ 1,600

The **accrual basis income** for the month would be:

Revenue ($37,600 + $1,150)		$38,750
Expenses:		
General ($30,650 + $950)	$31,600	
Amortization	300	31,900
Operating income		6,850
Loss on sale ($250 – $400)		(150)
Income for the month		$ 6,700

EXERCISES

E1. Cash Flow Statement Format
What are the major sections of a cash flow statement? Are these the same for all companies?

E2. Cash Equivalents
How is cash different from cash and cash equivalents?

E3. Cash vs. Accrual Income
Is income the same as cash? Explain.

E4. Define Cash Flow

Explain to someone who has never been exposed to accounting the concept of a cash flow statement. What is it intended to measure? How is it prepared?

E5. Cash Change Effects

Paramount Corporation's cash flow statement for 2007 showed the following:

Cash from Operations:	$ 84,600
Dividends declared and paid:	6,300
Cash flow from Investing:	(21,750)
Cash flow from Financing	(12,900)

(a) What was the change in CCE for the year?

(b) How would the cash flow statement have been different if the dividends had been declared but not yet paid?

(c) Suppose that the company has sold a delivery van for $5,200. The van had a net book value of $6,700 at the time of sale. What would be the effect of this sale on the cash flow statement?

E6. Deduce Cash Effect

Suppose that Staples Ltd. showed the following information:

End of 2006: Non-current assets, net	$271,400
End of 2007: Non-current assets, net	$341,150

Amortization expense for 2007 was $22,600. The company sold three vehicles at the end of 2007 for $34,600. These vehicles had accumulated amortization of $27,450. The vehicles had cost $48,000. The company replaced these with four new ones at the end of 2007.

(a) Was there a gain or loss on the sale of the three vehicles? What was the amount?

(b) Assuming that no other non-current assets were bought or sold, what was the apparent amount spent on the new vehicles?

(c) What are the cash flow statement effects of these non-current asset changes?

PROBLEMS

P1. Cash vs. Income

Why is it possible for a company reporting significant net income to go out of business? What information is provided by the cash flow statement that is not provided by the income statement?

P2. Cash Flow Statement Preparation

Following are two years of account balance data for ProFormance Works Ltd. Prepare an income statement for 2007, a cash flow statement for 2007, the closing entries, and then prepare the balance sheet as at the year ending 2007.

Additional information:

(i) The change in warranty liability was entirely due to the amount of warranty expense estimated for the year.
(ii) The change in pension liability was entirely due to the amount of pension expense estimated for the year.
(iii) No capital assets were sold during the year.
(iv) Dividends of $5,000 were declared and paid.

ProFormance Works Ltd.

	2007	2006
Accounts payable	42,250	47,200
Accounts receivable	46,950	43,350
Accumulated amortization—building	68,400	61,900
Accumulated amortization—vehicles	40,500	34,100
Bank loan (5 years)	21,500	0
Building at cost	134,200	130,650
Cash (deposits and on hand)	11,250	7,350
Current income tax liability	1,100	1,550
Vehicles at cost	80,700	57,300
Warranty liability	13,100	12,250
Bank overdraft	31,600	27,050
Inventories	74,750	59,300
Investment in subsidiary	3,250	9000
Land	40,000	40,000
Mortgage (due 2010)	79,400	89,250
Pension liability	16,050	11,800
Prepaid insurance	150	700
Retained earnings	43,550	48,550
Share capital	19,000	14,000
Cost of goods sold	178,350	
Amortization expense—building	6,500	
Amortization expense—vehicles	6,400	
Income tax expense	3,850	
Warranty expense	850	
Administrative expenses	81,950	
Pension expense	4,250	
Interest expense	4,250	
Revenue	301,200	

P3. Balance Sheet Preparation from Cash Flow Statement

Below are the balance sheet (2007) and the cash flow statement (for 2008) for WunderWerks Inc. Prepare the balance sheet as at October 31, 2008.

WunderWerks Inc.
Balance Sheet
As at Fiscal Year-End, October 31, 2007

Assets		Liabilities	
Current Assets:		Current Liabilities:	
Cash	$ 6,030	Demand Loan	$ 28,300
Term Deposits	15,000	Trade Payables	39,120
Receivables	68,200	Salaries Payable	6,690
Inventories	142,600	Income Tax Payable	14,230
Office Supplies	440		88,340
Prepaid Expenses	40,830		
	273,100	Non-Current Liabilities:	
		Mortgage	728,400
Non-Current Assets:		Machinery Loan	164,900
Land at Cost	588,000	Warranty Liability	16,820
Buildings	812,000	Pension Liability	112,450
Accum. Amort.—Bldg.	(162,000)		1,022,570
Machinery	336,000	Shareholders' Equity:	
Accum. Amort.—Mach.	(54,000)	Share Capital	210,500
	1,520,000	Retained Earnings	471,690
			682,190
TOTAL ASSETS	$1,793,100	TOTAL LIAB. & EQUITY	$1,793,100

WunderWerks Inc.
Cash Flow Statement
For the Year Ending October 31, 2008

OPERATIONS:		
Net income for the year	$164,800	
Adjustments for expenses and revenues not involving cash:		
Amortization expense—building	42,000	
Amortization expense—machinery	18,000	
Warranty expense	5,400	
Estimated pension expense	45,480	
Changes in non-cash working capital:		
Receivables	(22,500)	
Office supplies	170	
Inventories	(12,650)	
Prepaid expenses	13,570	
Trade payables	9,230	
Salaries payable	4,290	
Incomes taxes payable	(2,350)	$ 265,440
INVESTING ACTIVITIES:		
Acquisitions of non-current assets:		
Building	(386,000)	
Machinery	(42,000)	
	(428,000)	
Sales proceeds		
Land (cost $190,000)	190,000	
Building (cost $134,000)*	86,000	
	276,000	(152,000)
FINANCING ACTIVITIES:		
Dividends declared and paid	(24,000)	
Share issue	48,000	
Machinery loan	28,200	
Mortgage payments	(62,800)	(10,600)
Change in cash and cash equivalents		$ 102,840

Reconciliation of cash and cash equivalents:	
Increase in cash	$ 48,220
Increase in term deposits	50,070
Decrease in demand loan	4,550
Increase in cash and cash equivalents	$102,840

*The building sold for its net book value.

Additional information:

i. The change in warranty liability was entirely due to the amount of warranty expense estimated for the year.
ii. The change in pension liability was entirely due to the amount of pension expense estimated for the year.

P4. Cash Flow Statement Preparation

Tok Supplies Ltd. had the following summarized balance sheets at the end of 2007 and 2008. Using these and the additional information below, prepare the cash flow statement for 2008.

	2007	2008
Cash equivalent assets	$ 37,323	$ 45,414
Other current assets	322,335	428,301
Non-current assets, net	746,982	834,678
Total assets	$1,106,640	$1,308,393
Cash equivalent liabilities	$ 23,751	$ 29,232
Other current liabilities	236,466	307,719
Non-current liabilities	457,533	456,228
Share capital	156,600	208,800
Retained earnings	232,290	306,414
Total liabilities and equity	$1,106,640	$1,308,393

Additional information:

(i) Net income in 2008 was $100,224.
(ii) Pension expense resulting in a non-current pension liability was $22,968.
(iii) For the first time in the company's history, dividends of $26,000 were declared, $4,000 of which were still unpaid (within other current liabilities) at year-end.
(iv) The company sold machinery that had cost $65,250 for $17,900. Accumulated amortization on this machinery was $45,153.
(v) Amortization expense for the year was $98,397.
(vi) Non-current assets were acquired for $206,190.

P5. Cash Flow Statement Preparation

Below are two years of account balance data for Western Hardware Limited. The 2006 account balances are post-closing, whereas the 2007 account balances are pre-closing. Prepare a cash flow statement for 2007. (Hint: You need first to calculate 2007's net income.)

	2007	2006
Cash (deposits and on hand)	$ 4,725	$ 3,675
Temporary investments	0	4,500
Accounts receivable	23,475	21,675
Inventories	31,125	29,650
Prepaid insurance	75	350
Investment in subsidiary	6,250	0
Building at cost	67,100	65,325
Accumulated amortization, building	34,200	30,950
Vehicles at cost	40,350	28,650
Accumulated amortization, vehicles	19,350	17,050
Land	20,000	20,000
Overdraft line of credit	15,800	13,525
Accounts payable	21,125	23,600
Current income tax liability	550	775
Bank loan (due 2007)	10,750	0
Loan from shareholder (due 2007)	7,500	8,750
Mortgage (due 2009)	32,200	35,875
Pension liability	8,025	5,900
Warranty liability	6,550	6,125
Share capital	9,500	7,000
Retained earnings	21,775	24,275
Revenue	150,600	
Cost of goods sold	82,750	
Amortization expense, building	3,250	
Amortization expense, vehicles	3,200	
Income tax expense, current portion	1,925	
Warranty expense	425	
Gain on vehicle sale	100	
Administrative expenses	40,975	
Pension expense	8,550	
Interest expense	3,850	

Additional information:

(i) During the year, a vehicle trailer that had cost $1,300 was sold for $500. At the time of sale, it had accumulated amortization of $900. Vehicle trailers are considered part of the Vehicles at Cost account.

(ii) The change in warranty liability was entirely due to the amount of warranty expense estimated for the year.

(iii) The change in pension liability was due to estimated pension expense for the year of $8,550, less a pension payment of $6,425 to a retired employee.

(iv) A dividend of $2,500 was declared and paid.

P6. Balance Sheet Preparation from Cash Flow Statement

Below are the balance sheet (2005) and the cash flow statement (for 2006) for Nasim Manufacturing Inc. Prepare the balance sheet as at June 30, 2006.

Nasim Manufacturing Inc.
Balance Sheet
As at Fiscal Year-End, June 30, 2005

Assets		Liabilities	
Current Assets:		Current Liabilities:	
Cash	$ 3,015	Demand Loan	$ 14,150
Term Deposits	7,500	Trade Payables	19,560
Receivables	34,100	Salaries Payable	3,345
Inventories	71,300	Income Tax Payable	7,115
Office Supplies	220		44,170
Prepaid Expenses	20,415		
	136,550	Non-Current Liabilities:	
		Mortgage	364,200
Non-Current Assets:		Machinery Loan	82,450
Land at Cost	294,000	Warranty Liability	
			8,410
Buildings	406,000	Pension Liability	56,225
Accum. Amort.—Bldg.	(81,000)		511,285
Machinery	168,000	Shareholders' Equity:	
Accum. Amort.—Mach.	(27,000)	Share Capital	105,250
	760,000	Retained Earnings	235,845
			341,095
TOTAL ASSETS	$896,550	TOTAL LIAB. & EQUITY	$896,550

Nasim Manufacturing Inc.
Cash Flow Statement
For the Year Ending June 30, 2006

OPERATIONS:		
Net income for the year	$64,400	
Adjustments for expenses and revenues not involving cash:		
Amortization expense—building	21,000	
Amortization expense—machinery	9,000	
Warranty expense	2,700	
Estimated pension expense	22,740	
Loss on sale of land	45,000	
Gain on sale of building	(27,000)	
Changes in non-cash working capital:		
Receivables	(11,250)	
Office supplies	85	
Inventories	(6,325)	
Prepaid expenses	6,785	
Trade payables	4,615	
Salaries payable	2,145	
Incomes taxes payable	(1,175)	$132,720
INVESTING ACTIVITIES:		
Acquisitions of non-current assets:		
Building	(193,000)	
Machinery	(21,000)	
	(214,000)	
Sales proceeds		
Land (cost $95,000)	50,000	
Building (cost $67,000)	70,000	
	120,000	(94,000)
FINANCING ACTIVITIES:		
Dividends declared and paid	(12,000)	
Share issue	24,000	
Machinery loan	14,100	
Mortgage payments	(31,400)	
Pension payments	(14,550)	(19,850)
Change in cash and cash equivalents		$18,870

Reconciliation of cash and cash equivalents:	
Increase in cash	$ 6,110
Increase in term deposits	10,485
Decrease in demand loan	2,275
Increase in cash and cash equivalents	$18,870

P7. Cash Flow Statement Preparation

Below are two years of account balance data for OmniHorizon Limited. The 2005 account balances are post-closing, whereas the 2006 account balances are pre-closing. Prepare a cash flow statement for 2006 and define the accounts used in the calculation of cash and cash equivalents.

	2006	2005	Change
Cash (deposits and on hand)	$8,140	$2,820	$5,320
Short-term deposits	$1,400	$1,200	$200
Temporary investments	$0	$6,300	($6,300)
Accounts receivable	$32,865	$30,345	$2,520
Inventories	$43,575	$41,510	$2,065
Prepaid insurance	$105	$490	($385)
Investment in subsidiary	$8,750	$0	$8,750
Building at cost	$93,940	$91,455	$2,485
Accumulated amortization, building	($47,880)	($43,330)	($4,550)
Vehicles	$56,490	$40,110	$16,380
Accumulated amortization, vehicles	($27,090)	($23,870)	($3,220)
Furniture at cost	$14,050	$11,325	$2,725
Accumulated amortization, furniture	($3,650)	($3,195)	($455)
Land	$28,000	$28,000	$0
Overdraft line of credit	$26,145	$18,935	$7,210
Accounts payable	$29,575	$33,040	($3,465)
Current income tax liability	$770	$1,085	($315)
Dividends payable	$3,000	$0	$3,000
Bank loan (due 2008)	$24,050	$9,000	$15,050
Loan from shareholder (due 2008)	$10,500	$12,250	($1,750)
Mortgage (due 2011)	$45,080	$50,225	($5,145)
Pension liability	$11,235	$8,260	$2,975
Warranty liability	$9,170	$8,575	$595
Share capital	$14,700	$11,000	$3,700
Retained earnings	$30,790	$30,790	
Revenue	$210,840		
Cost of goods sold	$115,850		
Amortization expense, building	$4,550		
Amortization expense, vehicles	$4,480		
Amortization expense, furniture	$730		
Income tax expense	$2,695		
Warranty expense	$595		
Gain on vehicle trailer sale	$140		
Loss on furniture sale	$175		
Administrative expenses	$57,365		
Pension expense	$11,970		
Interest expense	$5,390		

Additional information:

(i) During the year, a vehicle trailer that had cost $1,820 was sold for $700. At the time of sale, it had accumulated amortization of $1,260. Vehicle trailers are considered part of the Vehicles account.

(ii) The change in warranty liability was entirely due to the amount of warranty expense for the year.

(iii) The change in pension liability was due to estimated pension expense for the year of $11,970, less a pension payment of $8,995 to a retired employee.

(iv) A dividend of $3,500 was declared.

(v) Furniture costing $1,300 was sold for $850. At the time of sale, it had accumulated amortization of $275.

INTEGRATIVE PROBLEMS

IP1. Cash Flow Statement Preparation and Analysis

Parkview Cleaners Ltd. has just finished its third year of operation.

(a) Prepare a cash flow statement for 2006 from the information given below.

(b) How did Parkview Cleaners manage its cash during fiscal 2006?

(c) If you were the management of Parkview, how would you explain the company's performance?

Parkview Cleaners Limited
Statement of Income
Year Ended March 31, 2006

Revenues		119,000
Expenses:		
Office	27,000	
Salaries/Wages	72,000	
Utilities	6,000	
Amortization	17,250	122,250
Income Before Income Tax		(3,250)
Income Tax Expense		0
Net Income		(3,250)

Parkview Cleaners Limited
Balance Sheet
As at Fiscal Year-End, March 31, 2006 and 2005
($000s)

Assets	2006	2005
Current Assets:		
Cash	21,000	49,000
Term Deposits	4,000	0
Receivables	77,000	81,000
Total Current:	102,000	130,000
Non-Current Assets:		
Buildings	155,000	155,000
Accum. Amort.	(23,250)	(15,500)
Equipment	95,000	82,000
Accum. Amort.	(26,500)	(17,000)
Total Non-Current	200,250	204,500
Total Assets	302,250	334,500
Liabilities		
Current Liabilities:		
Demand Loan	36,000	110,000
Trade Payables	42,000	17,000
Income Tax Payable	5,000	3,000
Total Current	83,000	130,000
Non-Current Liabilities:		
Mortgage	110,000	110,000
Long-Term Loans	18,000	10,000
Total Non-Current	128,000	120,000
Shareholders' Equity		
Share Capital	70,000	60,000
Retained Earnings	21,250	24,500
Total Equity	91,250	84,500
Total Liab. & Equity	302,250	334,500

IP2. Cash Change Effects

In the course of a fiscal year, a company's accounting decisions will affect its cash position as given by the cash flow statement. Discuss how the following decisions would affect the balance sheet, the income statement, and/or the cash flow statement in any given year:

(a) Air Canada adds four Boeing jets to its fleet and finances the acquisition through a share issue rather than long-term debt.
(b) MacMillan Bloedel acquires and harvests 10,000 hectares of timber land.
(c) The Delta Hotel adds a private banquet facility space and arranges long-term debt financing to pay for the expansion.
(d) General Motors ceases operations at one of its Canadian assembly plants.
(e) SPAR Aerospace renegotiates some of its short-term demand loans into long-term debt obligations.
(f) Bell Canada accepts a regulatory ruling to scale back a rate increase and retroactively pay subscribers fees collected in excess of the regulatory ruling rate.

IP3. Journal Entries and Statement Preparation

Chiu & Company, Ltd., a privately owned medical clinic, reported the following balance sheet:

Chiu & Co., Ltd
Balance Sheet
As at June 30, 2006

Current Assets:			**Current Liabilities:**	
Cash		$14,100	Operating (Demand) Loan	$9,200
Supplies		18,400	Accounts Payable	92,300
Receivables*		210,200		
Non-Current Assets:			**Non-Current Liabilities:**	
Lab Equipment	294,000		Bank Loan	412,000
Accum. Amort.	(29,400)	264,600		
Examination Room Equipment	255,000			
Accum. Amort.	(25,500)	229,500	**Shareholders' Equity:**	
Office Equipment	66,000		Share Capital	350,000
Accum. Amort.	(6,600)	59,400	Retained Earnings	69,500
Building	144,000			
Accum. Amort.	(7,200)	136,800		
Total Assets		$933,000	**Total Liab. & Equity**	$933,000

* Uncollected billings to provincial health care. Ten percent of these were prior month billings.

In July, the following events transpired:

(i) Diagnostic lab equipment having a useful life of 10 years was purchased for $12,000 cash at the end of July.
(ii) Patient billings (billed to provincial health care) totalled $194,900.
(iii) A doctor was hired at a salary of $77,500 plus full dental and health care coverage benefits.

(iv) The examination rooms were repainted at a cost of $4,000. The bill is not payable for 45 days.
(v) The office computer, having cost $6,000 and having a book value of $3,000, was traded in for a better model costing $7,000 at the end of July. The trade-in value was $1,000.
(vi) 90% of June's billings to health care were collected and the balance of May's billings were collected.
(vii) $3,000 of supplies were used and not replenished.
(viii) One-quarter of the operating loan was repaid.
(ix) A $4,000 payment on account was made to suppliers.
(x) Salaries of $240,000 for July were to be paid August 3.
(xi) The building is depreciated over 20 years; all other non-current assets are depreciated over 10 years. All are depreciated using the straight-line basis (effectively, divide the number of years into the historical cost of the asset to determine the annual amortization expense).

(a) Prepare journal entries (if any) for the events.
(b) If no receivables are collected before payroll is due, will the company meet payroll?
(c) What is the net income for July (ignoring taxes)?
(d) How has the working capital ratio changed from June?
(e) Prepare a cash flow statement for July.
(f) Comment on the company's change in position from June to July.

EXPLORATIVE QUESTIONS

EQ1. Cash vs. Income

Why do you suppose stock market analysts seemingly pay closer attention to income figures of publicly traded companies than to their cash flows?

EQ2. Cash Flow Statement Analysis

If you were to review a company's financial statements and the company's cash flow statement showed a reduction in cash, is this cause for alarm? What else might you look for to comfortably recommend investment in such a company?

EQ3. Cash vs. Income

Which do you think warrants more attention: managing income, or managing cash flow? Would your answer change depending on whether the business in question was publicly traded, a sole proprietorship, or a privately held company?

SOLUTIONS

EXERCISES

E1. There are usually three major sections on a cash flow statement:

- cash generated from (used by) operations;
- cash provided from (used by) financing activities (including dividends); and
- cash used in investing activities.

All companies will use a cash flow statement that follows the above format.

E2. Cash is not the same as cash and cash equivalents (CCE). CCE includes near-cash assets and near-cash liabilities; that is, items that represent ways of holding cash (e.g., marketable securities) or getting cash (e.g., a bank demand loan).

E3. Income is not the same as cash. Revenues and expenses constitute income. But not all revenue is received in the form of cash (i.e., some is on account/credit) and not all expenses are paid in cash (i.e., some are paid on account/credit).

E4. Management of a company's cash is a different problem altogether from earning income. The income statement reveals how the company accounts for its revenues and expenses on an accrual basis; that is, whether or not cash has been received for such revenues or paid for such expenses. Therefore, the cash flow statement is a means of showing how a company has managed its cash.

In the accounting perspective, cash is not simply cash in the bank; it is also cash that has been invested in short-term investments that could be retrieved in a hurry if need be. There is also "negative cash," meaning ways of getting and owing cash quickly (e.g., bank overdrafts). In effect, then, cash is really cash and cash equivalents. Income and cash flow should move in the same direction. Generally, a company earning good income will also be improving its cash flow. If it is not, this is cause for attention since the company would be posting good earnings, but these earnings are obviously not in cash and it needs cash to pay its bills.

To prepare the cash flow statement, the starting point is to take net income for a period and adjust it for items that did not involve cash receipts and payments. This adjustment process produces a figure showing the net amount of cash inflow or outflow. For example, if accounts receivable increased in a period, this means that sales were generated but not for cash. So, the income figure would be reduced by the increase in accounts receivable to adjust it for those revenues involving only cash. Similarly, if the company had a tax expense (which would have been deducted in calculating net income), but did not pay these taxes as yet (and called it tax payable), such an expense would be added back to net income since cash was not dispensed. Other adjustments would include any changes in non-current assets (either using up cash or freeing up cash), changes in financing activities such as borrowing more money (which would not have shown up on the income statement except in the form of interest expense), and paying dividends, if any, which also would not have appeared on the income statement.

E5. (a) $84,600 – $21,750 – $19,200* = $43,650 *$12,900 + $6,300

(b) Cash Flow from Operations would be $6,300 higher since there would be a current liability of Dividends Payable. Dividends declared of $6,300 would still be deducted in the Financing section but would be offset by the current liability. If dividends are declared but not paid, $6,300 of cash outflow is saved. Hence, compared to the current cash flow statement, the change in CCE is increased by $6,300.

Alternatively, it is possible to ignore altogether any dividends declared (and unpaid); hence the change in CCE is $6,300 greater than is currently the case. It is also possible to have the following in the Financing section:

Dividends Declared	($6,300)
Adjustment for Changes in Dividends Payable	$6,300

Again the change in CCE is $6,300 higher than the current cash flow statement reveals.

(c) There would be a loss on sale of $1,500. Such a loss would be deducted in the determination of net income. The loss would, therefore, be added back to net income in the Operating section of the cash flow statement, since it was a non-cash reduction of net income. The sale proceeds of $5,200 would be added to cash flow in the Investing section.

E6. (a)

Selling price:	$34,600
Net book value of assets: ($48,000 – $27,450)	$20,550
Gain on sale:	$14,050

(b) Let X equal the value of new vehicles purchased:

$271,400 – $48,000 + $27,450 – $22,600 + X = $341,150

X = $112,900

c)

Operating section:	Add back $22,600
	Deduct $14,050
Investing section:	Add $34,600
	Deduct $112,900

PROBLEMS

P1. Despite strong earnings, a company may be cash poor. This, in itself, is not disastrous unless the company cannot meet its debt obligations as they come due. It is one thing to earn income but quite another to manage earning and spending cash. It is this cash management ability that the cash flow statement shows and that the income statement cannot show.

P2. Income Statement

ProFormance Works Ltd.
Income Statement
Year Ending July 2007

Revenues		$301,200
Cost of Goods Sold		178,350
Gross Profit		131,850
Operating Expenses:		
Amortization—Building	6,500	
Amortization—Vehicle	6,400	
Administrative	81,950	
Warranty Expense	850	
Pension	4,250	99,100
Income Before Interest & Tax		23,750
Interest Expense		4,250
Income Before Tax		19,500
Income Tax Expense—Current		3,850
Net Income		$ 14,800

Closing Entries

Retained Earnings	286,400	
Cost of Goods Sold		178,350
Amortization Expense—Building		6,500
Amortization Expense—Vehicles		6,400
Income Tax Expense—Current Portion		3,850
Warranty Expense		850
Administrative Expenses		81,950
Pension Expense		4,250
Interest Expense		4,250
Revenues	301,200	
Retained Earnings		301,200

Balance Sheet

ProFormance Works Ltd.
Balance Sheet
As at Year Ending July 2007

ASSETS		**LIABILITIES**	
Current		*Current*	
Cash	$ 11,250	Accounts Payable	$ 42,250
Accounts Receivable	46,950	Bank Loan	21,500
Prepaid Insurance	150	Income Tax Payable	1,100
Inventory	74,750	Overdraft	31,600
Total Current	133,100	Total Current	96,450
Non-Current		*Non-Current*	
Investment in Subsidiary	3,250	Pension Liability	16,050
Land	40,000	Mortgage	79,400
		Warranty Liability	13,100
Buildings	134,200		
Accum. Amort.	(68,400)	Total Non-Current	108,550
Vehicles	80,700		
Accum. Amort.	(40,500)	**EQUITY**	
Total Non-Current	146,000	Share Capital	19,000
		Retained Earnings	58,350
		Total Equity	77,350
Total Assets	$282,350	Total Liabilities & Equity	$282,350

ProFormance Works Ltd.
Cash Flow Statement
For the Year Ended 2007

OPERATIONS:		
Net income for the year	$14,800	
Adjustments for expenses and revenues not involving cash:		
Amortization expense—building	6,500	
Amortization expense—vehicles	6,400	
Estimated warranty expense	850	
Estimated pension expense	4,250	
Changes in non-cash working capital:		
Accounts receivable	(3,600)	
Inventories	(15,450)	
Prepaid insurance	550	
Accounts payable	(4,950)	
Current income tax liability	(450)	8,900
INVESTING ACTIVITIES:		
Acquisitions of non-current assets:		
Building	(3,550)	
Vehicles	(23,400)	
	(26,950)	
Sales proceeds		
Investment in subsidiary	5,750	(21,200)
FINANCING ACTIVITIES:		
Dividends declared and paid	(5,000)	
Share issue	5,000	
Bank loan	21,500	
Mortgage	(9,850)	11,650

Change in cash and cash equivalents (defined as Cash less Bank Overdraft)	($650)

CCE (2006) = $7,350 – $27,050 = ($19,700)
CCE (2007) = $11,250 – $31,600 = ($20,350)
Change in CCE ($650)

P3.

WunderWerks Inc.
Balance Sheet
As at Fiscal Year-End, October 31, 2008

Assets		**Liabilities**	
Current Assets:		Current Liabilities:	
Cash	$54,250	Demand Loan	$23,750
Term Deposits	65,070	Trade Payables	48,350
Receivables	90,700	Salaries Payable	10,980
Inventories	155,250	Income Tax Payable	11,880
Office Supplies	270	Total	94,960
Prepaid Expenses	27,260		
Total	363,700	Non-Current Liabilities:	
		Mortgage	665,600
Non-Current Assets:		Machinery Loan	193,100
Land at Cost	398,000	Warranty Liability	22,220
Buildings	1,064,000	Pension Liability	157,930
Accum. Amort.—Bldg.*	(156,000)	Total	1,009,750
Machinery	378,000		
Accum. Amort.—Mach.	(72,000)		
Total	1,612,000	**Shareholders' Equity:**	
		Share Capital	258,500
		Retained Earnings	612,490
		Total	870,990
TOTAL ASSETS	$2,004,800	TOTAL LIAB. & EQUITY	$2,004,800

With a selling price of $86,000 (from the cash flow statement) that was equivalent to its net book value, the building thus had accumulated amortization of $48,000 since the building cost was $134,000. So, $162,000 + $42,000 (amort. expense) – $48,000 = $156,000.

P4.

Tok Supplies Ltd.
Cash Flow Statement
For the Year Ended 2008

OPERATIONS		
Net income	100,124	
Amortization	98,397	
Loss on sale	2,197	
Pension expense	22,968	
Other current asset changes	(105,966)	
Other current liability changes (incl. dividends payable)	71,253	$188,973
INVESTING ACTIVITIES		
Acquisitions of non-current assets	(206,190)	
Sale proceeds	17,900	(188,290)

FINANCING ACTIVITIES		
Dividends declared	(26,000)	
Non-current liability changes	(24,273)	
Share capital	52,200	1,927
Change in cash and cash equivalents		2,610
Cash and cash equivalents, 2007		13,572
Cash and cash equivalents, 2008		$16,182

P5. Net income for 2007 is $5,775. This is revenues (including the gain) less all expenses (including cost of goods sold).

Western Hardware Ltd.
Cash Flow Statement
For the Year Ended 2007

OPERATIONS:		
Net income for the year	$5,775	
Adjustments for expenses and revenues not involving cash:		
Amortization expense—building	3,250	
Amortization expense—vehicles	3,200	
Warranty expense	425	
Estimated pension expense	8,550	
Gain on sale of vehicle trailer	(100)	
Changes in non-cash working capital:		
Accounts receivable	(1,800)	
Inventories	(1475)	
Prepaid insurance	275	
Accounts payable	(2475)	
Current income tax liability	(225)	15,400
INVESTING ACTIVITIES:		
Acquisitions of non-current assets:		
Investment in subsidiary	(6,250)	
Building	(1,775)	
Vehicles*	(13,000)	
	(21,025)	
Sales proceeds		
Vehicle trailer	500	(20,525)
FINANCING ACTIVITIES:		
Dividends declared and paid	(2,500)	
Share issue	2,500	
Bank loan	10,750	
Mortgage	(3,675)	
Loan from shareholder	(1,250)	
Pension payments	(6,425)	600
Change in cash and cash equivalents		($5,725)

*$28,650 + New acquisitions – 1,300 = $40,350; New acquisitions = $13,000

CCE (2006) = $3,675 + $4,500 – $13,525 =	($5,350)
CCE (2007) = $4,725 + $0 – $15,800 =	($11,075)
Change in CCE	($5,725)

P6.

Nasim Manufacturing Inc.
Balance Sheet
As at Fiscal Year-End, June 30, 2006

Assets		Liabilities	
Current Assets:		Current Liabilities:	
Cash	$ 9,125	Demand Loan	11,875
Term Deposits	17,985	Trade Payables	24,175
Receivables	45,350	Salaries Payable	5,490
Inventories	77,625	Income Tax Payable	5,940
Office Supplies	135	Total	47,480
Prepaid Expenses	13,630		
Total	163,850	Non-Current Liabilities:	
		Mortgage	332,800
Non-Current Assets:		Machinery Loan	96,550
Land at Cost	199,000	Warranty Liability	11,110
Buildings	532,000	Pension Liability	64,415
Accum. Amort.—Bldg.*	(78,000)	Total	504,875
Machinery	189,000		
Accum. Amort.—Mach.	(36,000)	Shareholders' Equity:	
Total	806,000		
		Share Capital	129,250
		Retained Earnings	288,245
		Total	417,495
TOTAL ASSETS	$969,850	TOTAL LIAB. & EQUITY	$969,850

* With a gain of $27,000 on the sale of a building, and a selling price of $70,000 (both figures from the cash flow statement), the building that was sold must have had a net book value of $43,000 and hence accumulated amortization of $24,000 since the building cost was $67,000. So, $81,000 + $21,000 – $24,000 (from building sold) = $78,000.

P7.

CCE (2005) = ($2,820 + $1,200 + $6,300) – $18,935 =	($8,615)
CCE (2006) = ($8,140 + $1,400 + $0) – $26,145 =	($16,605)
Change in CCE	($7,990)

OmniHorizon Ltd.
Cash Flow Statement
For the Year Ended 2006

OPERATIONS:		
Net income for the year	$7,180	
Adjustments for expenses and revenues not involving cash:		
Amortization expense (4,550 + 4,480 + 730)	9,760	
Warranty expense	595	
Pension expense	11,970	
Gain on sale	(140)	
Loss on sale	175	
Changes in non-cash working capital:		
Accounts receivable	(2,520)	
Inventory	(2,065)	
Prepaid insurance	385	
Accounts payable	(3,465)	
Current income tax liability	(315)	
Dividends payable	3,000	$ 24,560
INVESTING ACTIVITIES:		
Acquisitions of non-current assets:		
Investment in subsidiary	(8,750)	
Building	(2,485)	
Vehicles*	(18,200)	
Furniture**	(4,025)	
Sales proceeds		
Sales proceeds, vehicle	700	
Sale proceeds, furniture	850	(31,910)
FINANCING ACTIVITIES:		
Dividends declared	(3,500)	
Pension liability	(8,995)	
Bank loan	15,050	
Mortgage	(5,145)	
Shareholder loan	(1,750)	
Share capital	3,700	(640)
Change in cash and cash equivalents		$ (7,990)

*$40,110 + New acquisitions – $1,820 = $56,490; New acquisitions = $18,200
*$11,325 + New acquisitions – $1,300 = $14,050; New acquisitions = $4,025

INTEGRATIVE PROBLEMS

IP1. (a)

Parkview Cleaners Ltd.
Cash Flow Statement
For the Year Ended, March 31, 2006

Cash Flow from Operating Activities:	
Net Income	$ (3,250)
Amortization	17,250
Decreases (Increases) in Current Assets	4,000
Increase (Decreases) in Current Liabilities	27,000
	45,000
Cash Flow from Financing:	
Long-Term Loans	8,000
Share Capital	10,000
	18,000
Cash Flow from Investing Activities:	
Acquisition of Equipment	(13,000)
Net Increase (Decrease) in Cash and Cash Equivalents	50,000
Reconciliation of Cash and Cash Equivalents Change:	
Cash plus Term Deposits less Demand Loan, beginning of year	(61,000)
Cash plus Term Deposits less Demand Loan, end of year	(11,000)
	$ 50,000

(b) Cash and cash equivalents seemed to be reasonably well managed, increasing by $50,000. Most of this increase was due to being able to defer cash payment by increasing Trade Payables as well as to obtaining additional financing. The company controlled its cash expenditures, restricting them to purchases of new equipment.

(c) The company showed poor earnings because of substantial amortization charges. The company has obviously improved its cash position but is still not in the clear. This should be cause for worry to both the management and the company's creditors. It is somewhat surprising that the company was actually able to secure more trade credit given its precarious cash position. If the company's short-term debts were suddenly called, the company could be forced to liquidate. Since it has no inventories, this would mean that it would have to sell off its receivables (known as factoring) at less than 100 cents on the dollar.

It is clear that the company has improved its cash position, but it is also clear that it is carrying too many receivables and needs to collect on some of these. Additional financing will be difficult to secure if the company cannot somehow improve its working capital.

The focus of this company now should be on ensuring that debt is repaid as it becomes due. This means making credit-worthy sales and collecting on that credit.

IP2. (a)

Balance Sheet:	There is an equivalent increase in assets and share capital.
Income Statement:	The purchase has no effect.
Cash Flow:	Investing activities are increased (use up cash) while financing activities also increase (bringing in cash); net effect is zero (called "grossing up").

(b) Balance Sheet:

- With regard to the acquisition, if the purchase was paid for in cash, there would be no net effect on assets although the accounts would show different balances; if it was financed, assets and liabilities would increase.
- With regard to the harvesting, assets would be decreased due to depletion but would be increased due to creating inventories of harvested timber.

Income Statement:

- With regard to the acquisition, there would be no effect.
- With regard to the harvesting, depletion expense would be increased.

Cash Flow:

- With regard to the acquisition, investing activities increase, showing a usage of cash; if the acquisition was financed, financing activities increase, showing an inflow of cash.
- With regard to the harvesting, depletion expense would be increased and must be added back to cash flow from operations as a non-cash expense.

(c)

Balance Sheet:	There would be an equivalent increase in assets and liabilities.
Income Statement:	There would be no effect.
Cash Flow:	Investing activities increase (using cash) and financing activities increase (bringing in cash); net effect is zero (called "grossing up").

(d) Ceasing operations in itself has no effect on any financial statement.

(e)	Balance Sheet:	This is a re-arrangement of liabilities only; there is no net change.
	Income Statement:	There is no effect.
	Cash Flow:	If the demand loan is considered part of CCE, CCE decreases while financing activities increase, showing an inflow of the same amount; net effect on the total change in CCE is zero.
(f)	Balance Sheet:	Cash is reduced or accounts payable are increased.
	Income Statement:	An extraordinary expense is created, thus reducing income.
	Cash Flow:	If cash is paid, CCE is reduced but there is no effect on the cash flow statement other than the magnitude of the change in CCE to be explained; if accounts payable are used, the increase in the current liability saves the company cash and would be added back to net income.

IP3. (a) Explanations are excluded since they are given in the question.

		Debit	Credit
(i)	Lab Equipment	12,000	
	Cash		12,000
(ii)	Accounts Receivable	194,900	
	Revenue		194,900
(iii)	No transaction.		
(iv)	Maintenance Expense	4,000	
	Accounts Payable		4,000
(v)	Accum. Amort., Office Equip.	3,000	
	Loss on Trade-In	2,000	
	Office Equip.	7,000	
	Office Equip.		6,000
	Cash		6,000
(vi)	Cash	191,282*	
	Accounts Receivable		191,282
	* (10%)($210,200) = $21,020 collected from May (90%)($210,200 – $21,020) = $170,262		
(vii)	Supplies Expense	3,000	
	Supplies		3,000
(viii)	Operating Loan	2,300	
	Cash		2,300
(ix)	Accounts Payable	4,000	
	Cash		4,000

		Dr.	Cr.
(x)	Salaries Expense	240,000	
	Salaries Payable		240,000
(xi)	Amortization Expense	5,725	
	Accum. Amort., Office Equip.		550
	Accum. Amort., Exam. Room		2,125
	Accum. Amort., Lab Equip.		2,450
	Accum. Amort., Building		600

(b) The company will not meet payroll because the balance in cash is \$181,082 = (\$14,100 + \$191,282 – \$6,000 – \$12,000 – \$2,300 – \$4,000).

(c) Net income = \$194,900 – \$3,000 – \$240,000 – \$2,000 – \$4,000 – \$5,725 = (\$59,825)

(d) June: Current Assets = \$242,700
Current Liabilities = \$101,500
Current Ratio = \$242,700/\$101,500 = 2.39

July: Current Assets = \$410,300
Current Liabilities = \$339,200
Current Ratio = \$410,300/\$339,200 = 1.21

(e)

Chiu & Co., Ltd.
Cash Flow Statement
For the Month Ended July 31, 2006.

Net Income (Loss)		\$(59,825)
Non-Cash Items		
Amortization	5,725	
Trade-In Loss	2,000	7,725
Working Capital Changes		
Receivables	(3,618)	
Supplies	3,000	
Payables	240,000	239,382
Cash from Operations		187,282
Investing Activities:		
Office Equipment	(7,000)	
Lab Equipment	(12,000)	
Proceeds from Trade-In	1,000	(18,000)
Financing		0
Net Change in CCE		\$169,282

CCE, beginning of period:	\$4,900
CCE, end of period:	174,182
Net Change:	\$169,282

CCE is defined as cash less operating loan.

(f) While the company reported a loss for July, its more immediate concern is having sufficient cash to meet payroll when it comes due August 3. In such a case, it would seem that the company's only solution at this point is to seek an additional operating loan to cover the salaries payable while still keeping some cash on hand. Keep in mind that the problem is short-lived, since it is due to collect on receivables from patient billings. The operating loan is feasible and could be backed by the receivables. Since the receivables are due from a provincial treasury, payment is almost guaranteed and the receivables should thus provide adequate security. With the salaries paid, the working capital will not improve substantially since cash will be reduced and the operating loan increased.

That problem aside, the company's more inherent problem is a salaries expense that is clearly out of line with billings. Salaries are not usually subject to considerable variation. The hiring of the additional doctor, albeit not a transaction in itself, will have increased the monthly salaries expense by $6,458 ($77,500/12 months), not enough to account for the amount of the loss for the month. June's billings were also inadequate to cover the salaries expense (which must have been $240,000 – $6,458 = $233,542). June's billings were $189,180 ($210,200 – ((10%)($210,200)). So, at minimum, June saw a loss of $44,362 not including any other expenses. The simple problem, then, appears to be overstaffing or inadequate billings for the staff on hand.

EXPLORATIVE QUESTIONS

EQ1. Stock analysts seem to focus on the growth and earnings potential of companies. This is reflected in companies' ability to consistently generate strong or growing returns (i.e., income). Cash flow and income are generally positively correlated; that is, they move together. Over time, this has to be the case, since a prudent company will eventually collect on its receivables (getting cash from revenues) and sell its inventories (freeing up cash), while paying its debts (using cash to pay for expenses).

Stock market analysts do not pay attention only to income figures. A variety of analytical techniques pay close attention to balance sheet items as well. (These techniques are discussed in Chapter 10 of the text.) The clients of stockbrokers are interested in two things primarily: (1) increases in wealth brought about by an increase in the value of their stocks; and (2) increases in wealth brought about by receipt of dividends. The first of these is usually attained as a company shows improved earnings. The second of these is attained by the company's ability to pay cash. Naturally, then, cash management is important to stock analysts and brokers.

A company with strong earnings growth is worthless to a shareholder if the company is cash poor and declares bankruptcy.

Income reporting has become a focus of media attention since it is easy to understand. Stock analysts rely on income figures but do not use them solely to evaluate a company's affairs.

EQ2. If a cash flow statement showed a reduction in cash, it would not necessarily be cause for alarm. In any given period, a company might embark on an ambitious acquisition of assets. Assets make future growth possible. A company may also be spending cash on inventories in anticipation of a peak sales period ahead. This is not unusual in companies subject to seasonal sales. A company may also be paying down its debts hoping to improve its creditworthiness.

A reduction in cash may be cause for alarm for a variety of reasons. If inventories have been increasing without corresponding increases in income, the company is likely stockpiling inventory and unable to sell it. The company may also be granting credit extensively, thus building up accounts receivable. Long-held receivables bring into doubt the creditworthiness of some customers and raise the question of whether management is simply trying to post strong sales at the risk of defaulting receivables.

The gist of this discussion is that you must look at the various components of the cash flow statement to determine whether cash has been poorly or well managed. Even then, the cash flow statement doesn't tell the whole story and, for that reason, note disclosure exists to help statement readers understand particular activities affecting cash.

EQ3. It is not a question of which warrants more attention, managing cash or managing income. They are not substitutes for each other, nor are they polar opposites. What is more important to a reader depends on the characteristics of that reader. If you are a creditor, cash flow is considerably important to you. But your lending decision is not solely based on cash in the bank. After all, if a company had all the cash it needed, it would not likely need to borrow from you. Your lending decision will be based, in part, on the earnings potential of the company. Presumably, if the company can generate earnings, it will be able to generate cash since, ultimately, cash is the basis of exchange.

If you are a customer, you may be more concerned about cash flow rather than income since you may be seeking trade credit. For a company in a cash squeeze, trade credit is unlikely.

If you are from the Canada Revenue Agency, you are more likely concerned with income measurement for tax assessment. If taxes are owed, they ultimately have to be paid in cash and the worst-case scenario is for a company to declare bankruptcy. The Canada Revenue Agency should also be concerned with cash management, but it has the regulatory clout to be less concerned since it will be first in line in front of other creditors, in the event of bankruptcy, to lay claim to the proceeds from the liquidation of assets.

All told, this is a question of perspective. What is important depends on your relation to a company.

As to whether the business in question is a sole proprietorship, partnership, or corporation, cash is equally important to any form of business organization. Typically, however, cash management is more important to proprietorships or partnerships, since business income *is* personal income and, as such, there must be adequate cash to withdraw to meet the personal obligations of the owners. In corporations, business income is usually after paying salaries of employees. This could include paying salaries to owner–employees. In such a case, business income *is not* personal income and cash management is therefore not as important. But if the owners of a corporation are relying on dividend income, then cash management is quite important since dividends are paid out of cash, not income.

CHAPTER 5
STANDARDS AND PRINCIPLES SURROUNDING THE FINANCIAL STATEMENTS

LEARNING OBJECTIVES

After completing Chapter 5, you should:

- be aware of current historical developments in accounting;
- know what generally accepted accounting principles (GAAP) are;
- know why GAAP exist;
- understand, in principle, how GAAP affect financial statement use and preparation; and
- fundamentally understand that accounting for business organizations is different in form from accounting for non-business organizations.

CHAPTER SUMMARY

5.1 Chapter Introduction: Accounting Standards and Principles

- Generally accepted accounting principles (GAAP) are a system of principles and rules that govern how financial accounting information (not managerial accounting information) is calculated and presented.
- This does not mean that all financial accounting practices are completely regulated. Many accounting techniques are not governed by rules but are accepted as proper; there are other accounting problems to which rules would be difficult to apply and which therefore call upon professional judgment.
- Some of these principles are illustrated in assessing balance sheet values and accounting for corporate groups and not-for-profit organizations.
- To understand the development of GAAP requires a brief knowledge of accounting's history. This will help you understand why GAAP exist.

5.2 Using Principles to Produce Accounting Information

- GAAP encompass generally accepted and practised methods and concepts. This means that they do not fit every accounting circumstance.
- In accounting for a company, though, the accountants must decide which GAAP apply and how to apply such GAAP.
- Incorporated companies in Canada are obligated to adhere to the practices and methods set forth by the GAAP, but are allowed to exercise professional judgment in those rare areas of reporting where the GAAP are less clear.
- Various users rely on statements prepared in accordance with GAAP to make various decisions, such as lending to the company in question, buying that company's stock, evaluating the performance of senior officers of the company, or perhaps simply deciding whether or not to do business with the company.

- The underlying objective of financial reporting is to satisfy the need for information used in decision making.
- This decision making could be by managers, shareholders, potential investors, creditors, stock analysts, government regulators, and other interested parties.
- In deciding which GAAP to use and how, several decision criteria should be kept in mind:

    (1) The information provided in the statements should be relevant to the user, be delivered in a timely manner, and be material in nature. Professional judgment must be exercised in what constitutes materiality. Information is material if its omission or misstatement would influence or change a decision. Clearly, not every minute transaction needs to be described in detail.

    (2) The cost of preparing information should not exceed its benefit. The difficulty in using this as a decision criterion lies in determining the benefit derived by the users.

    (3) Selecting a GAAP may involve assessing the tax consequences associated with the principle. Tax treatment differs depending on accounting methods chosen.

    (4) The information gathered and the methods chosen may reflect the extent of internal control—that is, information—desired.

    (5) A company's unique circumstances may render certain GAAP more appropriate than others.

- GAAP try to reflect both practice and desired practice. The backbone of GAAP hinges on the following:

    (1) In measuring income, a tool often used to gauge corporate performance, the principles of recognition of income determining events (revenues and expenses) and that of matching should be employed. Matching is the practice of ensuring that the appropriate expenses are charged against the revenues that these expenses helped generate. In this way, income is properly determined.

    (2) Values used on financial statements should be conservative and reflect what was actually incurred or paid. This means that where there may be room for judgment, assets, income, and revenues should not be overstated, and liabilities, expenses, and losses should not be understated.

    (3) Information presented through the statements should be fair. What constitutes fair includes whether such information has been faithfully represented—that is, if its substance is reported, not just what is legally required. This means that statement preparers are obligated to present a sequence of events surrounding a financial transaction if that transaction is not, by itself, sufficiently clear.

- Fairness also requires consistency and comparability. You should be able to take the financial statements of the same company over two different time periods and compare the financial performance. If there have been accounting policy changes, these should be brought to your attention to signify that comparability may require more in-depth analysis.
- Furthermore, you should also be able to compare the performance of two different companies. Do recognize that complete comparability between companies is unlikely since each faces a different set of facts, objectives, and constraints.
- Naturally, users—and notably, auditors—expect that any information be verifiable; that is, that supporting evidence of the information presented is available to an independent observer.

5.3 An Example of Applying Accounting Principles to a Company

- The chapter uses the example of the Canadian Pacific Railroad to discuss some of the issues associated with choosing and applying accounting principles.

5.4 Financial Accounting Standards and Their Development

- The *CICA Handbook* is the most authoritative source of GAAP in Canada. However, it is not the only source of generally accepted accounting principles.
- Included in the *Handbook* is a discussion on the scope and contents of financial statement preparation and "Recommendations" on how to deal with various accounting topics.
- GAAP grew out of a desire to establish financial reporting standards to ensure fairness and comparability. The *Handbook* is now the means by which uniform accounting practices are introduced or revised to meet the changing needs of users.

5.5 International and Non-business Accounting Standards

- Up to this point, very little has been said about accounting for non-business organizations such as governments and non-profit organizations.
- The financial statements compiled by governments differ from those prepared by the private sector.
- The balance sheet is called a statement of assets and liabilities, and, since there are no owners, per se, there is no owners' equity section but rather a "fund balance" of liabilities over assets.
- The income statement is called a statement of revenues and expenditures, since the government is not in the business of earning income. This statement shows tax and other revenues received less cash expenditures and some accruals.
- The financial statements of not-for-profit organizations tend to be fairly simple because, as for government, there are no owners per se and income measurement is not an objective.
- The users of these statements are primarily concerned with the prudent use of money coming into the not-for-profit agency, rather than the net income and increases to retained earnings.
- The statements are generally heavily supplemented with financial and non-financial disclosure as to the organization's operations.

- Companies in various countries do not all subscribe to the same accounting standards as those in Canada.
- While the goal is to develop harmonized standards, particularly for companies operating in different countries, this is not the practice and you should not expect that the financial statements of an Asian company, for example, are comparable to a Canadian company since different accounting methods may have been employed in producing those statements.

5.6 The Annual Report and the Set of Financial Statements

- All public and private corporations are required to prepare an annual set of financial statements. Partnerships and proprietorships would also do so if for no other reason than to monitor their own progress.
- A standard set of financial statements includes:
  - a balance sheet;
  - an income statement;
  - a statement of retained earnings;
  - a cash flow statement; and
  - notes to financial statements (which help explain accounting policy choices, unusual information, detailed information of important accounts, and disclosure of other information such as segment earnings).
- An auditor's report commenting on the fairness of the statements presented is also usually attached.
- For public companies, this standard set is found in an annual report that, along with the financial standing and performance reports, provides qualitative information on the company's officers, products, and operating environment.
- Annual reports are more than just a means of conveying financial information; they are also an important marketing tool.

5.7 Notes and Other Supplementary Information

- Financial statements are generally augmented with supporting narrative and calculations.
- These financial notes and supplementary disclosures normally include, among other things:
  - accounting policy choices;
  - supporting calculations and information on items such as amortization and long-term debt;
  - significant issues, such as pending lawsuits or information obtained after the statements' dates;
  - segmented reporting; and
  - comparative figures for a number of prior years.

5.8 The External Auditor's Report

- The external auditor is a person or group whose job it is to verify the accuracy of financial statements.
- Auditors are to render a competent and unbiased opinion in their work.

- They are members of the CICA, the Society of Management Accountants of Canada, or the Certified General Accountants' Association of Canada.
- These organizations have established rules of professional ethics that prohibit an auditor from having a financial interest in the entities being audited, as well as rules governing other possible relations.
- Maintaining that lack of bias, or independence, cannot be easy since auditors must work closely with management. However, they are not appointed by management but rather by the shareholders, and it is to the shareholders that they report.
- The auditor only renders an opinion as to the compliance with GAAP of the financial statements. In no way does the auditor guarantee or interpret the financial statements (e.g., by saying, "This company is unhealthy.").
- The auditor relies upon the board of directors and management of the client company to provide accounting records, information, and financial statements.
- The accuracy of such statements will be confirmed and presented to shareholders.
- The presentation usually takes a standard format, expressing that the statements are the responsibility of management and that they are free of material misstatement, with reasonable assurance.
- The GAAP of materiality is raised here since the statements must be free of *material* misstatement. This means that something that would affect a user's decision one way or another has not been included or excluded.
- Note that the auditor cannot unequivocally assure the shareholders, but can only offer reasonable assurance. This is because, without being an active member of management, the auditor must exercise professional judgment and expertise.

5.9 The Nature of a Profession and Professional Ethics

- To be a member of a professional association, such as the CICA, affords you rights and privileges in the practice of your profession, such as the right to practise across provinces or the privilege to do a broader range of work than a non-professional could.
- As a professional, you are expected to adhere to a code of ethics in the execution of your duties and to objectively execute those duties.
- This ensures clients and financial statement users that professional and competent performance has been rendered.

5.10 Capital Markets

- For public companies, buying and selling ownership through shares is done via stock exchanges such as the Toronto Stock Exchange.
- Stocks or shares are not the only securities traded; so too are rights, warrants, options, futures contracts, and debt securities such as bonds and debentures.
- Rights, warrants, and options are means by which shares could be bought or sold under specific circumstances. They trade just like the shares themselves since they give the holder privileges.

- Futures usually refer to commodity futures contracts that commit the holder of the contract to either deliver, or take delivery of, a specified quality and quantity of a commodity at some future date. If you are selling corn, for example, you could enter into a futures contract to sell corn six months from now at a price agreed upon today; it wouldn't matter what the price of corn would be in six months.
- The difference between bonds and debentures is that bonds are secured against the assets of the enterprise that issues the bond, whereas debentures are not.
- Buyers and sellers are represented by brokers who act as intermediaries for the transactions, for which the brokers receive a fee.
- As for any other product, the demand for and the supply of securities determines prices.
- A stock exchange is based on the following principles:
  - *Personal trust:* between the broker and his/her client.
  - *Disclosure:* the publication of information regarding purchases and sales of securities and timely information regarding the activities of the companies that are listed on the exchanges.
  - *Regulation of members:* through strict trading, administrative, and financial rules applied to the various brokerage firms that trade on behalf of their clients.
- So, simply put, the capital market is the means by which savings (of investees) are channelled into investments (by enterprises) to sustain and stimulate economic development.
- There are five elements of capital markets that introduce the role of accounting information in such markets:

1. Securities Trading and Securities Prices

   - The trading of stocks or other securities is no different in principle than the trading of other products in other markets; that is, the laws of supply and demand apply in capital markets.
   - As a result, securities prices depend on the availability of and demand for securities.
   - Accounting information can affect this supply and demand.

2. Role of Information in a Capital Market

   - Securities trading (and hence prices) can be affected by buyers and sellers who enact trades because they either have cash to invest (buy securities) or need cash and thus sell securities.
   - These "liquidity traders" are simply looking to either put away cash or free up cash due to circumstances or reasons unique to them and not common to the broader market or social setting; that is, they trade because of information unique to themselves.

- Trading is also the result of market traders' reacting to general information such as political turmoil, currency crises, inflationary news, tax reforms, etc.

- This type of trading is based on the individual trader's reactions to and evaluation of general information.

- Finally, trading is also the result of traders' reacting to or preparing for information particular or specific to a security. A quarterly financial report to shareholders of General Motors may cause some to sell, for example.

- Trading of this type depends, in large part, on the financial statements or similar information released about particular companies.

3. Return and Risk

- There are two types of returns associated with holding a security: you get dividends or interest; and you either gain or lose depending on what happens to the price of the security (called a capital gain or loss).

- Capital market theory focuses on capital gains or losses.

- If security prices go up or down, there is naturally a risk associated with holding such securities.

- Risk can be either systematic (price varies with the overall market) or unsystematic (price varies due to confidence in, or characteristics of, the security itself).

- The role of accounting information is limited in its ability to help predict which way prices will go; prices have been found to follow what's called a "random walk"—where the next step will be is anybody's guess.

- There is some accounting information—such as those events which directly affect cash (e.g., a creditor's calling in a loan)—that have some predictive value, but it is usually the case that, although prices react to accounting information, how much they will react is speculative.

4. Aggregates

- Capital market theory suggests that risk can be diversified away by investing in a portfolio of securities (i.e., by not "putting all your eggs in one basket").

- Of course, systematic risk cannot be diversified away, unless you buy securities in different markets (since each type of market has different systematic risks), but unsystematic risk may be diversified away.

  - From an accounting perspective, it is assumed that investors hold portfolios, and, thus, the accounting decisions and financial results of an enterprise, in the aggregate, will not seriously disadvantage an investor.
  - It is presumed that an investor is free to rearrange his or her portfolio.

5. Market Informational Efficiency

  - Markets respond quickly to information.
  - This means that any information that is made public by an enterprise cannot be used to beat the market, since, by the time you have it, the market will have already adjusted and prices will have already changed, if they were going to be affected by the information.
  - This means that you cannot use information published in the business press to make unilateral gains.
  - Markets tend to respond very little to expected information, such as the usual losses reported by the Canadian airlines, since these losses were widely foreseen and made public by company, industry, and stock analysts alike.
  - Markets do respond to unexpected information, such as when significant market leaders like Nortel Networks announce under-target earnings and layoffs.
  - Accounting is only one source of information and, as such, has value only in addition to the value provided by other sources such as analysts and news media.

- The elements of capital theory simply hold that the role of accounting information is to add value to analysis, but this information is not the sole basis of analysis; that is, once again, financial accounting is part of a larger environment.
- Accountants make decisions about what to disclose based on the qualities of accounting information, such as understandability, relevance, reliability, conservatism, and comparability.
- However, the financial statements themselves often do not contain as much information as potential creditors or investors would like, so note disclosure (as discussed above) is required.
- Despite this, the problem that arises is that financial reports are too infrequent, since lending and investment occurs every day.
- Therefore, much of the news in financial statements is released before financial statements are printed, through press releases, securities exchange filings (information required by regulations), rumours, etc.
- One of the principles of stock exchanges is disclosure (mentioned above), requiring all publicly traded companies to immediately disclose material information to the public.

- What is material varies from one company to another, depending on financial size (assets, profits, debt, etc.), the nature of operations, and the like.
- Rumours about a company are expected to be confirmed or denied by company officials when trading has been affected by such rumours.
- Naturally, there is confidential information in any company, but trading on such information, to the disadvantage of those not privy to such information, is strictly prohibited until such information is fully disclosed to the public.
- The nature and intent of corporate disclosure is to make as much information as possible available as soon as possible.
- This information is intended to help those who have a reasonable understanding of business and economic activities make informed judgments.

5.11 Contracts and Financial Accounting Information

- Contractual business relationships give rise to what is called agency theory.
- In the accounting realm, this concerns interested parties' using accounting information in acting for another person.
- For example, the agents might be managers of a firm or lawyers appointed by the firm, and the principals would be the firm's owners and the firm itself, respectively.
- Agents are entrusted to act in the best interests of their principals.
- Agency theory focuses on the stewardship role of accounting; that is, on monitoring and controlling the actions of, say, management (the agents), on behalf of the owners (the principals).
- Accounting information is essentially produced as a result of the wishes of various parties to provide incentives and controls over each other's behaviours.
- Keep in mind that it is not always the case that the actions of management will coincide with the interests of the owners.
- As a result, accounting reporting provides incentive to the managers to act in the interests of owners and provides a basis for control of management by the owners.
- Principals and agents will demand whatever information is needed to ensure that the contractual relationship is maintained in good order.
- Financial accounting information can be used by the principals to monitor the agents' performance.
- The agents may be equally interested in the accounting information, and perhaps even in the methods of reporting revenues, for example, because they are appointed by the owners of the company, in effect.
- Think of an instance where a firm offers a profit-sharing plan or stock ownership to its managers. There is considerable incentive for the managers to show healthy earnings.
- You should thus be able to see what function auditors have to ensure fair reporting.
- Financial accounting information is a means by which principals and agents alike can be assured that the relationship between them is fair; that is, that the consequences and risks of the relationship can be fairly assessed.

- Agents can be assured that, as long as they act prudently and ethically, the principals are bound by the terms of the contracts between them.

EXERCISES

E1. Development of Standards What were the limitations encountered by users of early financial information? Name some of the historical ideas that have helped to bring us to a common understanding.

E2. Understand GAAP What are Generally Accepted Accounting Principles? What is their purpose and scope?

E3. Understand GAAP Explain why GAAP are, in fact, "generally accepted."

E4. Understand GAAP Are GAAP applicable to every accounting circumstance? What happens if GAAP do not or cannot apply to a particular circumstance?

E5. Applying Principles How must financial statement information be made useful to readers?

E6. Non-Business Accounting Are you likely to see a "bottom line" for the province of Manitoba's 2005/2006 fiscal year?

E7. Financial Statement Use Your neighbour is contemplating going into business for herself as an engineering consultant. As with most start-ups, she is short of cash and has approached her banker with her idea. The banker has asked her for a complete set of projected financial statements. As is typical with most would-be borrowers, her pride got in the way at the bank and she "neglected" to ask the banker what "complete" actually meant. She already knew about an income statement and a balance sheet and she thought that was a "complete" set of financial statements. She asks you over the fence one afternoon what the banker meant by "complete." What would you tell her?

E8. Financial Statement Use Of what use are financial statements?

E9. Financial Statement Use Go onto the Web and find an annual report of a Canadian company. What information will you find? For whom is the report intended?

E10. Annual Reports Are all forms of business organizations required to prepare annual reports? financial statements?

E11. Auditing Principles When financial statements are audited, who conducts the audit? What do the auditors guarantee?

E12. Financial Statement Notes What is meant by note disclosure?

E13. Auditing Principles If a professional accountant prepares your business's financial statements, and an auditor verifies that they have been fairly presented and are free of material misstatement, are you absolved of responsibility for the information contained within those statements?

E14. Auditing Principles Why do auditors only render an opinion? What does that opinion concern?

E15. Applying Standards Why would the accounting profession have professional standards yet allow professional judgment? That is, why do the standards exist and why is professional judgment allowed?

PROBLEMS

P1. Applying GAAP "GAAP are a set of rules and regulations that *all* companies must follow in preparing their financial statements." Is this true or not? Explain.

P2. Auditing Practice A junior auditor at a public accounting firm recently spent three extra days at a client's office counting every pencil, eraser, sheet of paper, paper clip, etc. He was very careful not to miss any office item so that the balance sheet values were absolutely accurate. Discuss what GAAP might have avoided this extreme case.

P3. Applying Principles Suppose that a company changed its amortization policy this year to a different policy than it had used in preparing last year's statements. Has comparability been jeopardized?

P4. Non-Business Accounting Do not-for-profit organizations follow GAAP? Why wouldn't they?

P5. Understanding Auditing West & Steers Ltd., an architectural firm managed by West and Steers but owned by a number of private shareholders, had a particularly unsuccessful year. The annual shareholders' meeting was coming up and Mani Steers was terribly worried that he would be removed as an officer of the company. Wilson West urged him not to worry, since the financial statements of the company would be audited before they were presented to the board. The auditor would make the company's statements "look better" than they otherwise would by leaving out the "little things" and would guarantee to the shareholders that the statements were prepared in accordance with GAAP. What should Mani be worried about here?

P6. Applying Standards If there is room for professional judgment in the field of accounting, should a user of financial statements be cautious?

INTEGRATIVE PROBLEMS

IP1. Applying Standards What is meant by professional judgment? How can there be room for professional judgment if GAAP exist?

IP2. Applying GAAP Explain how the following possible events would affect financial statement preparation in accordance with GAAP:

(a) A customer slips on ice in front of your place of business and files a legal suit for several million dollars against your company. The suit is not expected to be heard in court for more than a year.

(b) A temporary investment was made in the shares of another company based on a "hot tip." Your informant told you that by the end of the year, this stock would nearly double in value.

(c) The auditors of the company's statements also prepared the company's statements.

(d) A recent market appraisal of the property that your building sits on shows that, because of mineral deposits discovered nearby, your land is worth four times what you paid for it.

EXPLORATIVE QUESTIONS

EQ1. Financial Statement Notes Can a company use note disclosure to explain any departure from GAAP?

EQ2. Applying GAAP In the case of Canadian companies that have U.S. subsidiaries, are problems created by differences in Canadian and U.S. GAAP? How could these problems be addressed?

EQ3. Understanding Auditing Do you think the day will come when auditors will guarantee the accuracy of financial statements and their compliance with GAAP?

SOLUTIONS

EXERCISES

E1. Limitations on the use of early financial information included that only certain people were trained to read and write and that the lists merchants kept could only include that which could be easily counted. There were difficulties in administering large regions of conquered lands due to the lack of administrators who could read and write. Once the crusades and the development of the merchant banks began, there was a need for more exact recordkeeping. The biggest problem was that each country would have its own rules and ideas about the system to be used.

Historical ideas that have helped bring us to a common understanding include the following:

- methods of measuring and calculating;
- medium of exchange or currency;
- double-entry bookkeeping;
- auditing;
- the balance sheet;
- debits and credits;
- the concept of stewardship; and
- the concept of disclosure.

E2. GAAP are the compilation of all the legal rules, authoritative accounting standards, theoretical analyses, and judgment precedents that guide the preparation, verification (audit), and use of financial statements. GAAP grew out of the desire to establish financial reporting standards to ensure fairness and comparability.

E3. GAAP are generally accepted because they have been most useful, in general, in satisfying the needs of the parties involved in financial accounting. So, they have become generally accepted by virtue of their use. GAAP are mostly stable so that interested parties can get used to what to expect, but this does not mean that GAAP are fixed. They can change as demands for information change.

E4. GAAP do not fit every accounting circumstance, but they are flexible enough to be adapted to the circumstances of particular organizations. There may be special circumstances, such as legislative or contractual requirements, that require a departure from GAAP to a different basis of accounting, and this is certainly permissible. If such a departure is undertaken, professional judgment is expected to be exercised; that is, judgment based on experience in the profession in dealing with similar particular circumstances.

E5. To be useful, financial statement information must be: (1) understandable to a user who has a reasonable understanding of business and economic activities; (2) relevant to the decisions of users (what is material or not); (3) reliably presented in an unbiased, verifiable, and conservative manner; (4) comparable in that the statements have not used different accounting policies over time without adequate explanation, or in that they are reasonably similar, in preparation, to the statements of other organizations.

E6. You will see a "bottom line," but it will not be the "net income" figure you are used to seeing. What you will see is a figure called a budgetary deficit or surplus, depending on how good the year was, but no net income or net loss. The reason is that governments and not-for-profit agencies are not in the business of earning income.

E7. In addition to the balance sheet and the income statement, "complete" probably meant including the following:

- a statement of retained earnings, which is one of the sources of asset financing. The statement would show how retained earnings will change over time (increasing by income; decreasing by dividends). If your neighbour's business is not incorporated, she should have a statement of owner's equity, which shows how the capital account will change (increasing by income; decreasing by withdrawals).

- a cash flow statement describing the increases and decreases in cash and near-cash assets for forthcoming periods. Inform your neighbour that the banker is probably interested in her ability to generate cash rather than income, since cash pays back the bank's loans to her.

- notes to support the financial statements, which would likely be required to help explain background information to some of the figures in the statements.

E8. Financial statements have a variety of users from managers to creditors. The statements' purpose is to reflect on how a company's assets have been managed, how they have been financed, to what extent the owners of the company have increased or decreased their stake in the company, and how successful the company has been in using those assets to generate income.

Statements provide a basis for lending, investing, tax assessment, accounting policy, and management performance and review decisions, among others. They are the starting point, typically, for anyone who may have a financial or other (e.g., employment) interest in a company.

E9. An annual report will usually contain the following information:

- Summary performance of the company or its segments over a five- or ten-year period.
- A letter to shareholders, usually from the chief executive officer (CEO) and chair of the board. The letter usually highlights major initiatives and performance of the company over the year, briefly discusses the company's strategic focus for the next year, and may include advisement of any changes to the board.
- A company profile briefly discussing the company, its products, and, if it is a consolidated entity, its segments.
- A "management discussion and analysis" highlighting key performance figures and the results of key decisions such as asset acquisitions. If the company is a consolidated entity, segment performance is usually highlighted.
- A statement attesting that responsibility for the financial statements and internal control belongs to management.
- The financial statements, an auditor's report attesting to the fairness of presentation of the company's statements, and supporting notes.
- Corporate information such as high and low share prices over the year, the names of directors and management, and socially responsible actions as evidence of good corporate citizenship.

E10. Only public companies are required to prepare an annual report. Private companies, generally speaking, are required to file income statements with the Canada Revenue Agency and, usually, the provincial treasury for taxation purposes. Partners in a partnership and sole proprietors are required to submit a statement of business income to the Canada Revenue Agency for taxation purposes, since business income is considered personal income.

Required or not, it is important from a management perspective to know how your company is performing, and for that reason alone financial statements should be prepared at least annually.

E11. Audits are conducted by independent auditors, who are usually chartered accountants. Auditors do not have any vested interest in the companies they audit. They guarantee nothing; auditors only render an opinion as to the fairness of the financial information presented in the statements.

E12. Note disclosure and supplementary data is information provided to help explain the financial statements and to provide information above and beyond that contained strictly in the financial statements. Note disclosure might explain, amongst other things:

- what method of amortization is being used;
- the composition of inventories;
- the breakdown of long-term debt;
-
- a listing of assets that may have been grouped as "other" on the balance sheet;
- income tax calculations; and
- segmented reporting.

Supplementary disclosure might explain, among other things:

- quarterly financial information;
- prior year summary figures for comparison; and
- comparison between U.S. and Canadian accounting principles for entities operating in these countries.

E13. Regardless of whether statements have been professionally prepared and audited, the responsibility for the integrity and objectivity of the statements ultimately rests with management.

E14. An opinion is rendered since the auditor cannot be absolutely certain that the statements in question are free of material misstatement and that all GAAP have been followed. Because the auditor is not an active member of the company, it is quite possible for information to be excluded from or included in the statements so as to redirect a user's analysis. It is the obligation of the auditor to ensure that the risk of such is minimized and that, by the company's complying with GAAP, the user can rely upon the information contained in the statements.

E15. Professional judgment is required where accounting treatment or statement presentation does not follow GAAP as specified in the *CICA Handbook.* However, even when a standard or a clear tradition exists, trying to fit the accounting policy to the unique circumstances of a business may require professional judgment.

Standards exist to reduce the risk of error and impropriety. The collective wisdom of the profession is brought to bear on issues, and so removes the inefficiencies that would arise if everyone had to interpret every accounting issue on their own. Professional judgment has a place alongside standards, since judgment is required to determine if a standard applies to a given circumstance. Circumstances change, while standards remain relatively static. Judgments are needed to apply standards, especially when such standards require estimates and allocations or when the principle of materiality is threatened.

PROBLEMS

P1. The statement is not true. GAAP do not have to be followed by all companies. Public companies must prepare their statements in accordance with GAAP since the auditors will look for such compliance. Private companies, partnerships, and proprietorships do not have to follow GAAP; however, not doing so seriously undermines the reliability of the statements for use by creditors, investors, and the like.

Even where GAAP are followed in large part, departure from GAAP is permitted if the circumstances warrant. In such cases, professional judgment is expected to be exercised.

P2. The GAAP of materiality would have avoided such a case. This principle holds that items are material if omission or misstatement of such would influence or change a decision. It is unlikely that extreme accuracy for office supplies would, in fact, change a user's decision.

An argument could also be made that the benefit versus cost restraint also applies. The cost of getting this extra information (three days' salary plus the opportunity cost) versus the benefit of exact figures for office supplies is debatable. The evaluation of the nature and the amount of the benefit and the cost is, however, judgmental.

P3. Comparability will be jeopardized when *any* accounting policy changes. Inconsistency may lead to misconceptions arising from a change in policies. When such an accounting policy change is made, it is usually necessary to disclose the change, the reason(s) for the change, and the effects of the change, to maintain comparability. This would mean, then, that the change would be retroactively applied and that key figures of prior year statements would be recalculated to reflect the new policy. In this case, where the amortization policy has changed, amortization expense, income, and retained earnings may be recalculated.

P4. GAAP apply mostly to profit-seeking organizations. Since the financial statements of not-for-profits differ somewhat, GAAP do not readily apply. The CICA has urged not-for-profits to follow GAAP but this has not been widely accepted. Such organizations do not report income since they are not in the business of earning income. Nor do they report a conventional balance sheet since members do not own the organization, and, hence, do not have any equity in it. So, to follow some of the GAAP seems inappropriate.

P5. First of all, leaving out the "little things" is a question of professional judgment. What may be little to Wilson West may be material to shareholders, and the auditor has an obligation to make sure that there has been material disclosure. The auditor must exercise professional judgment in making the call between what is material and what is not. In doing so, there must be strict adherence to ethics and the principle of objectivity.

Secondly, an auditor may *assure* the shareholders that he or she has conducted the audit in accordance with generally accepted auditing standards. This is not the same as guaranteeing that the statements have been prepared in accordance with GAAP. While the audit may have been adequately conducted, in no way should or would an auditor *guarantee* that the financial statements have been prepared in accordance with GAAP, since the auditor is not an officer of the company and must rely on professional judgment and expertise. Even if such a guarantee were made, compliance with GAAP does not relieve Mani and Wilson of responsibility for the statements and the performance attested to in those statements.

P6. If standards do not govern every circumstance and professional judgment is permitted, then the possibility exists of reporting being less than fair and accounting policies being chosen that may present a less than fair account of the circumstances. How revenues are recognized, how amortization is calculated, or how inventories are valued can alter balance sheet and income figures. A user should, therefore, be cautious in using statements and should pay close attention to the disclosure of the various accounting policy choices made.

INTEGRATIVE PROBLEMS

IP1. Professional judgment is required where accounting treatment or statement presentation does not follow GAAP as specified in the *CICA Handbook*. The practice should, however, be explained in the notes to the financial statements along with a reason why GAAP have not been followed.

Professional judgment is exercised when a departure from GAAP is warranted and the statement preparer relies upon the informed opinion of a professional in the field, professional experience, the advice of committees within the CICA, and/or established principles for analogous situations.

The exercise of professional judgment may be necessary in those circumstances where the *CICA Handbook* has not made a recommendation or where following a recommendation of the handbook would result in misleading financial statements.

IP2. (a) The lawsuit must be noted as a contingent liability in the notes to the financial statements. If you are reasonably certain to lose the lawsuit and can estimate the damages to be awarded, you should accrue the liability.

(b) The temporary investment would be considered a current asset that should be recorded at cost. Regardless of what the intended value of the investment is, it is still recorded at cost. If its value does double and it is sold, then a capital gain would be realized.

(c) It is usually the responsibility of management to prepare the financial statements of a company to be verified by auditors. If the auditors are also management, they have then breached integrity and reliability. If the auditors are independent from management yet prepared the statements, they have likely done so in accordance with GAAP. However, to prepare the statements themselves raises questions as to their independence from the company, and, once again, integrity and objectivity are challenged.

(d) The market appraisal does not affect the carrying value of your land on the balance sheet. You may, however, as supplementary data, include the appraised value and the reason for the difference between it and historical cost.

EXPLORATIVE QUESTIONS

EQ1. A company cannot use note disclosure to explain *any* variation from GAAP. It is not acceptable to diverge from GAAP in circumstances where GAAP apply, even if note disclosure is made. Simply put, if you diverge from GAAP in a circumstance where the application of GAAP would have been appropriate, note disclosure does not normally validate that divergence. This response is clouded, however, by Section 1500.06 of the *CICA Handbook,* which permits such divergence from a recommended practice provided that the disclosure shows the effects of the practice that has been followed as compared with the recommended practice. If, however, you diverge from GAAP in circumstances where GAAP either do not apply or would result in misleading statements, then the divergence must be validated with note disclosure.

EQ2. There are certainly differences between Canadian GAAP and U.S. GAAP. These differences focus on methods of income determination and balance sheet valuation. For example, interest expenses incurred in the construction of assets are capitalized in the United States but expensed in Canada. For a Canadian company to address these differences is only a matter of courtesy to its U.S. shareholders. While such reconciliation is not necessary, it is a service to shareholders. Canadian companies are not required to do this, and, indeed, many do not. (Note, however, that in the case of Canadian companies whose stock (or whose subsidiaries' stock) trades on U.S. exchanges, such reconciliatory disclosure is required by the U.S. Securities and Exchange Commission.)

EQ3. It is unlikely that auditors would ever guarantee the accuracy of financial statements and their compliance with GAAP. One possible reason is that the auditors are neither the company's management nor its owners. They do not have access to decision making as it is happening. Nor do they have perfect information. As outsiders, they can never be 100% certain that the information they receive from the company, despite their tests and procedures, is accurate. Whether or not GAAP have been adhered to, for certain, is also debatable. Perhaps the auditor has overlooked an accounting policy change of which he or she was not informed.

A guarantee is an extreme request of an auditor. The question then arises as to what if a guarantee is offered but the audited statements prove to be flawed in some way. What remedy does or should the user have from the auditor? What compensation could or would the auditor then give the injured users? The point is, even if there were a guarantee, finding a remedy for the injured parties is an academic issue. What would be a suitable remedy? Would the auditor pay it personally? Would the auditors need to take some form of malpractice insurance, the premiums for which would cover claims on the guarantee?

Put yourself in the position of an auditor who is asked to guarantee someone else's work. Would you do it?

CHAPTER 6
REVENUE AND EXPENSE RECOGNITION

LEARNING OBJECTIVES

After completing Chapter 6, you should:

- understand why accrual accounting exists;
- recognize that economic events do not necessarily coincide with cash flow and that this requires special accounting treatment to fairly present as complete a picture as possible;
- know that adjustments and corrections may need to be made to records kept solely on the basis of transactions;
- know what an accounting policy is;
- understand some of the reasons for the existence of a choice in policy matters;
- appreciate that accounting policy choices satisfy important criteria of reporting;
- recognize the role of professional judgment, once again;
- know what a fiscal period is;
- know what guidelines have to be met in order to recognize revenue and what methods are available for recognizing revenue; and
- understand what expense matching is.

CHAPTER SUMMARY

6.1 Chapter Introduction: Revenue and Expense Recognition

- When ongoing business events are broken up into reporting periods, the financial nature of some of those events continues forward into the next reporting period.
- This means that the transactional information contained in the bookkeeping records does not necessarily best reflect the economic process of earning income.
- Accrual accounting is a means by which financial statements are able to reflect the fact that, at the time of preparation, there are transactions that have not yet been completed, but must still be recorded to show that they are part of a company's operations.

6.2 What Is Accrual Accounting?

- Accrual accounting goes beyond cash basis accounting. It attempts to paint a more complete economic picture than the simple cash basis, transactional method of accounting.
- This is not to say that cash flow is unimportant; sooner or later, every economic event involves cash.

- Accrual accounting allows us to separate the timing of the economic event from the cash flow associated with it.
- This means that we can record and represent economic events in financial statements either before or after cash is received or paid out.
- As an example, you might have earned income at your retail store this period, but might not actually pay for your heating, electricity, etc., until next period. Accrual accounting allows us to recognize the economic events (earning income and incurring an expense) on this period's financial statements, even though cash flow has not yet occurred.

6.3 Conceptual Foundation of Accrual Accounting

- You should see that accrual accounting attempts to recognize economic flows as well as cash flows.
- What accrual accounting attempts to do is *recognize* economic flows whether or not they have yet been *realized* by cash flow.
- The matching principle underlies many of the premises of accrual accounting.
- Matching simply means to ensure that revenues and expenses are measured comparably. That is, expenses are recognized in accordance with the revenues that those expenses helped generate.
- Revenues and expenses are economic flows and may occur before or after—or coincide with—cash flow.
- To help illustrate accrual accounting, consider the following:

(1) Revenues can be recognized at three possible points:

(i) as cash is received;
(ii) before cash is received;
(iii) after cash is received.

Examples of journal entries to recognize these revenues would be:

Dr. Cash
Cr. Revenue

Dr. Accounts Receivable
Cr. Revenue

Dr. Deferred Revenue Liability*
Cr. Revenue

* This liability would have been created when a customer made an advance payment or placed a deposit for goods/services yet to be rendered (see part (3)). Once the goods/services have been rendered, the liability is debited.

(2) Expenses can be recognized at three possible points:

(i) as cash is paid;
(ii) before cash is paid;
(iii) after cash is paid.

Examples of journal entries to recognize these revenues would be:

Dr. Rent Expense
Cr. Cash

Dr. Rent Expense
Cr. Rent Payable

Dr. Rent Expense
Cr. Prepaid Rent*

* Prepaid Rent is an asset that would have been created when cash was paid in advance for rent (or at least a promise of cash was made, resulting in a credit to something like Rent Payable instead of Cash.). As time passes, this asset is consumed and, hence, a rent expense is recognized. As a result, the asset is credited to reflect its consumption.

(3) In completing the recognition of expenses and revenues, four other groups of transactions are necessary

Having recognized revenues prior to receipt of cash, when the cash is received:

Dr. Cash
Cr. Accounts Receivable

Having recognized revenues sometime after receipt of cash, when the cash *was* received:

Dr. Cash
Cr. Deferred Revenue Liability

Having recognized expenses prior to payment of cash, when the cash is paid:

Dr. Rent Payable
Cr. Cash

Having recognized expenses sometime after payment of cash, when the cash *was* paid (or the promise of payment made):

Dr. Prepaid Rent
Cr. Cash (or Rent Payable)

6.4 Accounting Policy Choices

- The first question to be answered is "What is an accounting policy?"
- An accounting policy is a decision made in advance about how, when, and whether to record or recognize something.
- Since accrual accounting entails deciding when and how to recognize an event, accounting policy choices standardize, as much as possible, how a company would handle routine accrual decisions.
- Policy choices may encompass the following areas:
  - revenue recognition;
  - amortization method;
  - inventory valuation;
  - valuation of receivables;
  - capitalization of expenses;
  - amortization of intangibles;
  - cash and cash equivalents; and
  - treatment of subsidiaries.
- Policy choice may be nothing more than classifying an account as current or non-current.
- Once we have answered the question of what an accounting policy is, we can then ask "Why is there a choice?"
- There is choice because all possibilities are not predetermined. Reasons for making policy choices include:
  - The information value that arises from classifying accounts (e.g., is the debt due within a year or not for several years?).
  - Basic recordkeeping requires that policy choices be made about what constitutes a transaction, what accounts to use, and when and how a transaction should be recognized (remember the principle of consistency?).
  - In the interests of more complete and fair reporting, accrual accounting requires that choices be made to adhere to standards and to exercise professional judgment.
  - The simple fact that standards are not universally applicable or all-encompassing requires that choices be made to suit the circumstances of a particular company; that is, there is not necessarily one correct way of doing things in every circumstance and so policy decisions must be made.
- In making accounting policy choices, we should consider:
  - fairness;
  - matching;
  - consistency over time;
  - comparability to other companies;
  - conformance with standards and GAAP;
  - materiality;

    - cost of implementing the policy; and
    - conservatism.

- Historically, we know that more choice was possible in earlier times. As the standards developed, much of the freedom to choose was lost to an enterprise.
- We are now constrained by GAAP, standards, and legislation in some areas while in other areas we have quite a bit of choice.
- This, then, brings us back to the idea of professional judgment and professional standards.
- The text quotes the *CICA Handbook*'s "Introduction to Accounting Recommendations," which points out that:

  "No rule of general application can be phrased to suit all circumstances or combination of circumstances that may arise, nor is there any substitute for the exercise of professional judgment in the determination of what constitutes fair presentation or good practice in a particular case."

- This certainly seems to leave the ball largely in the court of the accountant, who must make the decisions about treatment of the items in the financial reports.
- Ultimately, the question that can be asked is whether or not it is possible to manipulate the numbers that are put into the financial statements to tell the story that the company wants told.
- Of course this is possible, since the line between fairness and choice is very narrow and can easily be stepped over.
- Appreciate that management objectives will affect policy choices.
- Under normal circumstances, cash flow will not be affected by changes in accounting policy.
- The only time we expect to see an effect on cash is if there is an income tax effect that increases or decreases tax payable and thus, eventually, affects cash.
- Of course, if we make a change to selling prices or to the way we collect money from our clients, cash will also be affected.
- Most financial statements usually contain a note as to the significant accounting policies that have been used. Keep in mind that the statements are meant for an audience with a reasonable understanding of business, economics, and accounting, and, as such, generally practised and expected policies (such as recognizing revenues at the time of sale) are not often disclosed.
- When accounting policy changes have been made, many require that the effects of such changes be applied retroactively; it is for this reason that you may encounter an instance where a company's annual report for one year may not show the same figures when that year's information is presented in subsequent years' summary performance data.

6.5 The Fiscal Period

- The fiscal period refers to the accounting year, typically. It is the time frame over which financial performance is measured.
- It is usually one year in length, but does not necessarily correspond to the calendar year.
- Companies can establish their fiscal year to end on any day of any month, but, once they do so, they are typically bound to that year-end for the life of the company.
- The reasons for choosing a fiscal year-end different from a calendar year-end vary, ranging from tax-related causes to the cyclical nature of the business.
- The difficulty that fiscal periods create is that, quite often, there are transactions that are incomplete as at the end of a fiscal period. The particularly troublesome of these transactions are those that involve revenues and expenses.
- It is thus necessary to endeavour to place revenues in the periods in which they are earned and match expenses to those revenues.

6.6 Revenue Recognition

- Part of what accrual accounting does is "cut off" long-lived or incomplete economic events at the beginning and end of a fiscal period so that their effects during that period can be estimated.
- There is always a trade-off between relevance/timeliness and accuracy/precision. because an event is usually most accurately measured at the point of cash flow. That point may not be the most informative point for users trying to evaluate the company's economic performance during a period, however.
- Herein lies the trade-off: If revenues and expenses are recognized earlier, hence making their information value more relevant, then they will not be as accurate (since accrual accounting involves estimates) as they would be if recognition were delayed until the event had been completed, such as with the flow of cash.
- Considerable emphasis is placed on income as a measure of the success of a company, notwithstanding the need to also examine cash flow.
- You should by now be aware that, if there are specific costs associated with generating revenue, these costs should be charged as expenses in the *same* period in which the revenues were generated (i.e., matched).
- Being that there are a host of activities associated with generating revenue (such as selling, delivery, obtaining inventory, and renting or buying store or office space), when should revenue be recognized as having been earned and expenses be appropriately matched?
- Revenue may be recognized when *all* of the following criteria have been met:
    - when the firm has exerted a substantial portion of its production and sales effort;
    - when the major portion of costs have been incurred, and the remaining costs can be estimated with reasonable reliability and precision;
    - when the revenue can be objectively measured; and
    - when eventual collection of cash can be reasonably assured.

6.7 Revenue Recognition Methods

- With the above four criteria in mind, revenue can be recognized at one of five different points for a transaction:

  - *At Time of Sale*—when delivery of a good/service has been made or at the time of passage of legal title.

  - *During Production*—when the process of earning revenue extends beyond one fiscal year, it may be appropriate to recognize revenue on the basis the percentage of the good/service that has been completed.

  - *At Completion of Production*—when the production of a product has been completed, but the product is not yet sold, revenue may be recognized as long as the sale of the product is virtually guaranteed, such as when the product is produced under contract.

  - *Upon Collection of Cash*—when there is doubt about collecting cash on a credit sale, or when the majority of cash is expected to come in over a long series of installments.

  - *After Cash Has Been Received*—when there is a money-back period associated with the sale of your product, it may be appropriate to defer recognition of revenue until after this period has lapsed.

6.8 Expense Recognition and Matching

- Expenses should be accounted for in the same fiscal period in which they helped generate revenue.
- Failure to do so will result in skewed income results from one fiscal period to the next.
- Accrual basis income, where expenses are indeed matched, produces different income results than cash basis income because of the fundamental difference in the two bases (i.e., the timing of cash flow).

6.9 Demonstration Problem: Revenue and Expense Recognition

- This section in the chapter provides an illustration of revenue and expense recognition at Nakiska Fabricating Inc. Note that there are many revenue recognition alternatives available to choose from.

6.10. Prepaid and Accrued Expenses

- Prepaid expenses are not expenses; they are assets. They are created when a company incurs an expenditure for an expense that will be recognized in some future period.
- For example, if an insurance premium is paid in full at the beginning of a coverage period, an insurance expense would be recognized each month as the insurance expires. But having paid the full premium in advance, an asset is created since value extends into the future.

- Accrued expenses are not expenses either; they are liabilities. They arise when payment will follow the incurrence of an expense.
- For example, if interest on a loan payable will be paid at year-end, then during the year, "accrued interest expense (or liability)" has risen along with interest expense.

EXERCISES

E1. Cash Basis vs. Accrual Accounting How does accrual accounting differ from cash basis accounting?

E2. Accrual Accounting Why does accrual accounting exist?

E3. Accrual Accounting What is matching?

E4. Revenue Recognition A customer enters your furniture store on April 30 and places an order for a piece of furniture that you will have to build. You quote her a $1,500 selling price. She leaves you a $200 deposit and you agree to have the item ready for her to pick up in 25 days. How much revenue can you recognize for April from this sale?

E5. Revenue Recognition Under what circumstance might it be prudent to recognize revenue only when cash has been received?

E6. Reporting Periods What is a fiscal period? What is an interim period?

E7. Reporting Periods If a company's fiscal year-end is April 30, 2006, what difference would it make to the company's balance sheet and income statement if it paid its insurance premiums April 1, 2006, versus July 1, 2006?

E8. Accrual Accounting Is accrual accounting income reliable?

E9. Cash Basis vs. Accrual Accounting Does cash basis income differ from accrual basis income?

E10. Revenue Recognition In which of the following events has revenue been earned:

(a) A customer pays $500 cash for a piece of furniture and takes the furniture home, promising to pay the other $400 of the purchase price within 30 days.
(b) A trade creditor forgives a debt your company has to that creditor as long as your company provides one month of free service.
(c) A customer pays you $1,000 for merchandise that she previously purchased on credit.

E11. Recordkeeping Practice Explain why accountants debit expenses and credit revenues when it is true that revenues increase assets while expenses decrease them.

E12. Accounting Policy Choices "It really doesn't matter what accounting policy choices a company makes since there is no effect on cash." Discuss the merit of this statement.

PROBLEMS

P1. Revenue Recognition In the following scenarios, indicate when you think revenues should be recognized.

(a) An urban office complex project by Triple Five Corporation
(b) Subscription sales by *The Economist*
(c) Videon's prepaid subscriptions
(d) Zachary's Leatherworks' custom orders received at the local Farmers' Market
(e) United Way's annual fundraising drive
(f) Leon's Furniture's "don't pay a cent" event, where the customer does not pay for the furniture purchase until the next season
(g) Crusty Jewellers' deferred billing for items purchased by holders of the Crusty credit card

P2. Revenue Recognition Superior Communications operates a TV mail order business. The business, which is not incorporated, rents office space in several Canadian cities and establishes a mailing address, and a toll free number. Under permission from record publishing companies, Superior then advertises, on TV, special promotions of the recordings of musical artists. These recordings are not typically sold in retail stores so the only way for a purchaser to buy the record is to order through Superior. When the order is received from the customer, Superior instructs the record company to ship the record directly to the buyer. Superior pays the record publisher 45 days after delivery. In this way, Superior does not have to keep any inventory. Credit cards and money orders are the only accepted means of payment to Superior. Superior also offers a 30-day trial period during which the customer may return the record, undamaged, if they are not satisfied. Superior then returns the returned merchandise to the record publisher for a credit.

(a) Identify when revenue could be recognized by Superior.
(b) When could the record publisher recognize revenues?

P3. Revenue Recognition and Matching Why is so much accounting attention given to revenue and expense recognition and matching?

P4. Revenue Recognition Bases Christine Beverage Ltd. is a Hong Kong-based producer of exotic fruit flavoured drinks. Each flat of 24 cans costs C$8 to produce. The product is then shipped to North America in caselots of 200 flats. Each shipment contains 250 caselots and costs C$240,000. Each flat sells for C$13 to the North American importer. All expenses are settled in cash.

In March, the company produced 75,000 flats, made one shipment, and collected C$520,000. In April, Christine produced 85,000 flats, made one shipment, and collected C$585,000.

(a) Assuming that there was an assured market for Christine's products, what would its income be for March using a production basis for calculations? What would it be for April?
(b) Assuming revenue was recognized when the product was shipped, what would income be for March? for April?
(c) Assuming Christine was conservative and recognized revenue when cash was collected, what would income be for March? for April?
(d) Would total assets as at April 30 be affected by the choice among the three recognition bases? Explain.

P5. Income Determination Township Creations is a one-person operation. Daryl Willows, the proprietor, creates miniature glass animals. His first set of glass animals has an Arctic theme (e.g., seals, penguins). He plans to create other sets around other themes (e.g., the jungle, the African plains, the boreal forest, the deserts). He plans to sell each set of animals for $200. He estimates that each set costs him $120 to produce and ship. Wanting to establish credibility in his field, Willows offers a one-year, money-back guarantee against faulty workmanship. He estimates that 16% of sets sold this year will be returned. He doesn't intend to try to re-sell returned sets since there must have been something wrong with them for customers to return them in the first place. He thinks this figure is testament to his high-quality work. In 2005, Willows sold all 25 sets he made.

(a) How much income could he recognize in 2005? in 2006?
(b) Can you determine the cash inflow each year? What is the cash outflow each year, assuming that he is correct in his returns estimate?

P6. Revenue Recognition Hippo Farm Software Ltd. sells software to the industrial catering industry. The software records meal consumption using swipe cards at high volume catering locations such as military canteens and student housing cafeterias. Hippo Farm charges the following fees for the use of its software by its clients:

(i) a master licence fee of $15,000 payable upon acceptance of a three-year licence agreement;
(ii) a $1,500 per day installation fee for initial setup and installation of the software on a client's site;
(iii) an annual maintenance fee of $12,000 payable in advance by a client;
(iv) a $0.07 subscription fee for each meal consumed payable monthly by a client.

How and when should each of these fees be recognized?

INTEGRATIVE PROBLEMS

IP1. Expense Capitalization and Revenue Recognition Timeless Computer Corporation has developed a mini computer-based system that can be used by law firms for client billings, payroll, and the like. Timeless expensed the $250,000 in development costs as they were incurred. However, now that the system is finally functional, the company's accountants are questioning whether these costs should have been capitalized.

In July 2006, Timeless convinced Roger, Oxford, Bonner, and Underwood (ROB-U), a local law firm, to test the system under no obligation to purchase and without incurring any costs. Timeless provided a complete system, hardware included. Running this test cost Timeless $10,000.

The test was a success and, on August 1, the law firm agreed to purchase the system for $75,000, paying a $12,000 deposit, provided that Timeless made certain revisions to the system to comply with certain office practices at ROB-U. The balance would be due upon delivery. The system was priced to yield a margin of $10,000. Timeless spent $4,500 in August and another $3,000 in September modifying the system to meet ROB-U's requests, after which the system was 85% complete. Another $9,750 was spent in October and it finally delivered the completed system to ROB-U on November 1 and collected full payment. All contract costs, as they were incurred, were paid in cash.

Timeless realized that any further sales would mean taking a base system and modifying it to meet the needs of a particular client. Naturally, Timeless would not make such modifications unless the client had contracted to purchase and had made a deposit.

Timeless expected to sell another 20 systems in the next four years before the technology improvements in systems hardware would render its system a dinosaur.

Prior to deciding what to do about the capitalization of development costs, consider the following additional information:

Cash	$ 6,750
Contract Development Costs	55,250
Development Costs	250,000
	$312,000
Contract Receipts	$ 12,000
Share Capital	300,000
	$312,000
Retained Earnings	$ 0

(a) What are the different ways that revenue could be recognized in this case? How would you suggest revenues be recognized?
(b) Should the development costs be amortized?
(c) How should development costs be amortized?
(d) Based on your suggested revenue recognition basis and your method of amortization, prepare an income statement for the year ended September 30, a balance sheet as at September 30, and a cash flow statement for the year.

IP2. Revenue Recognition Policy ProSports Fitness provides training facilities to its members. It also allows members' guests to use the facilities for $2.50 per visit if accompanied by a member. The annual membership fee is $99 payable in advance for unlimited use throughout the year.

The strongest membership recruitment drive is in the winter. The following membership information is available:

	November	December	January
New members	40	60	20
Renewals	100	40	20
Expirations (including those who renewed)	100	80	20
Guest visits	30	35	15
Total membership	720	740	760

The club manager notes that a major part of her staff's efforts are aimed at recruiting new members and obtaining renewals, and processing new applications and renewals. In other words, the majority of service has been provided *before* a new member joins the club or an existing member renews.

Monthly costs total $14,000, including $6,000 for salaries and $2,500 for promotions and advertising.

(a) How would you recommend revenues be recognized?
(b) What is the effect on income of alternative points of recognition?

EXPLORATIVE QUESTIONS

EQ1. Matching Principle You have been selected for the arduous task of preparing the financial statements for the year-end of the Guest Speakers Seminar Series, a not-for-profit university organization. As you examine the organization's source documents and recordkeeping over the past year, you find that some recent bills have not yet been paid. The organization doesn't produce an income statement *per se* since it is not in the business of earning income. Therefore, you do not have to report expenses, only expenditures. Cheques were already written to pay for those unpaid bills. You decide to tear up those cheques and write new ones after the year-end of the organization. This way, the financial statements might not look so bad. Are revenues and expenses being properly matched? Is this ethical?

EQ2. Understanding Accrual Accounting By now you should appreciate that accrual accounting tries to present a broader picture of earnings and financial position than does the cash basis. However, accrual accounting still fails to measure wealth in the same way an economics perspective would. Why do you suppose, then, that stock analysts still put so much faith in the financial statements of a company?

SOLUTIONS

EXERCISES

E1. Accrual accounting recognizes, in the accounts, economic flows, such as asset acquisitions, revenue generation, and expense incurrence, regardless of whether a cash flow coincides with such economic flows. Cash basis accounting only recognizes, in the accounts, an economic event that coincides with the outflow or inflow of cash.

E2. Accrual accounting exists to more completely portray a company's financial performance and position. Implicitly, accrual accounting forces us to make estimates and exercise professional judgment but this does not make financial reporting unreliable.

E3. Matching is the process by which expenses that are incurred to generate revenues are recognized in the accounts in the same period in which the revenues are generated, rather than waiting until the expenses are actually paid in cash.

E4. You cannot recognize any revenue, since you have not yet provided the item and you have not incurred any significant portion of costs associated with this sale. The deposit is not considered revenue. It is considered a deferred revenue liability. When the customer pays for the item in full and takes delivery, revenue of $1,500 can be recognized and the liability can be eliminated since you have performed your end of the deal.

E5. Waiting until cash has been received to recognize revenues would be advisable when there is serious doubt as to actual cash collection in a credit sale.

E6. A fiscal period is an accounting period, usually one year in length. This does not have to correspond to the calendar year. Interim periods are accounting periods that are less than one year in length.

E7. If it paid its insurance premiums before its fiscal year-end, it would have a prepaid asset on its balance sheet. If it waited until after year-end, it would have an accrued liability on its balance sheet. When the premium is actually paid makes no difference to the year-end income statement, since an insurance expense should be recognized for the year, regardless of when it is actually paid.

E8. Accrual accounting income is reliable; it is not, however, the complete story. As in the discussion of the cash flow statement in Chapter 4, you cannot ignore cash flow. A profitable company (according to reported earnings) is not necessarily a healthy company (depending on cash flow).

E9. Cash basis income will usually differ from accrual basis income unless it so happens that cash is collected in the same period in which revenue is recognized and cash outflows occur in the same period as expenses are incurred to generate those revenues.

E10. Events (a) and (b) are instances where revenue has been earned since they both increase the wealth of the company in return for something. In (a), the customer has received the furniture and the vendor has received cash and a promise to pay the balance. In (b), your company receives a waiver on a debt in exchange for providing a service. The service, incidentally, is not really free: it is apparently worth the value of the debt because both parties have agreed to this exchange.

Item (c) is not an instance where revenue has been earned since the customer is simply paying you what he/she owes you. When the original promise was made to pay you, and when you provided goods or services in return, was when the revenue could be deemed as earned. A cash inflow of this type is not necessarily revenue.

E11. If you look at the income statement as being a part of the equity of a business, it will facilitate your understanding of this point. Equity accounts on the balance sheet usually carry a credit balance representing the owners' claims against the assets of the business. Revenues are credited since they increase that claim (increasing a credit balance), and expenses are debited since they decrease that claim (decreasing a credit balance). Revenues do increase assets such as cash and expenses do decrease assets such as cash. In order for the balance sheet to balance, the claim against those assets (equity) must be adjusted for revenues and expenses. This is done via the statement of owner's equity or the statement of retained earnings, depending on the organization of the business.

E12. Accounting policy choices generally do not involve cash. The circumstances in which policy choice changes do involve cash are usually policies dealing with pricing, or receivables collections, or those that affect income tax payable and, therefore, ultimately cash. Furthermore, just because an accounting policy does not affect cash does not mean it is not important. Policies classifying debt as short term vs. long term, or policies specifying whether inventory is calculated on a first-in first-out basis or a last-in last-out basis, have important analytical consequences even though they do not directly affect cash.

PROBLEMS

P1. (a) Upon occupancy, if tenants have been contracted for occupancy. Otherwise, at the time of closure of leasing agreements. Any advance payments should be considered unearned revenues.

(b) Upon delivery each week or each month.

(c) Upon provision of service each month.

(d) When cash is received. If a deposit is taken for work yet to be completed, it should be considered unearned revenue.

(e) When cash is received, since people make pledges that they do not necessarily honour.

(f) When the sale is made.

(g) When the sale is made, but just postponing the invoicing.

P2. (a) At all of these points, Superior will have satisfied the four revenue recognition criteria:

(1) When the order is received;
(2) when the order is placed with the publisher (Superior having done its part);
(3) when the publisher ships the record; or
(4) after the 30-day trial period.

(b) At all of these points, the record publisher will have satisfied the four revenue recognition criteria:

(1) When the order is received from Superior, assuming the major sales effort has been in establishing distributorships such as Superior;
(2) when an order is shipped;
(3) when payment is received from Superior; or
(4) after the 30-day trial period.

P3. Recognition and matching principles are widely accepted to truly reflect asset, liability, and income figures. Without proper accrual-based figures, these values could be manipulated from period to period. For example, by using cash basis accounting, it could be possible to show poor performance, for tax reasons, by not collecting cash from customers in credit sales: no cash, no revenues, minimum tax.

A simple analogy of accrual accounting is this: if you want to price a product (and receive revenues), you need to know what it cost you to make (incurring an expense). That is, the cost is matched to the price. Whether or not cash changes hands with the cost incurrence or the price received is irrelevant.

P4. (a), (b), and (c)
For March:

Basis of Revenue Recognition

Flats	Production	Shipment	Cash
Produced	75,000		
Shipped (250 × 200)		50,000	
Collected ($520,000 / $13)			40,000
Revenue	$975,000	$650,000	$520,000
Cost of Goods			
Sold ($8/flat)	600,000	400,000	320,000
Shipping ($4.80/flat)	360,000	240,000	192,000
Income	$ 15,000	$ 10,000	$ 8,000

For April:

Basis of Revenue Recognition

Flats	Production	Shipment	Cash
Produced	85,000		
Shipped (250 × 200)		50,000	
Collected ($585,000 / $13)			45,000
Revenue	$1,105,000	$650,000	$585,000
Cost of Goods			
Sold ($8/flat)	680,000	400,000	360,000
Shipping ($4.80/flat)	408,000	240,000	216,000
Income	$ 17,000	$ 10,000	$ 9,000

(d) The following assets are affected by the basis of revenue recognition:

(1) Cash (unaffected)
Inflows with all three methods: $520,000 + $585,000 = $1,105,000
Outflows with all three methods:
Production: ((75,000 × $8) + (85,000 × $8))
= $1,280,000
Shipping: (2 × $240,000) = $480,000
Total: $1,280,000 + $480,000 = $1,760,000
Net cash flow with all three methods: $655,000

(2) Accounts Receivable

(i) Production basis:

Revenues:	$2,080,000
Collections:	1,105,000
Receivables:	$ 975,000

(ii) Shipment basis:

Revenues:	$1,300,000
Collections:	1,105,000
Receivables	$ 195,000

(iii) Cash basis:

Revenues:	$1,105,000
Collections:	1,105,000
Receivables:	$ 0

(3) Inventory

(i) Production basis:

Inventory*:	$1,280,000
Cost of Goods Sold:	1,280,000
Inventory, Ending:	$ 0

(ii) Shipment basis:

Inventory*:	$1,280,000
Cost of Goods Sold:	800,000
Inventory, Ending:	$ 480,000

(iii) Cash basis:

Inventory*:	$1,280,000
Cost of Goods Sold:	680,000
Inventory, Ending:	$ 600,000

* ($75,000 + $85,000)($8)

(4) Prepaid Shipping

(i) Production basis:

Prepaid Shipping:	$480,000
Shipping Expense:	768,000
Accrued Liability:	$288,000

(ii) Shipment basis:

Prepaid Shipping:	$480,000
Shipping Expense:	480,000
Prepaid Shipping:	$ 0

(iii) Cash basis:

Prepaid Shipping:	$480,000
Shipping Expense:	408,000
Prepaid Shipping:	$ 72,000

The above calculations show that total assets are, indeed, affected by the revenue recognition basis.

P5. (a) 2005 income:

Sales (25 @ $200)		$5,000
Cost of Goods Sold:		
Beginning Inventory	$ 0	
Production (25 @ $120)	3,000	3,000
Warranty Provision		800
Income		$1,200

To make provision for returned sets, you could debit an account such as Warranty Provision and credit Warranty Provision Liability.

All the returns from 2005 sales are not necessarily returned in 2005. Therefore, each sales return would be accounted for in the year in which the return was made. For every sales return made in either 2005 or 2006, cash is credited and the Warranty Liability account is debited.

So, 2006 income depends on 2006 sales and 2006 sales returns and estimates of sales returns.

(b) His cash inflow depends on his sales each year and whether these sales are for cash or credit. His cash outflow depends on how many sets he produces each year plus a cash refund of $200 per set returned. The number of returns, in turn, depends on the number of sets sold. Cash flow, then, cannot be determined with the information given.

P6.

Master licence fee: Recognized in full at delivery (point-of-sale) since all the revenue recognition criteria could be satisfied. Practically, this means at the time of signing the licence.

Installation fee: Recognized in full at delivery (shipment, so to speak); that is, when the software has been successfully set-up and installed.

Maintenance fee: The advance payment should be treated as deferred revenue and, each month, 1/12 of this should be recognized as revenue (at delivery) since Hippo Farm will have satisfied all the recognition criteria at each month-end.

Subscription fee: Recognized in full at delivery (shipment, so to speak); practically, this means recognizing revenue each month-end. Even though Hippo Farm has a three-year licence with each client, the monthly volume of meal consumption cannot be measured in advance. Therefore, the revenue recognition criteria are not satisfied on this basis alone.

INTEGRATIVE PROBLEMS

IP1. (a) There are three possible ways of recognizing revenues in this case:

(i) Percentage of completion basis;
(ii) At completion of a contract; or
(iii) Upon cash collection.

Considering the criteria that must be satisfied in revenue recognition, all of the above methods could be defended. Which one you suggest might depend on the quality of the systems (to enable recognition before actual completion), the nature of the contract (terms and dates of delivery and penalty clauses that might cause revenue recognition to be at a specific point in time and no sooner or later), or the creditworthiness of clients.

(b) The development costs should be amortized because they added value to the system design and the ultimate system product.

(c) Amortization could be calculated in the following ways:

(i) \$250,000 / 20 systems = \$12,500 per system sold
(ii) \$250,000 / 4 years = \$62,500 per year straight-line basis
(iii) Matched to the proportion of completion:
e.g., if 85% complete, (85%)(\$12,500) = \$10,625

(d)

Timeless Computer Corporation
Income Statement
For the year ended September 30, 2006

	Percentage of Completion	Completion of Contract	Collection of Cash
Revenue	\$63,750*	\$ 0	\$12,000
Expenses:			
Contract Costs	55,250**	0	10,400A
Amortization	10,625E	12,500	2,000≅
Total	65,875	12,500	22,900
Net Income	\$(2,125)	\$(12,500)	\$ (400)

* (85%)(\$75,000)
** (\$75,000 – \$10,000)(85%)
E (85%)(\$12,500)
A (\$12,000 / \$75,000)(\$75,000 – \$10,000)
≅ (\$12,000/\$75,000)(\$12,500)

Timeless Computer Corporation
Balance Sheet
As at September 30, 2006

	Percentage of Completion	Completion of Contract	Collection of Cash
Assets:			
Cash	$ 6,750	$ 6,750	$ 6,750
Accounts Rec.	51,750*	0	0
Contract Work	0	55,250E	44,850A
Development Costs	239,375	237,500	248,000
Total	$297,875	$299,500	$299,600
Liabilities:			
Deposits	$ 0	$ 12,000	$ 0
Contract Liability	0	0	0
Accounts Payable	0	0	0
Equity:			
Share Capital	300,000	300,000	300,000
Retained Earnings	(2,125)	(12,500)	(400)
Total	$297,875	$299,500	$299,600

* $63,750 revenue – 12,000 deposit.

E Contract costs to date:	
($75,000 – $10,000) – $9,750 =	$55,250
Contract costs expensed this period:	0
Contract work in progress	$55,250

A Contract costs to date:	
($75,000 – $10,000) – $9,750 =	$55,250
Contract costs expensed this period:	10,400
Contract work in progress	$44,850

Timeless Computer Corporation
Cash Flow Statement
For the year ended September 30, 2006

	Percentage of Completion	Completion of Contract	Collection of Cash
Operations:			
Net Income	$ (2,125)	$(12,500)	$ (400)
Non-Cash expenses	10,625	12,500	2,000
	8,500	0	1,600
Non-Cash Working Capital:			
Contract Work		(55,250)	(44,850)
Accounts Rec.	(51,750)	0	0
Deposits	0	12,000	0
Decrease in cash:	$(43,250)	$(43,250)	$(43,250)

Proof:
Before contract sale:
Cash = \$6,750 – \$12,000 + \$55,250 (contract expenses paid in cash)
= \$50,000
After contract sale:
Cash = \$50,000 + \$12,000 – \$55,250 = \$6,750

Alternative Proof:

Cash Receipts:	\$12,000
Cash Payments:	55,250
Decrease:	\$43,250

IP2. (a) Revenues may be recognized when the four criteria discussed in your text have been met. In this case, while the club manager has spent considerable effort in recruiting new members and renewing old ones, the club has not provided any goods or services at the time when a customer pays for a membership. The customer does not pay for the club manager's efforts to get the customer. Rather, he or she pays for the use of facilities. Furthermore, most of the costs associated with making the facilities available to customers after they have paid have not been incurred at the time of payment. The \$14,000 in monthly costs are neither incurred nor paid every time a customer joins the club.

It would seem prudent, then, to treat the membership fee as unearned revenue (a liability) and recognize revenue at the end of each month, when monthly expenses have been incurred and the customer has had access to the facilities. At that point, all of the revenue recognition criteria will have been met. As for the efforts of the manager and her staff in recruiting and renewing members, the salaries expense and promotions expense account for their troubles. Promotions expenses are usually considered a period cost since it is not clear that these expenditures create economic value. Whether or not members join or renew, their efforts would continue (i.e., be an expense of every period). Therefore, their costs should not be justification for revenue recognition at the time of receipt of membership payment.

Revenues from guest visits could be recognized at the time cash is received, since the club will not honour that customer at a later date and will have, therefore, provided the use of its facilities the same day visit payments are received.

(b) The only other possible points of revenue recognition seem to be either when a member joins (or renews), that is, when a sale is made, or when cash is received (which may be some time after a member joins (or renews)). In the former case, the company would not be matching revenues to expenses since it has yet to provide a service to the member. If revenues were so recognized, income would be overstated at any given point in time, since revenues have been recognized but expenses have not yet been. In the latter case, waiting until cash is received is being more conservative. If cash is received shortly after a member joins, then the same problem of matching revenues to expenses occurs. If cash is not received for some time, then, again, a matching problem occurs except this time it is one of matching expenses with revenues. If this sort of revenue recognition is practised, it is quite possible that income would be understated at any given time if members are slow to pay for their memberships.

Given that the membership is payable in advance, it would appear that recognizing revenue would occur when the sale is made and when cash is received, since both should occur simultaneously. In this case, income will appear "lumpy" during the year, being better in the months with strong recruitment drives and lower in those months where new memberships (or renewals) are low.

EXPLORATIVE QUESTIONS

EQ1. Not-for-profit organizations report revenues and expenditures. Waiting to pay the bills after the year-end will certainly improve the look of the financial statements. The cash position and the excess of revenues over expenditures (this is not income) will both look better. You should realize that matching has not occurred, however. Chapter 5 discusses not-for-profit accounting in somewhat more detail.

Whether or not such a practice is ethical is obviously debatable. If accrual accounting were practised, recognizing the expenses, and not just the expenditures, would better reveal the obligations of the organization. In not-for-profit organizations, donors want to see how their contributions are being spent. It would seem proper, then, to show them how their contributions have been spoken for. If you were to pay the bills after year-end and not recognize the expense, ask yourself whether you would be misled by such a practice as a user of financial statements.

EQ2. As you should know by now, accrual accounting uses historical costs, not current values. It, therefore, fails to measure increases in wealth incurred by the changing values of assets (known as capital gains). In this regard, accrual accounting fails to measure what economic theory would.

You should also know by this point that accrual accounting produces income and cash flow figures that could differ considerably. Yet, cash flow is rather important to financial analysts.

Despite these shortcomings, stock analysts put considerable faith in financial statements because, in part, they represent a conservative evaluation of the company. For example, even if the historical cost of an asset on a company's balance sheet is far below its current value, there is no capital gain unless that asset is sold. And if it were sold, it wouldn't be on the balance sheet to worry about. Increases in wealth, in the economic sense, represent *potential* increases in wealth in the accounting sense. That is, shareholder wealth would be increased if an asset was sold and a capital gain was realized.

Another reason stock analysts might put faith in financial statements is that the statements reflect management decision making. How and when management chooses to recognize revenues or expenses is reflected in the statements. Or how receivables are handled is reflected in the statements. These sorts of decisions interest the stock analyst and help him or her evaluate the soundness of a company's management.

Yet another reason for use of financial statements by analysts is that statements are the only quantitative insight outsiders may have into the company. Shareholders employ stockbrokers to evaluate their investments in dollars and cents, in part. Stock analysts, therefore, need some sort of means by which they can do this. Shareholders, be they investors or speculators, take a risk. When a risk pays off or goes sour, they want to be able to count their winnings or their losses. Statement information allows them to do that.

So, you can see that stock analysts may have a variety of reasons for wanting statement information. The reasons above are, by no means, exhaustive, but offer, perhaps, some thoughts on how accrual accounting is valuable, even if it fails to measure wealth in the traditional economic sense.

CHAPTER 7
RECORDKEEPING AND CONTROL

LEARNING OBJECTIVES

After completing Chapter 7, you should:

- appreciate the value of complete and accurate records;
- understand management's responsibility in maintaining control over the assets of an enterprise;
- be able to identify various methods of cash and inventory control; and
- understand what the two most widely used contra accounts are and why they exist within the practice of accrual accounting.

CHAPTER SUMMARY

7.1 Chapter Introduction: Recordkeeping and Control

- As you saw in Chapters 1 and 2, recordkeeping has a transactional base.
- However, not all economic events present themselves as transactions and, therefore, records need to be adjusted.
- Some of these adjustments are a matter of routine, such as recording amortization on an asset; others are less routine, such as recording inventory shortages or delinquent accounts receivable.

7.2 Accounting's "Books" and Records

- Good recordkeeping:
  - allows a business to keep track of how the business is performing. Any business owner will attest to this need;
  - permits comparisons with other businesses as well as with the business itself over time; and
  - simplifies the management of legal and control issues, such as the need to provide information about assets lost in a fire (e.g., for police and insurance purposes) or lost due to theft (e.g., for control of cash handling purposes).
- Recordkeeping systems should be specific to the company based on the needs of that company. There is no *one* correct way to set up a recordkeeping system.
- Records cost money. The expectation, however, is that the informational value of the records to the business exceeds the cost of preparing and maintaining those records.
- Recordkeeping begins with recording transactions, posting them to accounts, preparing financial statements, auditing these statements, and releasing them to interested parties.
- This is the accounting cycle.
- To begin the cycle, source documents are prepared. Examples of these include purchase orders (to evidence receipt of merchandise), cheques (to evidence payment for goods or services), and sales invoices (to evidence transactions with customers).

- There are many additional source documents used by various companies.
- These source documents give rise to recording transactions.
- Transactions are recorded as journal entries in a general journal, showing how the particular accounts are affected by transactions. That is, the dollar values affecting individual accounts are recorded as either debits or credits to the accounts, depending on whether a particular account is being decreased or increased.
- The general ledger is a collection of all the various accounts. It is simply a place to record the effects of transactions on the accounts.
- Once transactions are recorded in the general journal, they are "posted" to the general ledger accounts. This simply means transferring account debits or credits from the general journal to the appropriate general ledger accounts.
- A trial balance is simply a listing of all the general ledger accounts and it is done to prove that, after all transactions have been recorded during a period, the sum of debits equals the sum of credits; in other words, to prove that the value of debits equals the value of credits, to various accounts, in every transaction.
- This trial balance, then, can be used to prepare the financial statements.

7.3 Internal Control

- The value of good records extends beyond simply using them to generate financial statements. Records allow management to run a business effectively and efficiently, permitting control over the organization's resources.
- Recordkeeping to meet decision-making needs, physical protection of assets from theft or damage, insurance coverage, and proper supervision of staff are all elements of what is termed internal control.
- Internal control is a responsibility of management.

7.4 Top Management's Responsibility for Internal Control

- Top management sets the internal control tone for the entire company; top management is instrumental in ensuring that adequate and thorough internal controls not only exist but are also put into practice.
- Ultimately, having effective internal controls is simply an effective management strategy.

7.5 Internal Control of Cash

- Due to its liquid nature, cash is the asset that is most easily stolen. In order to protect cash, internal control principles require proficient recordkeeping and the segregation of duties such that the people who handle cash are not the same as those who keep the records of cash.
- Controls in this area include using locked-in sales registers such as the ones you would see at your local supermarket with a numbered transaction on the register tape for each sale. Multiple copy sales receipts that are pre-numbered and matched with the cash receipts can also be used.
- Once again, the concept of stewardship arises under internal control. Management has a responsibility to safeguard the handling and recording of assets, one of which is cash.

7.6 Control of Sales Taxes Collected and Employee Deductions to Be Remitted

- Virtually every company must charge and collect sales taxes from its customers.
- In doing so, the company is simply acting as a collection arm of the provincial or federal governments.
- At the same time, a company is charged taxes on all its purchases.
- In the case of GST, as an example, the GST paid by a company on its purchases can offset the GST collected from customers and yet to be remitted to the federal government.
- That is, if $1,000 of GST is collected from customers, and $650 of GST is paid due to purchases by the company and for the company, then the company must effectively remit the difference of $350.
- So, sales taxes represent a liability to a company since the company has collected taxes that have to be remitted to the governments.
- In the case of employee payroll deductions or withholdings, again, the company is simply acting as a collecting arm for various parties such as government (income tax withholding, Canada Pension Plan (CPP) withholdings, and Employment Insurance (EI) withholdings), unions (union dues collected), or life insurers (insurance plan deductions)
- All these payroll deductions create a temporary liability until these entities are paid these deductions.
- Payroll creates even further liabilities in that, not only do employees make CPP and EI contributions, but the employer must as well.
- That is, there also arise "Employer CPP Payable" and "Employer EI Payable" liability accounts.
- These create an expense such as "Payroll Benefits Expense."
- Further, employers may make contributions on behalf of employees to medical or dental plans, or the like.
- These additional liabilities further increase "Payroll Benefits Expense" with offsetting liabilities such as "Benefits Payable."

7.7 Control Accounts and Contra Accounts

- A control account is an aggregated total of a group of other accounts, or simply an account unto itself. For example, Accounts Receivable is a control account representing the sum total of individual customer accounts receivable.
- For the purposes of an introductory accounting course, there are two contra accounts: accumulated amortization and allowance for doubtful accounts.
- Contra accounts serve to diminish the value of asset, liability, or even owners' equity accounts.
- Accumulated amortization is a rolling count of the amount of amortization that builds up on an asset.
- It is an account that offsets the value of the asset being amortized (depreciated).
- The historical asset value less accumulated amortization gives you net book value.

- As introduced in Chapter 4 and discussed further in Chapter 8, when an asset is sold, a gain or loss might be incurred. The gain or loss is a function of whether or not sale proceeds are in excess of net book value (hence, a gain) or whether they are less than net book value (hence, a loss).
- Occasionally, an asset is disposed of without any sale proceeds. In such a case, the asset is said to be "written off," meaning that a "loss on disposal" (an expense on the income statement) equivalent to its net book value would be recognized.
- Allowance for doubtful accounts is a rolling count of the amount of credit sales deemed to be uncollectible.
- Recognizing the bad debt is considerably different from writing off the bad debt.
- Recognizing the bad debt means creating a bad debts expense in the period of the sale; this does not directly affect accounts receivable until every attempt has been made to secure payment from the bad account.
- Writing off the bad debt means directly removing it from accounts receivable once default of payment has been reasonably assured.
- The allowance for doubtful accounts account offsets the accounts receivable account on the balance sheet.

7.8 Demonstration Problem: Contra Accounts

- The chapter provides a demonstration problem to better illustrate the accumulated amortization and allowance for doubtful accounts contra accounts.

7.9 Inventory Control

- Much of the working capital of a business may be tied up in inventory. It is necessary, then, to ensure that inventory will not be subject to obsolescence, spoilage, or theft.
- There are three methods of inventory control:

(1) Perpetual Inventory

- This is the most thorough of the inventory methods and requires that the inventory account be kept current at any point in time.
- In order to calculate the inventory and/or cost of goods sold, use the following calculation in either inventory units or dollar cost:

  Beginning inventory value
  + Record of purchases of inventory
  – Record of inventory sold
  = Ending inventory

- If this does not match a physical count at the time this calculation is performed, there is an error in the records or some of the inventory was misplaced or stolen.

(2) Retail Method

- This uses the selling value of the inventory, rather than the cost value, to charge the inventory delivered to the selling area (department). Each department begins a period with a total selling value of inventory and then subtracts the revenue from sales of the inventory as each sale is made. At any point in time, it is possible to calculate the inventory value that should be on hand and find out if it matches a physical count. Inventory valuation is made more difficult, however, because of the existence of markups and markdowns, which require more detailed records.

(3) Periodic Method

- No records are kept of expected quantities or values of inventory. When you need a figure, a physical count is needed and cross-referenced to purchase invoices to obtain a cost value for the balance sheet. Since you are relying on a physical count to prepare your record of inventory value, you cannot determine if there has been theft or misplacement of inventory.

- In order to calculate the inventory and/or cost of goods sold, one would use the following:
  Beginning inventory (from physical count)
  \+ Purchases (from records)
  – <u>Ending inventory (from physical count)</u>
  = Inventory sold (deduced)

- Take a look at the inventory journal entries on page 459 of your text, the Bransworth Ltd. example. Had the *periodic inventory method* been used, the following transactions would have been recorded:

a. Purchases	Dr. Purchases "Expense"	114,000	
	Cr. Cash		114,000
b. Sales	Same entry as perpetual method.		
c. Cost of Goods Sold	No entry is made since no record is being kept of inventory changes. Cost of goods sold is deduced.		
d. Count Adjustment	Dr. Beginning Inventory "Expense"	23,000	
	Cr. Inventory Asset		23,000
	Dr. Inventory Asset	28,000	
	Cr. Ending Inventory "Expense"		28,000
	(This transfers beginning inventory to expense under the assumption that it is sold and records the counted amount of ending inventory)		
e. Collections	Same entry as perpetual method.		

- Compared to the perpetual method in your text, note the differences in the journal entries. Under the perpetual system, there are entries for each area; that is, purchases of inventory, sales of inventory, cost of goods sold, count adjustment for shortage, and collections.

- Using the periodic method, there are entries for the initial purchase of inventory, sales of inventory, the count adjustment that opens the asset and closes the inventory asset for the period, and collections. The cost of goods sold must be deduced since there is no detail.
- Remember that the methods make no difference to any of the accounts except for the inventory. No changes need to be made to cash, sales, accounts receivable, or accounts payable.
- Under the perpetual method, cost of goods sold is $100,000 with a shortage expense of $9,000 (as per the text). Under the periodic method, cost of goods sold is deduced to be $109,000, thus hiding the shortage loss:

  Beginning inventory ($23,000)
  + Purchases ($114,000)
  – Ending inventory ($28,000)
  = Inventory sold ($109,000)

- Income under both approaches will be the same after the inventory calculation, since revenues are unaffected by either approach and expenses are equal under either approach (perpetual: Cost of goods sold expense + Shortage expense = $109,000; periodic: Cost of goods sold expense = $109,000)

EXERCISES

E1. Inventory Control Why is it necessary to take a physical count of inventory at the end of each accounting period?

E2. Ledgers What is a "control" account?

E3. The Use of Internal Control "Internal control seems like such a vague concept. Do I control my employees with a firm hand? Do I make sure my costs are under control? What does internal control really mean?" Explain what internal control means in the accounting context.

E4. Inventory Method Choice Why is the perpetual inventory method a better form of control than the periodic method?

E5. Use of Contra Accounts What is a contra account? In the case of amortization, why not simply credit directly to the asset in question?

E6. Accrual Income Calculation From the following data, calculate accrual net income for the year ending December 31, 2006:

Collection from customers during 2006	$191,250
Accounts receivable, end of 2005	6,615
Accounts receivable, end of 2006	4,940
Allowance for doubtful accounts, end of 2005	425
Allowance for doubtful accounts, end of 2006	570
Bad debts written off during 2006	290
Payments to suppliers during 2006	78,670
Accounts payable, end of 2005	9,650
Accounts payable, end of 2006	11,130
Payments to employees during 2006	89,755
Wages payable, end of 2005	3,425
Wages payable, end of 2006	4,125
Inventory, end of 2005	17,600
Inventory, end of 2006	18,840
Bank loan (taken out September 1, 2006, at 7% per annum)	9,000
Income tax payable, end of 2005	0
Income tax payable, end of 2006	1,725
Income tax paid during 2006	2,220
Future income tax payable, end of 2005	0
Future income tax payable, end of 2006	880

E7. Payroll Remittance Payroll taxes were due to be remitted by Jonas Painting Ltd. on June 15, 2006. After a very busy May, the following information was available:

Employee Income Taxes Withheld	$9,410
CPP Payable, Employer Share	1,879
CPP Payable, Employee Share	1,879
EI Payable, Employer Share	?
EI Payable, Employee Share	?

On June 15, 2006, the bookkeeper sent a cheque to Canada Revenue Agency for the full amount owing. The next month, a Statement of Interest Penalty from Canada Revenue Agency was received for the amount of $1,638.88. Apparently, June's payment was received late and, as a result, a 10% penalty was charged.

What was the amount of EI payable, for both the employer share and employee share, for the June payment keeping in mind that the employer share is 1.4 times the employee share?

PROBLEMS

P1. Inventory Control In the interest of becoming more technologically advanced, Cromwell Corporation decided to update its computer systems. As the comptroller of Cromwell, you believed the first area that needed to be addressed was the inventory. So the first installation was a computerized perpetual inventory system. On the very first day of its use, Joe Cromwell, the president, came to take a look at the records. The first two transactions that came off the system were:

Purchases on account—1,000 units @ \$10/unit = \$10,000
Sales on account—250 units @ \$25/unit = \$6,250

Joe Cromwell examined the journal entries that the computer generated and told you he was a bit confused by the fact that there was no Purchases account, as there had been prior to the change.

(a) Prepare the journal entries that the computer would have generated.
(b) Calculate the balance of the inventory.
(c) Explain to Joe Cromwell why there is no longer a "Purchases" account.

P2. Inventory Control "I can't figure it out," your boss, Ivan T. Terrible, mumbled one Monday morning. Ivan owns Terrible T's, a T-shirt shop in the local mall. "We seem to be selling out our inventory of T-shirts almost as fast as we get them in but we don't seem to be making a profit." Ivan hands you a piece of paper with the following information:

Terrible T's—1/1/06 to 12/31/06	
Sales of T-shirts @ \$5/shirt (including 25% markup)	\$25,000
Inventory, January 1	\$1,000
Purchases of T-shirts during year	\$26,000
Inventory, December 31	\$500

"I've held all my costs down as much as I can. You figure it out and let me know."

(a) Explain to Ivan what has been happening.
(b) Make a suggestion to correct the problem and explain how this would improve the situation.

P3. Use of Internal Control Your company operates a drop shipping business selling hunting clothing and accessories. As a drop shipper, you receive orders and payment from customers by mail or telephone (credit card), and pass these orders on to the manufacturers who will ship the products directly to the customers. What internal control issues should be of concern to you?

P4. <u>Bad Debts and Write-Offs</u> You've decided to enter into a summer business with a friend of yours who is in the engineering faculty. The two of you plan to install underground sprinkler systems in residential and commercial properties. The summer progresses and you're amazed (and exhausted) by how much business your partner has drummed up. You're also concerned by the fact that some of your installations have been for questionable clients. You raise this concern with your partner, who says: "Not to worry, we can write off anybody who doesn't pay us. Don't worry so much, that means that it's tax deductible; we'll get it back from the government." Sure enough, two residential installations you had done were for customers who were moving and wanted to increase their property value with the sprinklers; they moved without paying you! Explain to your partner the error of his ways.

P5. <u>Bad Debts and Write-Offs</u> In fiscal 2005, Markham Aviation Services, Ltd. recognized bad debts in the amount of $27,000. This meant that it had by now made allowances of $79,000. In preparing its year-end statement of financial position, the company showed $296,000 in uncollected billings. Upon more careful scrutiny of the clients involved, it was learned that one of the clients had filed for bankruptcy and that Markham was certain not to see any of the $17,000 it was owed by this client. The company also decided that another two clients, who had been pursued for overdue payments already and had promised to pay the $23,000 as soon as they could, were, in fact, doubtful accounts.

(a) By how much will 2005 income be reduced?
(b) What is the value of net accounts receivable?

P6. <u>Transactions and Journal Entries</u> Whisper Bookstores Ltd. operates a chain of stores in retail malls. All accounting matters are handled by a central office. The following information was received by the accounting office for the month of July:

(i) The leases of two stores were up for renewal. Rent would be increased by $200 per month/per store effective the first of next month.

(ii) In response to a change in mall management, one store will have to be closed down by the first of next month.

(iii) A publisher, to whom Whisper owed $4,200 for inventory, went into receivership. The receiver is demanding immediate payment of the $4,200.

(iv) Whisper took out a three-year, 12% bank loan for $30,000 to purchase new store fixtures. The funds were advanced to Whisper July 16 but payments would not start until August 30.

(v) Total inventory at all stores was valued at $790,000 at the beginning of the month. Universal Product Code (UPC) scanning at the cash registers showed that the cost of sales during the month was $165,000. Purchases of inventory for the month amounted to $35,000. A physical count showed inventory amounting to $660,500.

Prepare journal entries for the items that are accounting transactions. If an item is not an accounting transaction, state briefly why that is so.

P7. Bad Debts Policy A company practises the following policy with respect to its accounts receivable: in years of general economic growth, it reduces its doubtful account allowance and in years of economic downturn, it increases its doubtful account allowance. What would be the rationale for such a policy and what are its consequences?

P8. GST Remittance Paragon Services Ltd, a mechanical contracting firm, elected to remit GST returns quarterly using the simplified method. The simplified method meant that a GST registrant collected GST at a rate of 7% and remitted GST at a rate of 5%. However, the registrant was not permitted to claim GST paid on any purchases for the business.

For the period January 1, 2006, to March 31, 2006, Paragon had sales of $410,540. The GST remittance for the quarter is due April 30, 2006. By that date, however, the company had not yet collected $49,370 of credit sales it made during the year's first quarter.

How much GST does the firm need to remit on April 30, 2006?

INTEGRATIVE PROBLEM

IP1. Inventory Policy Effects If a company changed inventory control methods, could income be manipulated? Could the balance sheet be manipulated?

EXPLORATIVE QUESTIONS

EQ1. Internal Control Policy What guideline should be used ultimately to design the specific controls that should be built into a control system?

EQ2. Recordkeeping Practice Accounting seems to use fairly elaborate and extensive recordkeeping procedures. Why do you think this is necessary?

SOLUTIONS

EXERCISES

E1. It is necessary to take a physical count of the inventory to ensure that all of the inventory you expect is there, or to determine what the amount of the inventory is. Without knowing the inventory, one cannot tell what the COGS should be.

E2. A "control" account exists when a subsidiary ledger is kept for various accounts of the general ledger. A subsidiary ledger may be kept for all of a retailer's customers who bought on account. In other words, the subsidiary ledger contains the individual accounts of all the credit customers. The general ledger account for Accounts Receivable would be the "control" account. That is, if all the individual customer accounts in the Accounts Receivable subsidiary ledger were added together, they should equal the amount shown in the general ledger account for Accounts Receivable.

E3. Internal control refers to systems or procedures a company might establish to ensure that assets, such as cash or inventory, are safeguarded, to ensure that accounting records are reliable, and to ensure that financial information is prepared in a timely manner.

For example, McDonald's Restaurants will count hamburger patties at the end of a day to ensure that the number of patties used (as given by the difference from the previous day's count) will equal the number of hamburgers sold (as given by the cash register records that total the various products sold).

E4. The perpetual inventory control system keeps track of what the ending inventory should be if it were to be verified by a physical count. It requires that purchases and sales of inventory be continuously kept. The periodic system requires that a count be taken to determine what inventory was sold. The problem with this method is that it doesn't tell you what the inventory should be, only what it is. Therefore, if inventory is lost or stolen, it inadvertently becomes part of the cost of goods sold figure that the periodic method deduces.

E5. Contra accounts are used to accumulate amounts that will diminish the value of an asset, liability, or owner's equity account. They are mostly used for expense recognition and amounts are not directly credited to assets, for example, so as to show the historical value of the asset. In the case of amortization, if the historical asset value is shown, and accumulated amortization is shown separately, the reader can ascertain the useful life left in the asset.

Contra accounts are an accrual accounting tool used to represent the true value of assets, liabilities, or owners' equity. The balance sheet values are historical and, because of the passage of time, as in the case of amortization, or because of new information, as in the case of a credit customer who subsequently goes bankrupt causing a bad debt, they may not reflect the most recent position of the company.

E6. Sales: Let X = Sales
$\$6,615 + X - \$191,250 - \$290 = \$4,940, X = \$189,865$
Purchases: Let X = Purchases
$\$9,650 - \$78,670 + X = \$11,130, X = \$80,150$
Cost of Goods Sold: Let X = Cost of Goods Sold
$\$17,600 + \$80,150 - X = \$18,840, X = \$78,910$
Wages Expense: Let X = Wages Expense
$\$3,425 + X - \$89,755 = \$4,125, X = \$90,455$
Income Tax Expense: $2,220 + $1,725 + $880 = $4,825

Revenues	$189,865
COGS	78,910
Wages Expense	90,455
Income Tax Expense	4,825
Net Income	$ 15,675

E7. $(X)(0.10) = \$1,638.88; X$ = Total Payroll Remittance = $16,388.80
$\$9,410 + \$1,879 + \$1,879 + Y = \$16,388.80; Y$ = EI Payable = $3,220.80
$2.4Z = \$3,220.8; Z$ = Employee Share = $1,342
Employer Share = $3,220.80 – $1,342 = $1,878.80

PROBLEMS

P1. (a) The journal entries that the computer would have generated would be:

Inventory	10,000	
Accounts payable		10,000
Accounts Receivable	6,250	
Revenue		6,250
Cost of Goods Sold	2,500	
Inventory		2,500

(b) The inventory balance would be 1000 – 250 = 750 units or $7,500.

(c) The Purchases account is no longer necessary under the perpetual inventory system. Any items received are directly debited to the Inventory account and any sales directly remove items from that account.

P2. (a) Ivan has sold $20,000 worth of inventory. He began the year with $1,000 worth and purchased $26,000 worth of T-shirts, so he should have an inventory left over of $7,000 at the end of the year. Instead, he has only $500 of inventory, meaning a loss of $6,500.

(b) Since his T-shirts are likely not unique and distinguishable, it does not seem to make sense to try a perpetual inventory control system. The key is to determine what caused the loss. One reason might be poor recordkeeping. For example, a defective shipment may have been returned but not recorded as such. Another reason may be shoplifting or some other theft (by employees). Yet another reason may be inventory that was damaged by staff and thrown out. Ivan may want to implement some controls along these lines before he changes his inventory control system.

P3. You should be concerned about how payment is received from your customers. You should probably have a policy of no cash payments. This would minimize customers who claim to have sent payment and accuse your staff of stealing the money from the envelope. This would also minimize the chance of theft by both your staff and possibly mail handlers. If payment is received by cheque or money order, then there is documentation to support any disputes or control problems that may arise. For credit card orders, the card limit and expiry date should be confirmed before the order is passed on to the manufacturer. To prevent fraudulent use of credit card numbers received by your staff, you could ensure that orders are sent only to the address of the cardholder. This may be achieved by working with the credit card company.

Inventory control is not really a concern to you because you do not stock inventory. But you should be concerned about the possibility of staff placing orders with the manufacturers for which there are no supporting customer orders. In other words, the manufacturer will invoice you for an order but you will have no revenues to support that order. If this is a concern, perhaps all orders to the manufacturers could be routed through one person, or someone could verify that all orders to the manufacturers are indeed supported by customers' orders.

P4. You can make a provision for bad debts. To recognize the bad debt, the entry is:

Bad Debts Expense	XXX	
Allowance for Doubtful Accounts		XXX

To actually write off the bad debt, the entry is:

Allowance for Doubtful Accounts	XXX	
Accounts Receivable		XXX

Recognizing the bad debt gives you an expense that may be deducted from income and, therefore, reduces your income tax. This does not entitle you to reimbursement from the government.

Recognizing it also reduces your net assets and your equity. So there is something to worry about in such cases. Writing off the debt in no way affects your assets or your income. After the write-off, net accounts receivable and income are as they were after the recognition.

P5. (a) $27,000 + $23,000 = $50,000 in bad debts expense for 2005.

(b)

$79,000	in Allowance for Doubtful Accounts plus
23,000	in new doubtful accounts less
17,000	in write-offs equals
$85,000	total Allowance for Doubtful Accounts.

$296,000	in Accounts Receivable less
17,000	in write-off less
85,000	in Allowance for Doubtful Accounts equals
$194,000	in net Accounts Receivable.

P6. (i) No transaction because the rent increase is not yet effective.

(ii) No transaction. Since the stores are part of a chain, and not subsidiaries, this is not a discontinued operation in the accounting sense. If the store's assets are transferred to other stores, then all that has happened is that assets have been re-shuffled within the company. Each store is not a separate entity, it is presumed, with separate liabilities and assets. Rather, each store is simply part of the larger chain. All assets and liabilities are the chain's, not the stores'. If the assets are sold, then there may be a gain or loss on the sale of those assets depending on the book values of those assets. In such a case, there would be an accounting transaction but we do not have enough information to prepare one.

(iii)

Accounts Payable	4,200	
Cash		4,200

(iv) Normally, interest would accrue on the loan on a monthly basis. In this case, the first payment is not one month after the funds were advanced. It is therefore necessary to create an interest adjustment for the period from when the funds were advanced to one month prior to the first payment. In other words, interest will accrue from July 16 to the end of the month and then, of course, accrue monthly thereafter.

July 16 to July 31 is 15 days. (15/365)(0.12)($30,000) = $147.95
At the end of July, then, the adjusting entry is:

Interest Expense	147.95	
Accrued Interest Payable		147.95

(v) Given that Whisper's cash registers can accommodate UPC scanning, it appears that the company has a perpetual inventory system. Following the system, ending inventory should be $790,000 + $35,000 – $165,000 = $660,000. If the physical count reveals that $660,500 worth of inventory exists, then there is a gain on inventory. The transaction would be:

Inventory	500	
Inventory Gain		500

Such a gain may have occurred if more inventory was received in purchases than was actually recorded or if more inventory was recorded as sold than was actually the case (double scanned, for example).

P7. In the good years presumably more customers are less likely to default, whereas in bad years more are likely to default on their accounts. The company may be trying to present a fair valuation of its net accounts receivable, given economic realities. Given equal sales in the good and bad years, in the good years, the company will have fewer bad debt expenses, since there is less of an allowance for doubtful accounts; this means a higher net income. In the bad years, the increased bad debts will drive net income down. When income rises in the good years, so too does the tax liability and in the bad years, the tax liability will be reduced. In the good years, net accounts receivable will be higher than in the bad years, thus improving working capital.

An important assumption made above was that revenues stayed the same in both the good and the bad years. This is not too likely, however. If revenues fall in the bad years, the increase in bad debts expense due to the increased allowance will not be as large as if revenues had remained constant; if revenues are down, accounts receivable are down, and, therefore, any increases to the allowance for doubtful accounts (and bad debts expense) are not as great as would be the case if revenues had not fallen.

P8. The amount not yet collected is irrelevant. Canada Revenue Agency does not make allowances for a company's credit collection policy or efforts. The simplified basis of GST remittance calculates GST owing as follows:

$$(\$410{,}540 \times 1.07) \times 0.05 = \$21{,}963.89$$

The 2-percentage-point difference needs to be accounted for as additional revenue to the company:

GST Collected = \$410,540 × 0.07	= \$ 28,737.80
GST Owed	= \$(21,963.89)
Additional revenue	\$ 6,773.91

INTEGRATIVE PROBLEM

IP1. Whether a periodic or a perpetual inventory control system is being used, net income will ultimately end up being the same. The significance, however, is in how that income is derived. The periodic method will hide any inventory losses or gains in the cost of goods sold figure. The perpetual method, on the other hand, will show losses or gains separately. The income statement resulting from the perpetual method thus provides more information that may be useful in meeting some of management's objectives with respect to internal control. If, however, a physical count is not done (as may be the case for monthly statement preparation as opposed to quarterly or yearly), the perpetual method will not show inventory adjustments for gains or losses and income will therefore differ from that which will result from using the periodic method.

The choice of inventory control methods will not affect the balance sheet. The only instance where the balance sheet may differ between the methods is if the perpetual system is used without a verifying count. The inventory figure may then be overstated or understated, depending on whether there were losses or gains to inventory.

EXPLORATIVE QUESTIONS

EQ1. The guidelines that one should use to build specific controls into a control system are those that will address the specific needs of the firm. This may not seem like much of an answer, but each firm differs in its needs. A control system designed for a manufacturer, which incorporates extensive materials inventory purchasing and usage controls, will be meaningless to a small law firm. The key is flexibility and utility. If inappropriate controls are in place, they will not be used and may as well not exist.

EQ2. Among other reasons, it is important that the information available to users of accounting information be verifiable. The books and records of accounting provide proof that what the statements reveal is, in fact, true and not fabricated by the company to make the company look worse or better than it actually is. This is where the role of the auditor comes in (discussed in detail in Chapter 5 of your text). The auditor exists to verify and ascertain that, in his or her opinion, the statements reflect GAAP and that the information contained in the statements is fairly presented and free of material misstatement. The auditor may check the recordkeeping system of a company to see that a transaction leaves a proper audit trail. So, one reason, then, may be to satisfy the needs of external users.

Another reason may lie in the need to satisfy owners or management that their assets, such as cash or inventory, are protected by some form of control. As a business owner, it hurts the rewards of your efforts to have assets unjustly diminished. Equally unfortunate would be for a business owner to be misled by fixed assets that have not been depreciated, for example, or by debts that have not been recorded. Imagine the surprise of the business owner whose management has "forgotten" to record a bank loan sought earlier in the year. From an internal use perspective, a sound recordkeeping system is essential, that is, unless management does not want to know how it's doing. The importance of recordkeeping to management and owners is that it provides a fair means by which progress can be measured. If accounting events are not recorded, the real harm is to management and owners. It is, therefore, in both of their best interests to ensure that a system of checks and balances exists.

Extensive recordkeeping systems exist, then, to provide information that is as accurate and timely as possible for internal or external users.

CHAPTER 8
ASSETS ACCOUNTING

LEARNING OBJECTIVES

After completing Chapter 8, you should:

- understand the historical cost basis valuation of balance sheet items;
- be able to show that most policy choices do not affect cash flow;
- know how the policy choices in the following areas affect reporting:
  - inventories;
  - depreciable assets;
  - intangible and leased assets; and
  - liabilities and equity.
- understand the various cost flow assumptions made to value inventory and cost of goods sold (or manufactured);
- know how to apply the lower of cost or market rule;
- understand the various methods of calculating amortization;
- appreciate how the consumption of intangible or leased assets is accounted for;
- know the difference between an operating lease and a capital lease;
- understand why provision is made for long-term accruals; and
- know what is meant by off-balance-sheet financing.

CHAPTER SUMMARY

8.1 Chapter Introduction: Accounting for the Left-Hand Side of the Balance Sheet

- Ultimately, an enterprise must recognize the constraints placed on it by the standards and principles of financial accounting. Accounting policy choice exists, but an enterprise must prepare the financial statements being mindful of the complexity of users' needs and the necessity of being fair.

8.2 Balance Sheet Valuation

- When you were introduced to balance sheets in Chapter 2 of the text, you should have questioned what values to use when preparing a balance sheet. Is an asset reported at what it is worth today, what was paid for it, or some other measure?
- There are a number of ways in which assets and liabilities could be valued:

Historical Cost:	This considers what was paid for the asset at the time of acquisition and what was promised as a liability at the time that the obligation was created.
Price-Level- Adjusted Historical Cost:	This takes into account the effect of inflation/deflation on the historical cost values of assets and liabilities.

Current or Market Value:	This approach values assets and liabilities according to what it might cost to replace an asset now (or for what an asset could be sold now) and what it would cost to replace an existing liability (or for what an existing liability could be discharged).
Value in Use:	This approach considers the value of an asset or liability to be the future cash flows that will be generated or the future cash outflows that could be avoided.
Liquidation Value:	The value of assets and liabilities is given by what they could be sold for (in the case of assets) or discharged for (in the case of liabilities) if the company were no longer able to remain a going concern.

- Despite all these alternatives, GAAP specify that historical cost values will be used in financial reporting. The reasons for this hinge upon reliability and conservatism.

8.3 Demonstration Problem: Current Market Value as an Alternative to Historical Cost

- The chapter considers various alternatives to historical cost accounting in the context of two real estate development companies, Oxbridge and Bramview. Make sure you understand the various alternatives, their strengths and weaknesses and the rationale for recommending each one.

8.4 The Cost of an Asset: The Basic Components

- This section is included to show how GAAP are applied to balance sheet preparation and interpretation.
- When valuing an asset using historical cost, you must also include all of the costs associated with making that asset available for use.
- For example, if you buy a building, the acquisition cost would include not only the purchase price, but also any real estate commissions paid and any legal fees paid in association with the purchase. Furthermore, if you had to repair or remodel the building to make it usable, this, too, would be added to the acquisition cost.
- What if you had to make payments to existing tenants in order to prematurely terminate their leases to get them out of your new building? This, too, would become part of the acquisition cost.
- What if a month after you bought the building you had to replace the heating system? This would be considered a maintenance expense and not part of the acquisition cost. Alternatively, what if you added on to the back of the building? This would be considered a betterment and added to the value (or cost) of the asset.

8.5 Cash and Temporary Investments

- By this point, you are well aware that cash is deemed to include not just cash, but cash equivalents as well.

- Cash, by itself, is that which is available for immediate use and not tied up in holding accounts or receivables.
- The cash balance in a company's books may not equate to the cash balance reported by the company's bank. This is the result of having outstanding deposits or cheques (which have been recorded by the company but have not yet cleared the bank).
- Since most company chequing accounts do not bear interest, cash is held unproductively if left in the bank as a demand deposit. For this reason, temporary investments are tools by which excess cash is put to work to earn interest.
- Stocks of other companies, bonds, term deposits, etc., are examples of financial instruments that are used to "park" cash.

8.6 Accounts Receivable

- If the accounts receivable arise from the day-to-day activities of the business, they are known as "trade" receivables. They are normally classified as current assets since they are usually collected within a year.
- They are valued at the lower of cost or market; cost is the amount pledged by a customer at the time of sale, and market is the amount expected to be collected.
- Market value can be less than cost and, if so, an allowance is made for that amount of receivables that will not be collected (called Allowance for Doubtful Accounts and covered in Chapter 7 of your text).
- Accounts Receivable is usually shown as net, that is, after deducting the Allowance for Doubtful Accounts.
- There are other kinds of receivables that may be shown on the balance sheet separately from the "trade" receivables. They are:
  - "Notes" receivable, which are contracts between buyers and sellers that have a payment schedule and an interest rate. These are usually the result of the sales of appliances, cars, houses, etc. These notes are shown at present value (i.e., future value is not included, only the interest that is due at present).
  - Loans to employees, officers and shareholders, or associated companies, or tax refunds that are due to the company. These are transactions that do not arise from revenue transactions. They are valued as normal trade receivables but are usually disclosed due to the peculiarities of their circumstances.

8.7 Inventory Valuation and Cost of Goods Sold

- At the end of a reporting period, figuring out the actual cost of inventory may be made difficult by the varieties and quantities of goods that you have on hand.
- A technique called specific identification may be used when your inventory consists of relatively few items that are somehow identifiable and distinguishable, such as by serial numbers.
- But for most inventories, to make inventory accounting manageable, we can *assume* a cost flow.
- We can assume that inventory costs followed one of three flows (or we can assume different flows for different types of inventory):

(i) FIFO: We can assume that goods were sold in the order in which they were acquired; that is, on a "first-in, first-out" basis. Ending inventory is then carried on the balance sheet at the most recent cost, and the cost of goods sold expense is based on older costs.

(ii) LIFO: We can assume that the goods that were sold were those goods that were acquired most recently; that is, on a "last-in, first-out" basis. Ending inventory is then carried on the balance sheet at older prices paid and the cost of goods sold expense is based on the most recent prices paid.

(iii) AVGE: We do not assume that costs follow any particular flow, but instead assume that the cost of each unit both sold and on hand is an average of the costs of all units bought.

- FIFO results in a balance sheet value that represents the most recent acquisition costs and is thus more indicative of the current replacement costs of the inventory, but it also results in a cost of goods sold expense figure that reflects older costs.
- For inventories that have a limited shelf life due to perishability, obsolescence, or fad, FIFO is considered an appropriate method of valuation.
- LIFO results in a balance sheet value that reflects older costs, which may be far removed from the current market value of that inventory, but it also results in a cost of goods sold expense figure that reflects the most recent costs associated with inventory.
- For inventories that are not highly distinguishable, such as a pile of coal, LIFO is considered an appropriate method of valuation, since all of the product is, in effect, the same (it would serve little useful purpose to try to remove a truckload of coal from the *bottom* of the pile).
- AVGE results in both inventory and cost of goods sold figures that fall in between those resulting from FIFO and LIFO.
- For inventories that are mixed together and indistinguishable, such as oil, AVGE is considered an appropriate method of valuation.
- In Chapter 7, you were introduced to the periodic and perpetual inventory control systems.
- FIFO calculations are not affected by the use of either of the internal control systems, but LIFO and AVGE are affected.
- In periods of rising prices, LIFO perpetual produces a higher inventory value than LIFO periodic, but still lower than either FIFO, AVGE perpetual, or AVGE periodic.
- In periods of rising prices, AVGE perpetual produces a higher inventory value than AVGE periodic, LIFO perpetual, and LIFO periodic, but lower than FIFO.
- In periods of rising prices, LIFO perpetual produces a lower cost of goods sold figure than LIFO periodic, but higher than FIFO, AVGE perpetual, and AVGE periodic.
- In periods of rising prices, AVGE perpetual produces a lower cost of goods sold figure than AVGE periodic, LIFO perpetual, and LIFO periodic, but higher than FIFO.
- If the costs of inventory purchases do not change during a period, then FIFO, LIFO, and AVGE would allocate similar amounts to cost of goods sold and ending inventory.

- If inventory costs fluctuate, however, there are differing effects to the balance sheet and income statement from using any of the three methods.
- Regardless of whether a periodic or perpetual inventory control system is used, if inventory costs are rising, FIFO reports a higher net income than LIFO or AVGE since it shows a lower cost of goods sold, and LIFO produces a lower net income than FIFO or AVGE.
- This is because, during rising prices, FIFO yields the highest inventory figure (and, hence, lowest cost of goods sold) and LIFO yields the lowest ending inventory figure (and, hence, highest COGS).
- So, if it is management's objective to maximize net income, FIFO should be used during rising prices and LIFO during falling prices.
- But if the objective is to minimize net income to minimize the income tax expense, then LIFO should be used during rising prices and FIFO during falling prices.
- In Canadian practice, LIFO is not permitted for income tax purposes.

8.8 Demonstration Problem: Inventory Costing

- This section of the chapter reviews how to calculate inventory costs and COGS under five different inventory costing methods. Ensure that you understand the impact to the financial statements of choosing one inventory costing method over another.

8.9 Lower of Cost or Market and Other Costing Methods

- Regardless of the inventory cost flow assumption made or the inventory control system used, GAAP require a departure from historical cost when valuing inventory if the replacement cost of inventory loses its value, or if the inventory loses its value, say, due to damage, obsolescence, or deterioration.
- This means that inventories must be recognized at the lower of cost or market.
- Market can either mean replacement cost, for inventories that are typically consumed in the course of business but not sold, or it can mean net realizable value, for inventory that is intended for sale.
- When the market value of inventory drops below the historical cost of that inventory, the value of that inventory should be written down; that is, the lower of cost or market rule should be applied to reflect conservatism.
- Such a write-down will cause an inventory loss expense to be deducted from income in the period of the write-down.
- In summary, you should appreciate that the choice of inventory cost flow assumptions and the choice of internal control methods have both balance sheet and income statement implications.

8.10 Amortization of Assets and Amortization Expense

- All long-lived assets, with the exception of land, have a limited life over which they will provide benefits to the user.
- To ensure a fair matching of revenues and expenses (accrual accounting), the use of these assets in earning revenues for a company must be recognized.

- Accrual accounting requires that the cost of an asset be allocated over its useful life (with the exception of land).
- For tangible assets, this has been called depreciation; for intangible assets, it has been called amortization; and for natural resource assets, it has been called depletion. Note, however, that the term *amortization* is increasingly being used regardless of the assets in question.
- As you have already seen in earlier chapters, recognizing amortization gives rise to an accumulated amortization account, since non-current assets must be carried at historical cost on the balance sheet.
- The net book value of non-current assets then becomes historical cost less accumulated amortization.
- Amortization is a process of cost allocation, not asset valuation; that is, amortization is not calculated to determine the value at which the asset should be carried on the balance sheet, but, rather, to show how that asset is being used over its useful life and what cost that use has.
- When amortization expense is recognized on tangible assets, the balancing credit is accumulated amortization for those assets.
- Accumulated amortization is not a fund of cash set aside to buy new assets when the old ones expired.
- Land is not amortized, since it is not normally subject to physical or economic decline as are other long-lived assets.
- If land should lose its economic value and/or utility due to unusual circumstances, such as an earthquake, the asset would not be amortized, but instead an extraordinary loss would be recognized.
- In the case of land that is directly used to earn revenue, such as land used for strip mining, the land would, indeed, be amortized (depleted).

8.11 Gains and Losses on Non-Current Asset Disposals and Write-Offs

- When non-current assets are sold, the proceeds are not considered as ordinary revenue since such transactions are not the mainstay of the business.
- Instead, a gain or loss is respectively recognized and added to or subtracted from income.
- The amount of the gain or loss is the difference between the proceeds from the sale and the book value of the non-current asset at the time of the sale.
- Gains and losses are book gains and losses; consider them as corrections for incorrectly estimating amortization to the time of the sale.
- Losses are added back to income on the cash flow statement to correct for insufficient amortization up to the time of disposal; that is, more amortization, in effect, is added back to income on the cash flow statement to reflect the fact that the sale value was not as great as book value.
- Gains are deducted from income on the cash flow statement to correct for too much amortization up to the time of disposal; that is, more amortization is deducted from income on the cash flow statement to reflect the fact that the sale value was greater than the book value.

- If you think of gains and losses in these terms, you should see that they do not involve cash, just as amortization does not involve cash.
- The only cash effect of non-current asset disposal lies in the proceeds received from the sale, and this is accounted for in the Investing section of the cash flow statement.
- When a non-current asset is disposed of, both the asset and its accumulated amortization are removed from the balance sheet.
- Similarly, when a non-current asset is written off or written down in value, the asset and its accumulated amortization are removed from the balance sheet and the loss is simply the book value at the time of the write-off or the amount of the write-down.

8.12 Amortization Bases and Methods

- There are a variety of amortization methods that may be used:

  (1) Straight-Line Amortization

  - An equal amount of amortization expense is recognized every reporting period during the asset's life.
  - If the asset will have a salvage value (a value for which it may be sold) at the end of its useful life, such a value must be estimated.
  - Amortization expense for a period $= \dfrac{\text{Cost} - \text{Salvage value}}{\text{Useful life}}$

  (2) Declining Balance Accelerated Amortization

  - The amount of amortization expense diminishes each period during the asset's life.
  - Normally, salvage value is not considered with this method.
  - Amortization expense for a period = (Book value)(Amortization rate)
  - As you can see from the formula, the amortization expense will become consecutively smaller, since book value will be decreasing.

  (3) Units of Production Amortization and Depletion

  - Rather than considering the useful life of an asset in terms of time, this method calculates amortization on the basis of asset use.
  - Once again, salvage value is considered and an amortization rate is calculated based on anticipated usage over the asset's life.

- The amortization expense for a given period is based on the actual usage multiplied by the amortization rate.
- Amortization rate = $\frac{\text{Cost} - \text{Salvage value}}{\text{Estimated usage over useful life}}$
- Amortization expense for a period = (Actual usage)(Amortization rate)
- Amortization expense is still an estimate, since the rate is based on estimated usage and estimated salvage value.
- Depletion is calculated using the units of production method.
- The only significant difference in recording amortization vs. depletion is that, with depletion, there is not a contra account to hold accumulated depletion since the asset is credited directly.
- Depletion refers to the physical consumption of the asset, not just the economic consumption.

(4) Decelerated Amortization

- This method exists to depreciate assets whose values are expected to decline more in the latter years of their lives than in the former.
- As a result, the amortization expense per period of the asset's life increases.
- This method is not widely used, since few assets increase in economic usefulness.

- The method of amortization chosen does not affect cash flow; amortization is a non-cash expense.
- The method of amortization does, however, affect the book value of assets and net income.
- In considering the effect on net income, more than the obvious amortization expense effect is important; the book value at the time of a sale of a non-current asset, as determined by an amortization method, will determine gains or losses on the sale of that asset.
- Such gains or losses are respectively added to or deducted from income.

8.13 Demonstration Problem: Amortization Methods

- The chapter demonstrates the impact of various amortization methods using the example of Asimov Petroleum Inc.

8.14 Other Assets, Intangibles, and Capital Leases

- Deferred charges sometimes appear as assets. They refer to payments made in the past that are expected to yield a future benefit. Organization or incorporation costs may be an example.
- Intangible assets such as patents, trademarks, goodwill, and research and development expenditures, among others, are other non-current assets that must be accounted for.
- Generally speaking, general research and development costs are usually expensed, whereas expenditures in other areas are usually capitalized as intangible assets.
- Intangible assets are amortized over their useful life; the definition of useful life may be cut and dried for assets such as patents (having a 20-year life), or it may be difficult to determine, as in the case of incorporation costs.
- In some cases, such as goodwill, accounting standards specify a maximum life over which the asset may be amortized.
- Recognizing an intangible asset or a capital lease affects the balance sheet by way of increased assets and, in the case of capital leases, increased liabilities, and affects the income statement by way of increased amortization recognition.
- Historically, companies did not have to report long-term lease obligations.
- Standards have evolved, however, in the interests of fairness, requiring that such leases be carried on the balance sheet.
- Capital leases are long-term lease obligations that are recorded as if the company owned the assets.
- In accounting for the leased asset, the asset is valued on the balance sheet at the present value of the stream of future lease payments and a simultaneous lease liability is created to show that the asset is not, in fact, owned.
- When lease payments are made, the liability is reduced.
- Accrued interest is recorded separately so as to distinguish the value of the liability itself from the cost of financing.
- The leased asset is amortized over the term of the lease, not necessarily the life of the asset.
- The particulars of capital leases are usually disclosed in the notes to financial statements; in fact, the lessee must report the minimum capital lease payments for the next five years in the notes to the financial statements.
- Operating leases are accounted for differently because they do not give the lessee continuing rights to the asset beyond one year, typically.
- The leased asset in this case is not carried on the lessee's books and lease payments are simply considered a rent expense.

EXERCISES

E1. Inventory Valuation Methods What are some advantages and disadvantages of FIFO and LIFO inventory cost flow assumptions?

E2. <u>Conservative Valuation</u> What does "market" refer to in the context of presenting inventory values conservatively?

E3. <u>Understanding Amortization</u> Why is amortization *not* a means of asset valuation?

E4. <u>Lease Obligations</u> "Lease, rent, or buy, it's all the same; we have the asset." Explain how the accounting treatment differs for those three forms of asset acquisition.

E5. <u>Asset Disposition</u> Prepare a journal entry for the following transaction: Strolisky & Associates, Inc., purchased a new company vehicle for $42,000, putting $6,000 down in cash, trading in an old vehicle for $14,000, and financing the balance. The old vehicle had a book value of $18,000 with accumulated amortization of $7,000.

E6. <u>Asset Valuation</u> In purchasing a piece of land, would razing costs be capitalized?

E7. <u>Understanding Receivables</u> How does a note receivable differ from an account receivable?

E8. <u>Policy Choices</u> You have just opened a hardware store with a partner. What are some of the accounting policy decisions that you will have to make?

PROBLEMS

P1. <u>Inventory Valuation Methods</u> What rationale or justification can you provide for using LIFO as a basis of inventory valuation and income determination?

P2. <u>Inventory Valuation Methods</u> The following inventory purchase and sale information is available for Tridon Suppliers, Ltd.:

Date	Purchased (units)	Price/ unit	Sold (units)
January 3	200	$9.00	
January 5			75
January 9			90
January 10	300	8.50	
January 14			220
January 16			95
January 17	200	8.25	
January 23			120
January 24			50

Tridon's opening inventory for the month was 75 units valued at $712.50.

(a) Assuming a periodic inventory control system, calculate the cost of goods sold and ending inventory values under the FIFO, LIFO, and average cost flow assumptions.
(b) Repeat part (a) above, assuming a perpetual inventory control system.
(c) Give examples of products or cite the circumstances under which each of the cost flow assumptions may be appropriate.
(d) If Tridon were trying to minimize its tax liability this year, what would be your suggested inventory policy?

P3. Asset Valuation Timberline Resources, Ltd., recently acquired 5,000 hectares of timber land from a private owner for a cost of $10,000,000. The company estimated that the land would yield 80 million board-feet of saleable lumber. A further $1,000,000 was spent clearing logging roads and establishing several site stations. The company commenced logging operations on June 1, 2005, and in the first year harvested 11,250,000 board-feet of lumber and sold 9,000,000 board-feet at a contract price of $800 per 1,000 board-feet. The operations cost of the first year's harvest and re-forestation program amounted to $1,209,375, with selling and administrative expenses totalling $675,000. When all the timber has been harvested, and new seedlings planted, Timberline estimates that it will be able to sell the land for $2,000,000.

(a) How would you give accounting consideration to the $1,000,000 spent on road clearing and site station establishment?
(b) Ignoring income tax, calculate the fiscal 2005 income.

P4. Amortization and Asset Disposition Advanced Payroll Systems, Ltd., uses a mini-computer to process payroll cheques for its client companies. Computer equipment is depreciated on an accelerated basis, since it tends to become technologically obsolescent in a very short period of time. It was not considered to have a salvage value. The company chose to depreciate its mini-computer on a declining balance basis at 30% in the first year and 40% in subsequent years. The mini-computer was purchased for $120,000 in 2001. In 2004 it was sold for $42,000. Assume that the computer was bought at the beginning of the fiscal year and sold at the end of the fiscal year.

(a) Was there a gain or loss on the sale of the mini-computer?
(b) Assume that the company used the straight-line amortization method over a five-year useful life. What would be the difference in the 2004 income if such a method had been used?
(c) Assuming the accelerated method is used, in what year will the mini-computer become worthless?

P5. Gains and Losses "We bought that bulldozer for $110,000 two years ago and we sold it for $115,000. To me, we made $5,000!" exclaimed the manager of a construction company. "Yet, you're telling me we made $16,000." Explain to the manager what accounting concepts he does not understand.

P6. Capitalization of Costs Should research and development costs be capitalized or expensed? What are the accounting implications of the former vs. the latter? What are the managerial implications of making a policy choice one way or the other on this issue?

P7. Accounting for Leases Wilford Contracting, Ltd., leases both heavy industrial equipment and office equipment. Up to this point, it has been management's accounting policy to consider payments made on these leases as rent expenses. The heavy equipment is maintained by Wilford, whereas the office equipment is maintained by the office equipment firm that contracted with Wilford to provide the equipment. In preparation for a private share issue, the company's books were reviewed.

(a) Should the company's accounting policy with respect to leases be changed? If so, how? What financial statements are affected and how?
(b) Is long-term leasing simply another means of financing?

P8. Conservative Asset Valuation Of the various methods of balance sheet valuation, why is historical cost recommended?

INTEGRATIVE PROBLEMS

IP1. Conservative Asset Valuation Bear Steel Products, Inc., manufactures commercial and residential steel doors and accessories, such as hinges, handles, guiding tracks, and the like. It sources its processed steel from the United States and sells its products there and in Canada. It must, therefore, be cognizant of world steel prices, exchange rates, and U.S. and Canadian inflationary pressures. During a recessionary period in the 1980s, both Canada and the United States saw moderate inflation. Like most businesses, Bear Steel struggled financially as the recession lasted longer than anticipated. It showed several months of operating losses, its credit sources dried up, it began to default on debt obligations, its customers defaulted on payments, and the company's short-term investments declined in value. While pursuing a zero-inflation policy and allowing interest rates to fall during the prolonged recessionary period, the Bank of Canada allowed the Canadian dollar to appreciate against the U.S. dollar. This was both a blessing and a curse to Bear Steel.

(a) Of what accounting issues would you remind the preparers and users of Bear Steel's financial statements?
(b) Why was the Bank of Canada's exchange rate management policy and monetary policy both a blessing and a curse?

IP2. Policy Decisions Diversified Containers, Ltd. rents a variety of steel containers used primarily in intermodal transport. It has several depots where it owns container storage facilities. These facilities include warehouses, storage yards, steel racking for storage, forklifts, stationary cranes, a variety of vehicles, unrented containers, and rented containers awaiting shipment or simply being stored.

(a) How would you classify the steel containers: as non-current assets, or as inventory?

(b) Since all the facilities are constantly in use, the company has depreciated its assets at a uniform rate of 10% per year. What, if anything, is wrong with such a policy? What would you suggest to correctly account for amortization?

(c) The company is considering long-term leasing or selling one of its port facilities to another intermodal container company that has better access to Asian ports. The other company is not particularly interested in purchasing the port facilities, but would do so for $14,320,000. It would, instead, prefer to lease the facility for 10 years at $2,195,000 per year. All maintenance and repair obligation in such a lease would be assumed by the lessee. Diversified could earn 9.5% on any invested funds. Would it be in Diversified's best interests to lease or to sell?

(d) One of Diversified's customers, an offshore auto parts supplier, recently filed for bankruptcy protection and subsequently wound up in receivership to have its affairs wound down. This forced Diversified to recognize an additional $240,000 in allowance for doubtful debt and to write off the receivable. Assuming a 32% tax rate, what income statement effect will this have in the period of the recognition? in the period of the write-off (assuming the recognition and write-off occurred in different periods)?

(e) Two of the company's warehouses were re-sided and re-shingled this year, thus extending their life. The total cost for the work carried out was $48,000. Assuming a 32% tax rate, what is the income statement effect if the cost was capitalized? if it was expensed? Should it be capitalized or expensed?

IP3. <u>GAAP and Asset Valuation</u> Explain how the following possible events would affect financial statement preparation in accordance with GAAP:

(a) A customer slips on ice in front of your place of business and files a legal suit for several million dollars against your company. The suit is not expected to be heard in court for more than a year.

(b) A new piece of machinery was purchased, but, when it was delivered, it was found not to fit through the building's doors. A separate entrance was constructed at considerable cost.

(c) A temporary investment was made in the shares of another company based on a "hot tip." Your informant told you that by the end of the year, this stock would nearly double in value.

(d) A recent market appraisal of the property that your building sits on shows that, because of mineral deposits discovered nearby, your land is worth four times what you paid for it.

EXPLORATIVE QUESTIONS

EQ1. <u>Policy Choices and GAAP</u> If a company is free to change its accounting policies, what's to prevent it from doing so from period to period to make company performance, and thus managerial performance, look better than it otherwise might?

EQ2. Policy Choices and GAAP When or how does a company's management know that it has chosen a sound combination of accounting policies? Should such a combination be static?

SOLUTIONS

EXERCISES

E1. FIFO:

Advantages:

- Reports a balance sheet value that represents the most recent acquisition costs and is thus more indicative of the current replacement costs of the inventory.
- Reports a higher net income when prices are rising (as is usually the case).

Disadvantages:

- It in effect violates the matching principle, since the cost of goods sold figure uses older inventory costs and is matched against current revenues.
- The higher income that FIFO reports is due to using older, lower prices in determining the cost of goods sold. In so doing, the resulting profit does not consider the costs of replacing that inventory at current prices. As a result, that profit is misleading because inventory will have to be replenished at higher, current prices.

LIFO:

Advantages:

- Matches current expenses with current revenues; cost of goods sold reflects the most recent prices paid.
- As a result of a fairer matching of expenses and revenues, LIFO allows you to see whether the current selling price is providing adequate cost recovery. The gross profit (Sales – Cost of goods sold) reflects increases in the cost of goods sold.

Disadvantages:

- Reports a lower income (this may not be a disadvantage, depending on management's objectives).
- Understates (assuming rising prices) the balance sheet figures since it reports ending inventory at the earliest prices paid.
- Can be used to manipulate income since to report a lower income for the period, management needs only to buy high-cost inventory before year-end to inflate cost of goods sold (with LIFO periodic).

E2. For inventories that are consumed in the regular course of business, such as office supplies, market usually means replacement cost. For inventories that are intended for re-sale, market means net realizable value (NRV); that is, market selling price. Market value becomes relevant when it has dropped below cost.

E3. Amortization is an accrual accounting requirement to match the cost of an asset over the period in which that asset will help earn revenue. Amortization is not a means of valuing an asset so much as it is a means of allocating the cost of that asset over its useful life. Once accumulated amortization is deducted from an asset's original cost, we get net book value. This value, however, is not necessarily the current value of that asset. Selling the asset may yield more or less than its book value. For that reason, amortization does not value an asset.

E4. If an asset is purchased, it appears on the balance sheet and must be amortized, thereby affecting income. If an asset is leased, and the lease is considered a capital lease, the asset appears on the balance sheet but there is, initially, an equal and offsetting capital lease liability. The asset is still amortized, thereby affecting the income statement, but there is an additional expense of interest. If an asset is rented, or leased under an operating lease, the balance sheet is unaffected and the income statement shows only rent expense and no amortization.

E5.

Dr.	Automobile (new)	42,000	
Dr.	Accum. Amortization	7,000	
Dr.	Loss on Sale*	4,000	
Cr.	Cash		6,000
Cr.	Loan Payable		22,000
Cr.	Automobile (old)		25,000

*When an asset is sold for less than its book value, a loss occurs. It is like an expense.

E6. Razing costs refer to the costs incurred to tear down an old building, or other structure/impediment, on a piece of property. The recorded value of the piece of land would be after adding the razing cost to the purchase price, since it is a cost incurred to prepare the asset for use and would, therefore, be capitalized.

E7. An account receivable arises from the granting of trade credit and is expected to be collected within a year from the time of the sale. Often, the credit period is, in fact, far less than a year (30-, 60-, or 90-day periods are common). A note receivable also arises from trade but the trade period is usually greater than one year. The contract, or note, specifies the period over which the amount in question is to be paid to the seller, along with the interest. Typically, with accounts receivable, interest is not charged until the account is in arrears. With a note receivable, interest typically starts accruing from the date of the contract.

E8. You will have to decide some of the following:

- when to recognize revenue: when a sale is made, or when cash is received, or when partial payment has been received, etc.;
- which assets to amortize and how amortization will be calculated;
- which cost flow assumption to use in valuing inventories and computing cost of goods sold;
- how to estimate bad debts;

- which asset expenditures to capitalize and which to expense;
- what to include as CCE;
- which liabilities to classify as current vs. non-current; etc.

This list is not exhaustive but gives you an idea of the types of accounting decisions that must be made.

PROBLEMS

P1. The use of LIFO is not confined to situations where the physical flow of goods follows a LIFO pattern. Justifications for its use may be found in reasons other than that it is representative of the physical flow of goods. Firstly, LIFO matches the "current" costs of acquiring or producing goods with the current revenues from selling them. Secondly, under GAAP, accounting recognition is rarely given to increases in the market values of fixed assets, so why should accounting recognition be given to increases in the market values of inventories? That is, why shouldn't inventories be valued at the lower, earliest prices paid? While the FIFO method results in higher reported income (assuming prices are rising), the difference in profit, as compared to LIFO, must be used to replenish inventory. So, under FIFO, the firm is not really better off by showing higher income, since the higher income is simply a result of using a lower cost of goods sold figure, nothing more.

P2. (a) Periodic Inventory:

FIFO: Ending inventory:	\$1,031.25; COGS:	\$5,681.25
LIFO: Ending inventory:	\$1,162.50; COGS:	\$5,550.00
AVGE: Ending inventory:	\$1,082.50; COGS:	\$5,629.00

(average price = \$8.66 = \$6,712.50 available/775 units)

(b) Perpetual Inventory:

FIFO: Ending inventory:	\$1,031.25; COGS:	\$5,681.25
LIFO: Ending inventory:	\$1,140.00*; COGS:	\$5,572.50
AVGE: Ending inventory:	\$1,048.75**; COGS:	\$5,665.18

* Ending inventory:

75 @ \$9.50 =	\$ 712.50
20 @ \$9.00 =	180.00
30 @ \$8.25 =	247.50
	\$1,140.00

** Weighted average after first purchase:
(75 @ \$9.50 + 200 @ \$9.00)/(75 + 200) = \$9.14
Weighted average after second purchase:
(110 @ \$9.14 + 300 @ \$8.50)/(110 + 300) = \$8.67
Weighted average after third purchase:
(95 @ \$8.67 + 200 @ \$8.25)/(95 + 200) = \$8.39
Ending inventory: 125 @ \$8.39 = \$1,048.75

(c) FIFO would likely be used for products that are perishable in nature, such as foodstuffs. It also seems appropriate for inventories that are time-dated due to obsolescence or novelty.

LIFO would likely be used where products are relatively indistinguishable from one another and do not have a limited shelf life. Such products might include, for example, home hardware products or office furnishings. LIFO is not permitted in Canada for tax purposes.

AVGE would likely be used where prior purchases are mixed with current purchases and are not particularly perishable. Such products might include oil, natural gas, sand, gravel, ore, etc.

(d) To minimize their tax liability, they would want to maximize their COGS (or minimize their ending inventory). In a period of falling prices, FIFO would achieve such an objective.

P3. (a) The components of the cost of an asset include all those costs necessary to make it suitable for the purpose intended. Therefore, the $1,000,000 spent on road clearing and site station establishment should be capitalized, since those costs were necessary to make logging possible.

(b)

Operations cost:	$1,209,375
Depletion:	1,265,625
Total cost of lumber produced	$2,475,000

Total cost per board-foot = $2,475,000/11,250,000
= $0.22/board-foot

* Depletion rate = $\dfrac{(\$10{,}000{,}000 + \$1{,}000{,}000) - \$2{,}000{,}000}{80{,}000{,}000}$
= $0.1125 per board-foot

Depletion = ($0.1125)(11,250,000) = $1,265,625

2005 income:

Sales		$7,200,000
Expenses:		
COGS**	1,980,000	
Selling/ Admin.	675,000	2,655,000
Income		$4,545,000

** 9,000,000 board-feet × $0.22/board-foot

P4. (a)

Year	Depreciable Amt. ($)	Rate	Amort. Exp. ($)	Net Book Value ($)
2001	120,000	30%	36,000	84,000
2002	84,000	40%	33,600	50,400
2003	50,400	40%	20,160	30,240
2004	30,240	40%	12,096	18,144

There was a gain on sale of $42,000 – $18,144 = $23,856.

(b)

Year	Depreciable Amt. ($)	Rate	Amort. Exp. ($)	Net Book Value ($)
2001	120,000	20%	24,000	96,000
2002	120,000	20%	24,000	72,000
2003	120,000	20%	24,000	48,000
2004	120,000	20%	24,000	24,000

There would have been a gain on sale of $42,000 – $24,000 = $18,000 if this method had been used.

	Declining Balance Method	Straight-Line Method
2004 income effect:		
Gain on sale	$23,856	$18,000
Amortization Expense	12,096	24,000
	$11,760	$(6,000)

If the straight-line method had been used, income would have been $17,760 lower in 2004 than if the declining balance method had been used.

(c) Continuing the table in part (a) above, you should find that the computer will become worthless in the year 2028, when it will be worth less than one cent. However, it will likely be removed from the books far sooner as its net book value becomes immaterial, relative to its cost, in the year 2014 when it reaches approximately $110. To carry the asset even that long is unlikely since it will become technologically obsolete sooner. If the asset was not sold, as in part (a) or (b) above, the company would likely record a loss on disposal when the computer was no longer needed.

P5. The concepts that the manager does not understand are recognizing the use of an asset and allocating its cost over its useful life (i.e., amortization) and gains on asset disposals. If you say that the company made $16,000 on the sale of the bulldozer, you are talking about a gain on sale. A gain on sale is realized when the selling price is greater than book value. For a $16,000 gain to be realized, the net book value must have been $99,000. Given a net book value of $99,000 after two years, amortization per year must have been $5,500, meaning that the asset had an estimated useful life of 20 years.

P6. Accounting standards require that general research and development costs be expensed, not capitalized. Product development costs, which are more specific in nature and are very likely to return future value, may be capitalized.

If R&D costs are capitalized, they will appear as an asset. Net assets will not increase since there must be a reduction in cash or an increase in a liability to finance the R&D expenditure. As an intangible asset, it must then be amortized over its expected useful life, whatever that may be and however that may be calculated. That means that income will be affected in years subsequent to the incurrence of the R&D cost.

If, however, R&D costs are expensed in the period in which they are incurred, income is affected in that year alone and the balance sheet will show a decreased asset (cash) and/or an increased liability to finance the cost. Retained earnings would then be reduced by decreased income due to the R&D expense.

The managerial implication is that capitalization will improve asset ratios and income performance, whereas expensing will reduce tax liability but may minimize true earnings potential.

P7. (a) The industrial equipment should be considered a capital lease, not a rent expense or operating lease as it is otherwise known, since Wilford, in effect, has all the rights and obligations of ownership. The office equipment should continue to be considered a rent expense or operating lease, since Wilford has no obligations beyond rent and reasonable care.

Recognizing the heavy equipment as a capital lease does affect the balance sheet and the income statement. A new asset and liability are created to show the lease obligation. The capitalization creates two new expenses: amortization of the capital lease, and interest expense. The previous rent expense is removed. Whether income will go up or down as a result of the capitalization depends on the size of the original rent expense, the length of the lease, and the present value of the lease payments.

Cash flow is unaffected, except by any change to current tax liability that would ultimately have to be settled. Any tax consequences are likely to affect the future portion of taxes, in any event, since tax rules would be followed giving rise to future income tax liability.

(b) Long-term leasing *is* another means of financing. Off-balance-sheet financing has the advantage of not affecting financing ratios, liquidity ratios, solvency warning ratios, and some performance ratios. Operating leases have no balance sheet effect and so it is wise disclosure practice to provide material information about such leases. Capital leases must, of course, be brought onto the balance sheet.

P8. The principal reason that historical cost is recommended is that cost is documented; there is transactional evidence such as invoices, receipts, or contracts (verifiability). The other reason is that historical cost is a conservative value since it represents what the asset or liability was worth to an entity at the time of the transaction.

The other methods of balance sheet valuation fall short of being conservative. Conservatism is one of the foundations of reliability.

Historical cost valuation is not without criticism since its application makes comparability to current values difficult. If assets appreciate, for example, then wealth has been created according to the economist but not the accountant. But such wealth would only be realized if the assets were sold, and the accountant then, and only then, recognizes such an increase (as capital gains). Valuation by any other method is a moving target whereas historical cost is stable. This stability ensures that comparability is best achieved.

INTEGRATIVE PROBLEMS

IP1. (a) The symptoms of financial struggle shown by Bear Steel threaten the continuance of the enterprise as a going concern. The *CICA Handbook* discusses a number of recognition, measurement, and disclosure issues related to the impairment of assets or other possible consequences of an economic downturn. Some of the issues that should be considered as both a user and a preparer of financial statements are:

- making changes in estimates for doubtful accounts;
- carrying temporary investments at the lower of cost or market;
- writing down receivables to net realizable value as soon as they are known not to be fully collectible;
- disclosing defaults on debts;
- disclosing significant contractual obligations such as supply contracts; and
- implementing a conservative revenue recognition policy, perhaps waiting until cash is received.

(b) By allowing the Canadian dollar to appreciate against the U.S. dollar, Bear Steel's cost of goods would decrease since its imported steel would then be relatively cheaper. However, since it has sales markets in the United States, its exports will suffer as its products become more expensive for U.S. buyers.

Allowing the interest rate to fall can only help Bear Steel if it restructures its debts to take advantage of lower rates. Lower interest rates mean increased business and consumer spending. But if a zero-inflation policy is being pursued, then Bear Steel should expect the exchange rate to be kept fairly high to discourage import-induced inflation. This means that it should be concerned about its export sales.

IP2. (a) The steel containers should be classified as non-current assets since they are not inventory to be sold to customers. Rather, they are rented or leased to customers and are simply considered to be requisite to the earning of revenue.

(b) Amortizing its storage facilities at a uniform rate is inappropriate since the assets involved (cranes, vehicles, racking, etc.) would all be expected to have different useful lives and therefore depreciate at different rates. The storage yards, for example, are not likely to depreciate at all since land does not usually diminish in value. The warehouses are likely to have a longer useful life than the containers or the racking since the latter are more subject to wear and tear.

Straight-line amortization may be appropriate on all the assets but at different rates to reflect their useful lives.

(c) The present value of $2,195,000 per year for 10 years at 9.5% is $13,781,962. So, it would be more profitable (by $538,038) to sell the port facilities to the other company for the price stated.

(d) When the additional bad debt is recognized, income will decrease by ($240,000)(1 – 0.32) = $163,200.

It does not matter in what period the receivable is actually written off because there will be no income statement effect since the only accounts that are affected are Accounts Receivable and Allowance for Doubtful Accounts.

(e) If the $48,000 was capitalized, the only income statement effect would be the additional amortization due to the work. The work could be seen as a betterment, not extending the life of the asset, or as an extraordinary repair, thus extending the life of the asset. If it was a betterment, the additional $48,000 is depreciated over the remaining life of the warehouses. If it is considered an extraordinary repair, then the $48,000 is depreciated over the extended, remaining life of the warehouses.

Whatever the case, the amortization charge will be far less than expensing the full $48,000. If this had been done, the income statement effect would be to reduce income by ($48,000)(1 – 0.32) = $32,640.

The expenditure should be capitalized, since it has, presumably, bettered the asset by either increasing its service potential or extending its life.

IP3. (a) The lawsuit must be noted as a contingent liability in the notes to the financial statements. If you are reasonably certain to lose the lawsuit and can estimate the damages to be awarded, you should accrue the liability.

(b) The separate entrance would be capitalized to the building if the entrance was not re-sealed. If the entrance was closed up after the machinery was in place, then the cost would likely be capitalized to the cost of the machinery, since it represented a cost incurred in making the asset operational.

(c) The temporary investment would be considered a current asset that should be recorded at cost. Regardless of what the intended value of the investment is, it is still recorded at cost. If its value does double and it is sold, then a capital gain would be realized.

(d) The market appraisal does not affect the carrying value of your land on the balance sheet. You may, however, as supplementary data, include the appraised value and the reason for the difference between it and historical cost.

EXPLORATIVE QUESTIONS

EQ1. Companies are free to change their accounting policies from period to period. GAAP, however, require that disclosure of accounting policy choices be made and, in the case of significant accounting policy changes, the effects of those changes be retroactively applied to ensure comparability. The onus, then, is placed upon the user of the financial statements to be cognizant of the accounting policy choices made. Remember that financial statements are intended for the sophisticated user who is presumed to have a reasonable understanding of business.

The question then arises as to whether or not it is in a company's best interests to change its policies from period to period. Wouldn't such fickle behaviour raise concerns as to what the company was up to? You should be cautious of a company that regularly changes its accounting policies. You should ask the question: whose interests are best protected by such behaviour—the shareholders', or the management's? Do not forget the principles of agency theory; management represents owners. But if management is also evaluated by the owners, management may or may not be interested in the general concepts of fairness, conservatism, and adherence to GAAP if such concepts do not improve management's contractual relationship with the principals of the company.

EQ2. What constitutes a "sound combination" of policies is uncertain, but perhaps the following would be a possible answer: A company's management will have chosen a sound combination of accounting policies when performance results meet or exceed objectives, when shareholders are reasonably satisfied with statement performance and reporting practices, when auditors are satisfied that there has been adequate disclosure and adherence to GAAP, when the statements meet creditor scrutiny, and when the stewardship objective, in general, has been met.

Accounting policies need not, and should not, be static. The environment of the company changes, as do the objectives of both shareholders and management. As long as adequate disclosure of policy changes has been made, there is no reason why changes cannot be made.

CHAPTER 9
LIABILITIES, EQUITY, AND CORPORATE GROUPS

LEARNING OBJECTIVES

After completing Chapter 9, you should:

- know what a corporate group constitutes;
- know what intercorporate investments are and what consolidated statements are; and
- understand and be able to prepare consolidated financial statements.

CHAPTER SUMMARY

9.1 Chapter Introduction: Accounting for the Right-Hand Side of the Balance Sheet

- This chapter covers a variety of topics that supplement material learned to this point.
- The chapter is broken into modules in order to be able to learn particular material independently of the rest of the chapter.

9.2 Current Liabilities

- Debts are shown at historical cost, not any "distressed" value, since an entity is deemed to be a going concern.
- For significant debts, particulars such as term to expiration, interest rate, or security pledged may be disclosed.
- Debts fall into one of two categories: current liabilities, or non-current liabilities.
- The classification of debt into the category of current liabilities affects the working capital position of a company.

9.3 Non-Current Liabilities

- In this latter category, you will find long-term accruals, such as pension liabilities, warranty liabilities, or future income taxes, to name a few.
- With such liabilities there is in fact no debt at the time of recognition, but they are estimated to account for the future consequences of earning income today.
- Accounting for income tax liability gives rise to something called future income taxes.
- Income tax is payable on income from operations, with a resulting income tax expense and an income tax payable.
- As simple as this sounds, the calculation of income tax is complicated by the fact that tax laws permit income to be calculated in a manner different from that permitted by GAAP.
- As a result, a company's calculation of tax expense and tax payable is likely to be different from that calculated by the tax collection authority.
- There are permanent differences between tax law and GAAP, such as what revenues and expenses can be included in income calculations.

- There are also temporary differences that result from timing differences; that is, where tax law would permit more of an expense to be recognized in a period, for example, than would the matching principle of accrual accounting under GAAP.
- These timing differences give rise to what is called future income tax. Future Income Tax is an account used to maintain the matching principle.
- A common reason for a temporary difference relates to the values permissible for amortization. Income tax law calculates amortization (called capital cost allowance or CCA) at different rates than might a company.
- Usually, CCA rates depreciate an asset faster than a company would in its earlier years and slower than it would in its latter years. As a result, taxable income tends to be reduced in the earlier years and, therefore, income tax expense and income tax payable are lower than by the company's calculations.
- An example serves to illustrate the practice:

  Christine Company has calculated its income before tax to be $60,000. The company faces a 35% statutory tax rate. In calculating the income before tax, Christine deducted $9,000 of amortization according to the straight-line method of amortization. Tax law, however, permits the company to expense $14,000 this year.

  Naturally, the tax payable would be different depending on how much amortization is expensed. According to Christine, its income tax expense would be $21,000 ($60,000 × 35%). Income tax payable, however, would be $19,250 (($60,000 + $9,000 – $14,000) × 35%).

  Income tax expense ($21,000) does not equal income tax payable ($19,250). Debits would not equal credits. As a result, a Future Income Tax account is created to hold the difference:

Income Tax Expense—future portion	1,750	
Future Income Tax Payable		1,750

  To recognize the current portion of the expense:

Income Tax Expense—current	19,250	
Income Tax Payable		19,250

- The above example serves to illustrate several key points:
  - The differences in amortization methods will not affect the useful life of the asset. The company's method and the CCA method will bring the value of the asset to its salvage value or zero at the end of its useful life.
  - The different methods simply cause a difference in how much amortization is deducted each year up to the end of the useful life (hence, a timing difference).

- The future portion is not a way to *avoid* paying taxes; it is only a means of deferring what is paid. By the end of the useful lives of assets, the differences in methods will have resulted in an equal amount of taxes paid.

- The future income tax expense allows a matching of expenses, the need for which is created by tax law as opposed to GAAP.

- The future income tax liability is not owed to anyone. It is not a current liability; consider it a liability created for adjustment purposes. In those latter years of the asset's life, where the amortization method used by a company results in a greater charge to amortization than the CCA would allow, the future tax liability is reduced:

	Dr	Cr
Future Income Tax Payable	XXX	
Income Tax Expense —future portion		XXX

- As you should be able to see, this means that the company cannot expense as much as it would like to, and, as a result, the credit to the expense serves to increase its taxable income.

- By the end of the useful life of the asset, the future tax liability would have been reduced to zero, as would the cumulative debits and credits to the future income tax expense account.

- This has been a simple introduction to income taxes and future taxes, and you should be able to see that the process becomes quite complicated when companies buy new assets and sell existing ones before their useful life has expired; hence a reason for specialized tax accounting.

9.4 Equity

- By this point, you should know that the equity section of the balance sheet differs for unincorporated vs. incorporated businesses.
- For corporations, share capital, in the equity section, shows the amounts contributed by the owners of the company.
- If a company has a variety of share classes, the share capital for each class must be disclosed. As well, a note to the statements should disclose the number of shares issued and the rights, limitations, or privileges attached to such shares.
- If shares have been issued by a company and subsequently repurchased by the company, they are called treasury stock. The *Canada Business Corporations Act* requires that such stock be cancelled and not re-issued.

- The purchase of treasury stock decreases the company's assets and equity; treasury stock is a contra equity account and the company is not entitled to any dividends, voting rights, or the proceeds from liquidation.

- The retained earnings figure in the equity section shows accumulated income less dividends declared.
- Dividends are declared payable by a company's board of directors and such a declaration creates a liability for the company.
- Companies with foreign operations show, in the equity section of their balance sheet, something called "foreign currency translation adjustment" or "cumulative translation adjustment."
- This figure is a result of converting foreign asset, liability, and income values to Canadian dollar amounts, and is simply a balancing figure to make up for differences in exchange rates used for conversion.

9.5 Complex Financial Structures

- The distinction between debt and equity financing can sometimes be blurred by hybrid securities.
- As an example, sometimes preferred shares can have a redeemable feature requiring the company to buy back the stock, thus causing the stock to behave like a debt.
- Similarly, a bond may be convertible to common shares, causing the bond to behave like equity.
- Off-balance-sheet financing is the acquisition of assets or services without reporting the incurrence of associated debt on the balance sheet.
- A good example of this is the operating lease (discussed in Chapter 8); the lessee can use the acquired asset but does not have to report the asset or the associated liability on the balance sheet.
- As a result, the *CICA Handbook* requires detailed reporting of operating lease payments in the notes to financial statements, such as the minimum operating lease payments for the next five years.

9.6 Corporate Groups: Intercorporate Investments

- Intercorporate investments are investments made by one company in the voting shares, non-voting shares, or debt of another company. These could be for a short term (as a place to park excess funds, if you will) or a long term.

  (1) Temporary Investments/Marketable Securities

  - The accounting for short-term investments is to treat them as current assets, since there is no intention to hold these investments for long or to use them to exert influence over the companies that issued these securities.

  - These investments are valued at the lower of cost or market value (net realizable value) to reflect conservatism.
  - When temporary investments are "written down" to reflect a market value below cost, the difference is considered an expense on the income statement.

(2) Long-Term Passive Investment

- The accounting for long-term investments depends on whether or not the investing company intends to exercise control of the other company.

- If the investing company buys less than 20% of the voting control in the investee company, the investment asset is kept in the records of the investor as a non-current asset at cost. Investment income *from* the investee is recorded as "other" income on the investor's income statement.

(3) Long-Term Active Investment

- If the investing company buys between 20% and 50% of the voting control in the investee, the "equity method" is used to record the investment, where the investment asset is initially recorded at cost and then adjusted for the investor's share of any investee income (or losses) and any dividends paid.

(4) Joint Venture

- Joint ventures—in which two or more partners contribute various resources to achieve a task such as new product development—are accounted for on the equity basis.

9.7 Corporate Groups: Consolidation

- In the case of the last two types of intercorporate investments, the financial statements of the "investee" are combined with that of the "parent."

(5) Acquisition

- If an investing company buys more than 50% of the voting control of an investee (now a subsidiary), the "purchase method" of consolidation is used to account for the investment.

- Consolidation means to prepare financial statements for a group of companies where parent–subsidiary relations exist.

- A consolidated entity, although presented as if it were a single entity, does not legally exist as a separate entity. Instead, it is a group of entities presented as one entity.

- If the purchase makes the subsidiary wholly owned, then, at the date of acquisition, the consolidated balance sheet must eliminate any intercompany balances such as receivables, investments, or payables before the balance sheet items may be added together.

- If the purchase makes the subsidiary partially owned (50%–99%), then, at the date of acquisition, the consolidated balance sheet must eliminate any intercompany balances as though the subsidiary were wholly owned.
- However, minority interest arises in this case. This is where the portion that is not owned by the parent becomes a liability to the parent upon consolidation. This appears as a liability on the consolidated entity's balance sheet.
- Upon consolidation, the consolidated balance sheet only shows the investor's equity. When the investee was purchased, the investor bought the net assets or equity of the investee. If you added the equity of the investee, you would be double counting the value of the purchase.
- The parent company, upon acquisition, will usually re-assess the carrying values of the subsidiary's assets and liabilities. This re-assessment is to assign fair market values to these accounts as at the date of purchase. The purchase price, then, is based on the percentage of these fair market values that the parent is buying (50%–100%).
- The price that the investor pays may be greater than both the book value and the fair market value of the investee's net assets. In such a case, the excess paid is termed goodwill.
- When preparing the consolidated income statement, the consolidated net income simply adds together the incomes earned since acquisition.
- As with the balance sheet, though, this combined figure must be adjusted for intercompany balances affecting incomes (see page 564 of your text) as well as, in the case of partly owned subsidiaries, the claim to earnings that minority owners have. As a result, consolidated net income will be less than the sum of the individual company's net incomes.

(6) Merger

- A genuine merger occurs when two similarly sized companies join resources without one buying the other to have any controlling interest.
- The "pooling of interests" method is used to account for mergers. The assets, liabilities, and equities of the merging entities are summed together.

EXERCISES

E1. Corporate Groups What are intercorporate investments?

E2. Corporate Groups The John Labatt Company is a consolidated legal entity. Discuss the validity of this claim.

E3. Corporate Groups What is meant by minority interest?

E4. Future Income Taxes What is meant by future income taxes?

PROBLEMS

P1. Understanding Future Income Taxes A shareholder of a publicly traded company recently charged that the auditors of the company's statements had been negligent in their duties, even unethical, for allowing the company to take advantage of future incomes taxes, effectively avoiding payment of taxes. Discuss this claim.

P2. Corporate Groups Your boss and his team of soon-to-be-retirees are considering one last masterpiece before they make golfing their only daily duty. They are planning to make a long-term investment in the shares of a supplier (known as backward integration). Explain to them the accounting significance of buying less than 20%, between 20% and 50%, and more than 50% of the supplier.

P3. Corporate Groups For Problem P2 above, record the transaction, assuming that your company paid $50,000 for 18% of the supplier's voting stock and that, after the purchase, the supplier earned net income of $12,000 and paid a $2,000 dividend.

P4. Corporate Groups For Problem P2 above, record the transaction, assuming that your company paid $75,000 for 32% of the supplier's voting stock and that, after the acquisition, the supplier earned net income of $12,000 and paid a $2,000 dividend.

P5. Corporate Groups Suppose that Groupe Laval, Inc., purchased 85% of the shares of Pacific Holdings, Ltd., for $1,200,000. At the time of acquisition, Pacific's assets showed a book value of $1,940,000 and liabilities were carried at $1,130,000. Groupe Laval deemed the assets to hold a fair market value of $2,090,000 and that the book value of the liabilities was also fair value.

(a) If consolidation takes place at the date of acquisition, how much does Groupe Laval pay for goodwill?
(b) What is the value of minority interest at this time?
(c) How is the purchase shown on Groupe Laval's non-consolidated financial statements?
(d) If, in the year after the acquisition, Pacific earned $90,000 in net income, does the consolidated net income increase by $90,000? Explain.

P6. Bond Issues Morning Star Inc., an infant software company of three years, desperately needed cash to support operating and expansion needs. Having recently issued more stock, the company felt that the bond market was the only plausible alternative. The company floated 9%, $1,000 face value bonds and raised $2.5 million, falling short on its $3 million issue.

(a) Was a discount or a premium recorded?
(b) Record the journal entry for the bond issue.
(c) When the discount or premium is amortized over the bond life, will interest expense on the bond be reduced or increased?

INTEGRATIVE PROBLEMS

IP1. Corporate Groups, Inventory Valuation, Asset Disposition, Change Effects Widdrington Industries, Ltd., acquired a distressed and cashless Devonshire Ltd., a competitor selling the same products, on April 1, 2005. The balance sheets of Widdrington as at March 31, 2005, and the consolidated entity at the date of acquisition and one year later are shown below:

Widdrington Industries, Ltd.
Balance Sheet
As at March 31, 2005
($000s)

Cash	525	Current Payables	715
Accounts Receivable, Net	415		
Inventory	645	Long-Term Debt	1,750.5
Buildings	1,250		
Accum. Amortization—Buildings	(187.5)		
Land	975.	Share Capital	1,110
		Retained Earnings	47
Total	3,622.5	Total	3,622.5

Widdrington Industries, Ltd.
Consolidated Balance Sheet
As at April 1, 2005
($000s)

Cash	75	Current Payables	1,060
Accounts Receivable, Net	535		
Inventory	790	Long-Term Debt	1,949.5
Buildings	1,800		
Accum. Amortization—Buildings	(242.5)		
Land	1,175		
Goodwill	34	Share Capital	1,110
		Retained Earnings	47
Total	4,166.5	Total	4,166.5

Widdrington Industries, Ltd.
Consolidated Balance Sheet
As at March 31, 2006
($000s)

Cash	145.2	Current Payables	845
Accounts Receivable, Net	395		
Inventory	870	Long-Term Debt	1,849.5
Buildings	1,800		
Accum. Amortization—Buildings	(360)		
Land	1,175		
Goodwill	32.3	Share Capital	1,110
		Retained Earnings	253
Total	4,057.5	Total	4,057.5

(a) What was the net book value of the buildings as carried on the books of Devonshire at the time of acquisition? At the time of the acquisition, the buildings were one year old and being amortized over 10 years.

(b) Net income for the year after the acquisition was $206,000. How much cash was generated from operations in the year ending March 31, 2006?

(c) Assume that Widdrington had to adjust the March 31, 2006, inventory figure downward by $60,000 to reflect a drop in market value. What is the effect on income and on cash flow for 2006 (assume a tax rate of 30%)?

(d) Assume that the company had used a periodic LIFO inventory control system. With the following information, what would be the March 31, 2006, ending inventory and 2006 cost of goods sold had a perpetual inventory control been used?

April 1, 2005, beginning inventory 3,950 units @ $200/unit =	$790,000
May 28, 2005, sale	1,150 units
July 12, 2005, purchase 2,500 units @ $250/unit =	$625,000
September 3, 2005, sale	1,100 units
November 17, 2005, sale	750 units
January 4, 2006, purchase 2,600 units @ $275/unit =	$715,000
February 24, 2006, sale	1,780 units

(e) Three months into the second year after the acquisition, Widdrington decided to sell the buildings it had acquired from Devonshire. It also had to sell the land on which the buildings were built. At the time the buildings were acquired, the land was worth the $100,000 that it was carried at in Devonshire's books and the properties had not appreciated or depreciated since that time. The properties and the buildings were sold for $506,250. Was there a gain or loss on the sale of the buildings? If so, how much?

IP2. Corporate Groups and Write-Downs White Water Raft Tours, Inc., acquired 90% of Canal Canoes, Ltd., earlier this year, paying $65,000 for net assets having a book value of $47,000 and an estimated fair market value (due to river tour rights) of $51,000. In the year since the acquisition, Canal Canoes has reported net income of $77,000 but has yet to pay a dividend. White Water has reported sales of $337,000, with cost of sales, selling, and general administrative expenses totalling $194,000. White Water is taxed at 32%. White Water has declared but not yet paid an $8,000 dividend.

(a) White Water has temporary investments carried at $25,000. It has learned, however, that these investments have been in the debt securities of a company that has recently been downgraded by the Canadian Bond Rating Service. As a result, the investments must be written down to reflect a market value of $20,000. Prepare the journal entry to record this write-down.

(b) At the end of the first year after the acquisition, what is:
(i) net consolidated goodwill (assume amortization at $500 per year)?
(ii) consolidated minority interest liability?
(iii) consolidated net income?
(iv) consolidated retained earnings (assume White Water's beginning retained earnings were $44,000 and Canal Canoe's were $39,000)?

IP3. Corporate Groups Westfalia Sod Farms, Ltd., acquired 90% of Rhine Nurseries, Ltd., on March 31, 2005, for $3,200,000. The non-consolidated financial statements are as follows:

Westfalia Sod Farms, Ltd.
Balance Sheet
March 31, 2006

ASSETS		LIABILITIES	
Current Assets:		Current Liabilities:	
Cash	$ 186,000	Accounts Payable	$ 415,000
Accounts Receivable	94,000	Bank Loan	75,000
Marketable Securities	440,000		490,000
Inventories	1,470,000	Non-Current Liabilities:	
	2,190,000	Mortgage Payable	1,990,000
Fixed Assets:			2,480,000
Investments*	3,425,000	EQUITY	
Buildings, Net	225,000	Common Stock	3,600,000
Land	1,100,000	Retained Earnings	860,000
	4,750,000		4,460,000
Total Assets	$6,940,000	Total Equities	$6,940,000

* Investments are strictly in Rhine Nurseries, Ltd.

Rhine Nurseries, Ltd.
Balance Sheet
March 31, 2005

ASSETS		LIABILITIES	
Current Assets:		Current Liabilities:	
Cash	$ 48,000	Accounts Payable	$ 40,000
Accounts Receivable	440,000	Bank Loan	90,000
Inventories	900,000		130,000
	1,388,000	Non-Current Liabilities:	
		Mortgage Payable	500,000
Fixed Assets:			630,000
Buildings, Net	125,000	EQUITY	
Land	2,600,000	Common Stock	2,700,000
	2,725,000	Retained Earnings	783,000
			3,483,000
Total Assets	$4,113,000	Total Equities	$4,113,000

Rhine Nurseries, Ltd.
Balance Sheet
March 31, 2006

ASSETS		LIABILITIES	
Current Assets:		Current Liabilities:	
Cash	$ 68,000	Accounts Payable	$ 25,000
Accounts Receivable	400,000	Bank Loan	90,000
Inventories	940,000		115,000
	1,408,000	Non-Current Liabilities:	
		Mortgage Payable	475,000
Fixed Assets:			590,000
Buildings, Net	115,000	EQUITY	
Land	2,800,000	Common Stock	2,700,000
	2,915,000	Retained Earnings	1,033,000
			3,733,000
Total Assets	$4,323,000	Total Equities	$4,323,000

Assume the following additional information:

- Rhine paid dividends of $150,000 in 2006;
- There were inter-company profits of $12,000 since the acquisition;
- Of Rhine's 2006 year-end accounts payable, $5,000 is payable to Westfalia; and
- Goodwill is amortized at $500 per year.

(a) What accounting method is Westfalia using to recognize its investment in Rhine?
(b) At acquisition, how much goodwill arises from consolidation? How much minority interest arises?
(c) Prepare a consolidated balance sheet one year after the acquisition.
(d) If Westfalia earned $700,000 in net income in the year since the acquisition, what is the consolidated net income for fiscal 2006?

IP4. Amortization Fisher-Morris Research Laboratories, Ltd., has acquired blood analysis equipment that it intends to use for 20 years. The controller of the company intends to amortize the $500,000 piece of equipment on a straight-line basis. The equipment will not be worth anything at the end of its life. Tax law, however, permits the company to amortize the equipment at 10% in its first year of operation and at a 15% rate on a declining balance basis for the next 19 years. The controller is about to prepare the financial statements for the first full year of operation of the equipment. Income before taxes was $240,000. The company pays tax at 32%.

(a) What difference does the tax law make to net income for the first year? for year five? for the entire 20-year period?
(b) What effect does tax law have on the balance sheet for the first year?
(c) The owners of Fisher-Morris feel that the accountant has stumbled onto a way to save the company income taxes. Is this true?

EXPLORATIVE QUESTIONS

EQ1. Amortization Policy Why would a company choose an amortization policy that yielded a rate different from the CCA rate?

EQ2. Amortization Policy Why do you suppose capital cost allowance exists?

EQ3. Warranties and Pensions For long-term accruals such as warranties or pensions, there is considerable difficulty in measuring what the appropriate expense should be in a given period. If an estimate is made, how is it made? If it is only an estimate, why make such a recognition? And since it is uncertain that such accrued liabilities will, in fact, actually be called, how long should such accrued liabilities be carried on the balance sheet?

SOLUTIONS

EXERCISES

E1. Intercorporate investments are investments made by one company in the voting shares, non-voting shares, or debt of another company. Such investments could be short-term or long-term. Short-term investments are valued at the lower of cost or market (net realizable value). Long-term investments are originally recorded at cost, but, depending on the extent of investment, the investment may or may not be adjusted to reflect non-consolidated and consolidated accounting policies.

E2. There is no such thing as a consolidated legal entity. The John Labatt Company is legally a group of separate companies with connected ownership. Consolidation exists to present the group of companies as if it were a single entity.

E3. When a subsidiary company is not wholly owned (100%), a portion of the subsidiary is still owned by people other than the parent. These others have an equity interest in the subsidiary as well as an interest in its income. These interests are called minority interests.

E4. A future income tax does not mean that the company postpones paying taxes in one year. What it means is that, because tax law differs from GAAP in several areas, it is possible for a company to pay taxes owed, in different periods. So, all taxes are not postponed, rather, a portion of those taxes is allowed to be paid in a subsequent period. The accounting mechanics behind future taxes is that future taxes are not actually paid in a subsequent period. Rather, a company's income is increased for tax purposes in subsequent periods to recover taxes that were deferred in a prior period.

PROBLEMS

P1. The claim is without substance. It is clear that the shareholder does not know what deferred taxes are. There is nothing illegal or unethical about deferred taxes. They arise due to differences in a company's accounting policies and tax accounting regulations. Deferred taxes do not imply any malicious practice whatsoever and the auditors are not guilty of negligence for permitting them to remain on the balance sheet. Deferred taxes simply allow a company to pay lesser tax in some years and more in other years (usually latter years).

P2. If they buy less than 20% of the supplier, they are considered to be passive investors and would not gain any influence or control over the supplier. The supplier will not be considered a subsidiary. The non-consolidated, cost-based method is used to record the investment, which means that the investment is recorded at cost as a non-current asset. Any dividends or interest received from the supplier are considered "other" income.

If they buy between 20% and 50%, they will be able to have some influence over the supplier but still not have a controlling interest. The non-consolidated, equity-basis method is used. The investment would originally be valued at cost but, as the supplier earns income, the value of the investment asset would increase by your company's share of that income. If the supplier paid a dividend, the investment asset would be reduced by your company's share of that dividend since the supplier's income had increased it.

If they buy more than 50% of the supplier, they will have voting control and the supplier will become a subsidiary. Consolidated financial statements will be necessary, likely using the purchase method. This means that your company will have to assign fair values to the assets and liabilities of the supplier and any excess paid over the fair value of your company's share of the net assets is considered goodwill. If your company does not buy 100% of the supplier, minority interest will arise. This is not bad; it simply means different accounting treatment than if 100% of the supplier had been bought.

Before the consolidated statements can be prepared, intercompany balances have to be eliminated. This means that the investment in the subsidiary is not included in the consolidated balance sheet since the investment paid for the net assets of the subsidiary and these net assets are added to your company's. To include the investment in the subsidiary would be double counting. Similarly, the subsidiary's equity is not included in the consolidated balance sheet, since the equity is, in effect, what your company is buying (i.e, Net assets = Equity). Once the intercompany balances have been removed, the fair values of the assets and liabilities of the subsidiary are added to your company's assets and liabilities, goodwill is added (if any), and minority interest is created.

It is worth mentioning what fair value means. The supplier's assets and liabilities would be recorded at historical cost. But in selling the company, the realizable value of these may be more or less than the historical cost would suggest. Therefore, a fair or current value is assigned to the supplier's assets and liabilities.

P3.

	Debit	Credit
Long-Term Investments	50,000	
Cash		50,000

To record the purchase of 18% of voting stock in XXX supplier.

	Debit	Credit
Cash	360	
Dividend Income		360

To record receipt of dividends from XXX supplier.

Since the cost basis method is appropriate for investment in under 20% of the voting stock, your company does not participate in the earnings of the supplier.

P4. Long-Term Investments 75,000
Cash 75,000
To record the purchase of 32% of voting stock in XXX supplier.

Long-Term Investments 3,840
Investment Income 3,840
To record investment income for 32% equity interest in XXX supplier.

Cash 640
Long-Term Investments 640
To record receipt of dividends for 32% equity interest in XXX supplier.

Since the equity basis is appropriate for investment in between 20% and 50% of voting stock, your company participates in the earnings of the supplier.

P5. (a) Groupe Laval will pay $1,200,000 for 85% of the fair value of Pacific's net assets:

Goodwill = $1,200,000 – (0.85)($2,090,000 – $1,130,000) = $384,000

(b) Minority interest would be 15% of the book value of Pacific. Book value is used since the minority holders are not doing anything differently and need not concern themselves with fair values:

Minority interest = (0.15)($1,940,000 – $1,130,000) = $121,500

(c) For Groupe Laval's non-consolidated financial statement, the purchase is shown as a long-term investment asset for $1,200,000. No goodwill or minority interest is shown since these arise only upon consolidation.

(d) Consolidated net income will increase by less than $90,000, since Groupe Laval purchased only 85% of Pacific. So, only 85% of Pacific's income is included in consolidated income. Goodwill would then have to be amortized, meaning that consolidated income is reduced further by the amount of the amortization expense. Lastly, consolidated income would further be reduced if any of the $90,000 was earned on intercompany sales. That is, any intercompany profits have to be eliminated, otherwise the consolidated income figure would include profits earned on sales within the consolidated entity.

P6. (a) Since the target amount of $3 million was not raised, a discount occurred. In other words, bondholders wanted an effective interest rate greater than the face value of 9% and were not willing to pay the full face value for the bonds.

(b)

Cash	2,500,000	
Bond Discount	500,000	
Bonded Debt		3,000,000

(c) Interest expense will be increased as the bondholders effectively demanded a higher interest rate than the company was hoping to pay.

INTEGRATIVE PROBLEMS

IP1. (a)

Consolidated Accumulated Amortization, Buildings:	$242,500
Widdrington Accumulated Amortization, Buildings:	187,500
Devonshire Accumulated Amortization, Buildings:	$ 55,000

Net book value of Devonshire's buildings as at acquisition:
($1,800,000 – $1,250,000) – $55,000 = $495,000

(b) Cash from operations
= Net income + Amortization + Goodwill amortization +
Decrease in net receivables – Growth in inventory – Decrease in payables
= $206,000 + $117,500* + $1,700** + $140,000 – $80,000 – $215,000
= $170,200

* Accumulated amortization, March 31, 2006:	$360,000
Accumulated amortization, April 1, 2005:	242,500
Amortization expense, 2006:	$117,500

** Assumed amortization period: 20 years.

(c) A Loss on Inventory would be noted of $60,000. Net income would drop by 70% of that or $42,000. Income tax expense and income tax liability would decrease by the other 30% or $18,000.

(d) Ending inventory:
(2,800 @ $200) + (650 @ $250) + (820 @ $275) = $948,000
Cost of goods sold:
(1,150 @ $200) + (1,100 @ $250) +
(750 @ $250) + (1,780 @ $275) = $1,182,000

(e) One year after the acquisition, Devonshire's buildings had depreciated by another $55,000. Net book value at acquisition (from part (a) above) was $495,000. So, one year after acquisition, NBV is at $440,000. Three months into the second year adds another $13,750 in amortization, bringing NBV to $426,500. If the land had not changed in value, then $506,250 – $100,000 = $406,250 is what must have been paid for the buildings. The resulting loss on sale is, therefore, $426,250 – $406,250 = $20,000.

IP2. (a) Recognizing a decline in market value below cost, the temporary investments should be written down:

Dr.	Investment Loss	5,000	
Cr.	Temporary Investments		5,000

(b) Net consolidated goodwill:

$65,000 was paid for net assets having a fair value of $51,000. Since White Water purchased a 90% interest, goodwill of $65,000 – (90%)($51,000) = $19,100 arose at consolidation. After one year's amortization, goodwill sits at $18,600.

Minority interest liability:

At consolidation, minority interest would have been (10%)($47,000) = $4,700. After one year and an income of $77,000, minority interest will rise by (10%)($77,000) = $7,700 to bring it to $12,400.

Consolidated net income:

The parent's net income is ($337,000 – $194,000 – $4,500 – $5,000)(1 – 0.32) = $90,780. The parent's share of the subsidiary's net income is (0.90)($77,000) = $69,300. Consolidated net income is thus $69,300 + $90,780 = $160,080.

Consolidated retained earnings:

Beginning retained earnings + Net income – Dividends = Ending retained earnings: $44,000 + $90,780 – $8,000 = $126,780.

IP3. (a) Westfalia is using the equity method for its non-consolidated balance sheet. The proof of this is as follows:

Original investment in Rhine:	$3,200,000
Participation in Rhine income:	
(90%)($400,000)*	360,000
Participation in Rhine dividends:	
(90%)($150,000)	(135,000)
Investment in Rhine after one year: (as shown on Westfalia balance sheet for 2006)	$3,425,000

* Rhine income = Retained earnings, 2006 – Retained earnings, 2005 + Dividends
= $1,033,000 – $783,000 + $150,000 = $400,000

(b) Westfalia paid $3,200,000 for 90% of net assets worth $3,483,000. So, goodwill from this purchase must be $3,200,000 – ((90%)($3,483,000)) = $65,300. Note here that, without information to the contrary, fair value is assumed to be book value.

Minority interest is (10%)($3,483,000) = $348,300.

(c)

Westfalia Sod Farms, Ltd.
Consolidated Balance Sheet
March 31, 2006
($000s)

ASSETS		LIABILITIES	
Current Assets:		Current Liabilities:	
Cash	$ 254	Accounts Payable	$ 435*
Accounts Receivable	489*	Bank Loan	165
Marketable Securities	440		600
Inventories	2,410	Minority Interest	373.3**
	3,593		
Non-Current Assets:		Non-Current Liabilities:	
Goodwill	64.8	Mortgage	2,465
Buildings, Net	340		3,438.3
Land	3,900	EQUITY	
	4,304.8	Common Stock	3,600
		Retained Earnings	859.5≅
			4,459.5
Total Assets	$7,897.8	Total Equities	$7,897.8

* $5,000 intercompany balance is eliminated.
** (10%)(Net assets of Rhine, $3,733,000) = $373,300
≅ Reflects amortization of goodwill.

(d) Consolidated net income = $700,000 (Westfalia) + $400,000 (Rhine)
– $12,000 (intercompany sales)
– $360,000 (investment income recorded by Westfalia—see part (a) above)
– $40,000 (minority interest in Rhine income)
– $500 (amortization of goodwill)
= $687,500

IP4. (a) The CCA does not change income in year one, year five, or any year. Income tax expense is not affected in any year, even when the CCA is less than amortization. To illustrate the point, see the table that follows.

Year	Amortization ($)	CCA ($)	Difference ($)
1	25,000	50,000	(25,000.00)
2	25,000	67,500	(42,500.00)
3	25,000	57,375	(32,375.00)
4	25,000	48,769	(23,769.00)
5	25,000	41,453	(16,453.00)
6	25,000	35,235	(10,235.00)
7	25,000	29,950	(4,950.00)
8	25,000	25,458	(458.00)
9	25,000	21,639	3,361.00
10	25,000	18,393	6,607.00
11	25,000	15,634	9,366.00
12	25,000	13,289	11,711.00
13	25,000	11,296	13,704.00
14	25,000	9,601	15,399.00
15	25,000	8,161	16,839.00
16	25,000	6,937	18,063.00
17	25,000	5,896	19,104.00
18	25,000	5,012	19,988.00
19	25,000	4,260	20,740.00
20	25,000	24,141	859.00
	Total: 500,000	Total: 500,000	Total: 0

To explain why income is unaffected, take year 3. If the income before tax was $240,000 and the tax rate was 32%, income tax expense and income tax payable would be $76,800.

With CCA, taxable income would be \$240,000 + \$25,000 (amortization) – \$57,375 (CCA) = \$207,625. Income tax payable would therefore be \$66,440. Future income tax is therefore (0.32)(\$240,000 – \$207,625) = \$10,360. The journal entry (excluding explanation) would be:

Income Tax Expense	66,440	
Income Tax Payable		66,440
Income Tax Expense	10,360	
Future Income Tax Payable		10,360

Note that total income tax expense comes to \$76,800, the same as it would be without using CCA.

Then take year 15, when CCA is less than amortization. Assuming the same income before tax of \$240,000 and 32% tax, income tax expense and income tax payable would be \$76,800. With CCA, taxable income would be \$240,000 + \$25,000 – \$8,161 = \$256,839. Income tax payable would therefore be \$82,188.48. Future income tax is therefore (0.32)(\$240,000 – \$256,839) = (\$5,388.48). The journal entry (excluding explanation) would be:

Income Tax Expense	82,188.48	
Income Tax Payable		82,188.48
Future Income Tax Payable	5,388.48	
Income Tax Expense		5,388.48

Note that total income tax expense comes to \$76,800, the same as it would be without using CCA.

So, if income tax expense, or any other expense, is not affected by future income taxes, net income will not be affected.

(b) Using CCA will not affect balance sheet totals in the first year, or in any year. The liabilities are affected in that their composition changes. In year 1, the tax payable liability is reduced by (0.32)(\$240,000 – (\$240,000 + \$25,000 – \$50,000)) = \$8,000. A future tax liability is created for \$8,000. Overall, liabilities are unaffected.

(c) The accountant will save the company income taxes by using the CCA. However, this will only last for the first eight years of the new equipment's life. This savings in taxes payable, however, is worth more than it appears since money has a time value. That is, the savings in the first eight years are worth more the earlier they are received because of interest. Over the 20 years, taxes payable will be the same as if CCA had not been used. However, the use of CCA permits the company to enjoy some savings in the first eight years, savings that could be used for investment purposes.

After the eighth year, the use of CCA will result in a greater tax payable than would have been the case if CCA had not been used. Whether the company chooses to use CCA or not, the tax authorities will and this will determine the tax liability, not the accountant's methods.

EXPLORATIVE QUESTIONS

EQ1. The CCA rate is that which must be used for income measurement for taxation purposes. Management's objectives with respect to reporting income may be such that they would choose an amortization policy that would yield a different income figure. The purposes for doing this could vary from wanting to show extraordinarily strong earnings to taking a Big Bath (discussed in Chapter 3).

Why CCA rates do not follow accepted accounting practices in this area (or vice versa) is not altogether clear. One reasonable explanation can be found in the matching principle, in that GAAP concerning amortization try to ensure the fairest matching of expenses to revenues. On the other hand, CCA rates may permit faster amortization, while still meeting the matching principle, to simply allow for a lower tax liability in the first years of an asset's acquisition; this would be done to encourage capital expenditures by businesses.

EQ2. CCA seems to complicate the accounting process. It would seem logical for companies to use CCA and no other amortization method. The choice of amortization methods leads to differing incomes. A company would, therefore, be able to manipulate its income by changing its amortization policy. This, of course, means taxes payable could be manipulated. CCA is a means by which all companies are to depreciate their assets for tax purposes only. In this manner, a company's choice of amortization methods is irrelevant for computing taxable income.

CCA is on a declining balance basis in Canada. This means that companies are permitted to reduce their taxes payable in the early years of an asset's life. This has the effect of encouraging depreciable asset purchases for commercial and economic growth reasons.

A possible reason that all companies do not simply use just CCA instead of some other amortization policy might lie in what reported performance should look like. CCA lowers taxable income in the early years of asset acquisition. If CCA were solely used, reported income would not be as high as it could be if another amortization method were used.

It is true that CCA does not change income if it is used for tax purposes while another method is used for reporting purposes. But if CCA is used for both tax and reporting purposes, then in the early years of assets' lives income will be lower. Management may want to show a better income figure in the early years of assets' lives to justify that the acquisitions are paying off, but high amortization early on would not allow them to do that.

Another possible reason for not using CCA for reporting purposes is that a company may view an asset as having more economic value in the latter years of the asset's life rather than in the early years. It might then want to use decelerated amortization for reporting purposes.

Whatever the reasons may be for using an amortization method other than CCA for reporting purposes, CCA exists to entice firms to acquire depreciable assets for growth.

EQ3. Before 1987, pensions were a form of off-balance-sheet financing since companies received the benefit of employees' services but could avoid reporting pension liabilities on their balance sheets. Since then, the *CICA Handbook* has required companies to disclose pension liabilities. Pension contributions by the company are determined by actuarial studies conducted by trustees of the pension plan (such as trust companies or pension trusts). These trustees have pension plan actuaries who will determine the present value of the plan benefits, compare that to the plan assets, determine whether a surplus or deficit exists, and then determine an appropriate pension plan contribution. If all of this is confusing to you, take solace in the fact that pension plan accounting is the subject of more advanced texts.

With respect to warranties, the amount of a warranties expense in a given period would likely be estimated according to the company's history of returned products or warranty service provided. This will usually be a percentage of sales or a percentage of cost of goods sold, since they are directly related to sales.

Both pension and warranty expenses are indeed estimates. But, just like amortization, these estimates are made in order to allow the fairest matching of expenses and revenues. The future liabilities they create may not, in fact, ever be a liability *per se* since they may not have to be paid or delivered upon. But, in the interests of conservatism and fairness, these liabilities must be recognized until they are discharged. As long as pension plans exist and product warranties are rendered, there will be respective liabilities shown on the balance sheets

CHAPTER 10
FINANCIAL ACCOUNTING ANALYSIS WRAP-UP

LEARNING OBJECTIVES

After completing Chapter 10, you should:

- have knowledge of some of the tools used in financial statement analysis;
- understand the mechanics of ratios;
- be able to interpret cash flow information contained in the cash flow statement; and
- understand what the effects of potential changes would be on the financial statements.

CHAPTER SUMMARY

10.1 Chapter Introduction: Analysis of Financial Accounting Information

- Up to this point in the text, you have been exposed to a variety of accounting principles and procedures.
- You know by this point that it is not sufficient, as an accountant, simply to prepare financial statements; you also must know how to analyze these statements and determine what effects changes in accounting policies (e.g., method of amortization) would have on a set of statements.
- The calculation of the numbers used in financial statement analysis is not the end point, but is part of information that can allow you to make some sort of an evaluation of how the company is doing.
- Judgment is used to take the information and make decisions about the company. As always, the more information you have, the better the evaluation and decision.
- The demand for information regarding financial position and performance of a company is great. You need to look at company information from year to year or in relation to other companies. You need to assess potential, relative to the risk. In doing so, you must remember the principles of comparability and consistency.

10.2 Investment and Relative Return

- The concept of return on investment is a result of the thought that an investment is made to earn a return. What we look at is the return in relation to the amount of the investment.
- The equation for the return on investment is:

$$\text{Relative return (return on investment)} = \frac{\text{Return}}{\text{Investment}}$$

The numerator is the amount of the return from making the investment, while the denominator is the amount of the initial investment.

- It seems quite easy to calculate the amount of the initial investment. It is the amount of the return that can be difficult to determine. What is return? Is it the net income? Is it the amount of interest that could be earned if invested elsewhere? Or is it the amount of cash that we receive from the investment? In many cases the numbers will be the same, but in other cases they can differ, making evaluation more difficult.
- You should then consider the effect that income taxes have on your evaluation. The calculation of income tax is far more complicated than will be explained here, but it is necessary to consider its effect to some extent.
- Corporations do not get to keep all the income that is earned. The final net income is likely to be far less than the operating income. When doing an evaluation of a company, remember that there is a difference between operating income and net income.
- The calculation of income tax is such an important item in the financial statements that you will usually find information about it in the notes to the financial statements, including the income tax rate for the company for that year.
- Scenario-building or "what if" analysis is quite common in business. Business owners and managers often need to know how financial performance or position would change if one course of action were taken instead of another.
- Effects analysis involves taking an event, a policy change, or an accounting method change, and determining what happens to financial figures if the change is implemented.
- Naturally, if income is being affected by such a change, then income tax must also be affected.
- A useful rule to remember is to multiply the before-tax effect on income by (1 – Tax rate). Doing so yields the effect of a change on net income.
- For example, if, as a result of recognizing revenues earlier, revenues increase in the current year by $10,000, then net income would increase by ($10,000)(1 – Tax rate).
- An example would serve to illustrate the process of tax calculation and its importance to analyzing changes:

Blodgett Ltd., a publishing company, has earned revenues for 2004 of $100,000. It has expenses of $50,000 and the tax rate for 2004 is 40%.

Revenue	$100,000
Expenses	50,000
Income before income tax	50,000
Income tax expense (40%)	20,000
Net income	$ 30,000

Looking at the "net of tax" method, we would show a column that reports the income as follows:

Revenue (net = $100,000 × (1 – 0.40))	$60,000
Expenses (net = $50,000 × (1 – 0.40))	30,000
Net income	$30,000

You can see that no matter which way we do this calculation, we arrive at the same net income.

If Blodgett wished to see the effect of recognizing $1,000 more in revenues (and no increase in expenses), net income would go up by $600.

10.3 Introduction to Financial Statement Analysis

- The purpose of financial statement analysis is to evaluate the financial performance or financial position of an enterprise.
- If the underlying information is reliable, an evaluation may be done that will mean something to the evaluator. If the underlying information is not satisfactory, the analysis may not be informative.
- Most importantly, it is necessary to know why an analysis is being done. You need to know what decision is being considered.
- The more information you can gather about a company in addition to its financial statements, the more able you are to exercise judgment. This means that in any analysis you are constrained by the breadth of information to which you have access. The more limited your information, the more cautious you should be about drawing conclusions.

10.4 Financial Statement Ratio Analysis

- There are many different ratios we can use to analyze a company. This text uses 20 different ratios, but more exist and are used.
- The first set of ratios are performance ratios, that is, they are concerned with how well the company has performed over the period.

(1) Return on equity shows how much return is being generated by the equity held within the company. The question here is which number to use for equity. You can use year-end equity or an average of the beginning and end of the year.

(2) Return on assets shows the company's ability to generate a return on the assets before you look at the financing of the assets. This will help determine whether or not it makes sense to borrow. Once again, you need to make a decision on which asset figure to use: the end of the year or the average.

(3) Sales return indicates how much of each sales dollar falls to the bottom line. This can help judge whether or not a product is priced fairly or if the company is in a very competitive industry.

(4) Common size financial statements merely require that you calculate all balance sheet items as a percentage of the total assets, and all income statement items as percentages of the total revenue. What this does is discount the effect of the size of the company. It allows comparison of companies of very different sizes and allows you to spot trends from year to year.

(5) Gross margin is a ratio examining the pricing of products as well as the product mix.

(6) Average interest rate has several variations depending on how interest expense is calculated.

(7) Cash flow to total assets is a measure of how cash is generated relative to size. This focuses on the actual cash rather than accrual income and is another ratio that can factor out the size of the company.

(8) Earnings per share shows how earnings are generated by common shares. As you can tell, this is a ratio that shareholders would want to see. It factors out company size and allows the investor to know how well the company has done relative to the shareholder's investment.

(9) Book value per share functions similarly to the EPS ratio, showing the portion of the shareholders' equity that can be attributed to the common shareholders according to the number of shares outstanding.

(10) Price-earnings ratio looks at the earnings and the market price of the shares and tries to relate them.

(11) Dividend payout ratio measures the portion of the earnings paid out to the shareholders.

- After looking at performance ratios we turn our attention to activity ratios. This second set of ratios involves both the financial position of the company and the performance, and measures how effectively a company is using specific resources.

(12) Total asset turnover measures the dollar sales volume of a company relative to its size.

(13) Inventory turnover looks at the level of inventories related to a volume of activity. It is frequently difficult to calculate this ratio since many companies do not disclose the cost of goods sold expense. Sales revenues, however, can be substituted for cost of goods sold.

(14) The collection ratio shows how many days it takes for the entity to collect a day's sales revenue. A large number here may cause you to call into question the method of the company's collection procedures.

- The previous two sets of ratios involve the financial position of the company, that is, how the company stands at a particular point in time. The next group of three ratios are financing ratios.

(15) Debt-equity ratio measures how much a company has borrowed relative to the shareholders' equity.

(16) Long-term debt/equity ratio assumes that long-term debt shows a company's risk and financing strategy better than including the accounts payable and such items as the future income taxes.

(17) Debt to assets ratio shows the percentage of the assets financed by borrowing.

- The last group of three ratios are liquidity and solvency warning ratios; that is, they measure how well a business can meet its current debts.

(18) Working capital (current) ratio shows whether or not the company has enough short-term assets to cover its short-term debts.

(19) Acid test (quick) ratio is an even more strict version of the current ratio that indicates whether or not the company could cover the current liabilities without having to sell inventory. If we went even further, we could calculate the "extreme acid test" ratio, which uses only cash and cash equivalents as the numerator.

(20) Interest coverage ratio shows us whether or not the company can generate enough cash to pay the interest commitment.

- You can see that ratios help put financial statement information into a format that can be used for comparison.
- As mentioned before, more than just the ratios are needed to evaluate a company. The entire annual report can provide extra information, telling shareholders about the company's operations and structure. The financial press and financial analysts' reports are other information sources.
- The notes to the financial statements need to be examined as well, since they will provide more explanation of some of the numbers in the financial statements. Those notes will also reveal the policies that are being followed by the company and provide detail for some of the statement numbers that are less clear by themselves.

10.5 Interpretation of Cash Flow Information

- As stated repeatedly in this guide, while earning income is a good thing for a business, cash flow may be just as important for that business.
- Cash is required to pay the bills or dividends. Remember that income is equal to revenue minus expenses and that revenue may well include accounts receivable.
- Remember that a cash flow statement shows how the company raised cash, what was done with it, and what its cash position is at the current time.
- If we look at the cash flow statement and combine it with the income statement and the balance sheet, we can learn a number of things about the business:

- We can compare the cash flow numbers to the company's assets, equity, etc.
- We can see the company's dependence on external cash sources versus the cash that can be generated internally.
- We can evaluate its ability to pay its debts and whether or not it has sufficient cash or cash-equivalent assets.
- We can see what its long-term financing and investing strategies are and how they relate to its ability to keep its assets working.
- We can evaluate its dividend payment policy and determine the quality of its income.
- We can look for manipulation of cash flow figures by comparing from year to year and look for potential problems that may be the result of a successful business.

10.6 Integrative Ratio Analysis

- The calculation of ratios is useful to analyze a company, but an integrative analysis can be used to connect multiple ratios.
- One useful integrative analysis is the "Scott formula." The Scott formula uses the idea of "leverage." Leverage is the consequence of borrowing money and using it to generate a return.
- Leverage can hurt—as well as help—a company.
- When borrowing is involved, ROE equals the sum of the rate of return of the project applied to the equity invested, plus the leverage return (the difference between the rate of return of the project and the borrowing cost applied to the amount borrowed.
- Return on equity = Overall operating return before interest cost + Leverage return
  = (Sales return before interest) × (Asset turnover) + (Operating return minus interest rate) × (Borrowing proportion)

  ROE = SR × AT + (ROA – IN) × D/E
- Here is an example set of figures to use to calculate the Scott formula:

Total assets	$500,000
Total liabilities	$200,000
Total equity	$300,000
Total revenue	$1,000,000
Net income	$50,000
Interest expense	$20,000
Income tax rate	40%
After-tax interest expense	$12,000

Next, calculate the various components of the Scott formula:

ROE = $50,000/$300,000 = 0.1667
SR = $50,000 + $12,000/$1,000,000 = 0.062
AT = $1,000,000/$500,000 = 2
ROA = $50,000 + $12,000/$500,000 = 0.124
IN = $12,000/$200,000 = .06
D/E = $200,000/$300,000 = 0.6667

Now, assemble the components into the formula:

$$\begin{aligned} ROE &= SR \times AT + (ROA - IN) \times D/E \\ 0.1667 &= 0.62 \times 2 + (0.124 - 0.06) \times 0.6667 \\ 0.1667 &= 0.124 + 0.427 \end{aligned}$$

- Remember that the two figures to the right of the equals sign must equal the number to the left of the equals sign. If the two parts do not add up, there may be the possibility of a problem with rounding or a more significant problem with your calculations.
- To analyze what the Scott formula reveals about the company, you need to look at both of the components that have been generated: the operating component of the return on equity, and the leverage component of the return on equity.
- The operating component shows how the profit margin and the turnover interact. This operating return is the return on assets. You can see that profit margin is not particularly high in this example, but the turnover is on the high side, resulting in a good return on assets.
- The leverage component shows how the borrowing by the company is working. In this case, positive leverage is being generated. The return on the assets is 12.4% while the effective interest rate is only 6%. Even though the debt-equity ratio shows that the company is financed more by investors than by debt, we still have a positive leverage effect.
- Putting the two components together, we can see that the leverage component of the equation is equal to about 25% of the total return on equity. At the same time we see that 75% of our return on equity has been earned through the efficient operation of the company.
- At this point it would be good to have at least the prior year's information so that we could see how the company has done in comparison with the prior year. In order to do an even more thorough analysis, it would be helpful to have information relating to other companies in the same industry. We would then be able to tell how our company is doing with regard to its competition. We can also see that this kind of analysis lends itself to comparing two companies of different sizes.
- The Scott formula does have a significant limitation and that is that it does not take risk into account. It does not consider any of the ratios that reflect liquidity, solvency, cash flow or working capital.

10.7 Future Cash Flows: Present Value Analysis

- You have already seen that cash flow is very important to a company. How we look at cash flow is significant when we are analyzing a company.
- A typical occurrence in business is that an amount of capital may be borrowed or lent out. The fee that is paid for the amount borrowed or lent out is interest. This leads to the principle of the time value of money.
- Annual interest = Principal (the amount borrowed or lent) × Interest rate
- Amount due at the end of a year (or future value) = Principal × (1 + Interest rate)

- If no payments are made and the loan is for a longer period:

  Principal × (1 + Interest rate)^n, where n is the number of periods over which the principal is borrowed or lent.

- In other words, because interest exists, money has different values at different times.
- Money in hand today, which can be invested to earn interest, has more value than money to be received later, since the latter wasn't available for you to invest and earn interest.
- You can look at this idea another way by thinking about what you lose if you wait until some time in the future before you get your money. In other words, because of interest, and the opportunity to earn such, you should be prepared to accept less money now in exchange for a greater sum in the future. This is called present value analysis.
- Suppose you will be given $1,000 a year from now. What is its worth if you were to receive it today? Assuming the going interest rate is 5%; the present value of receiving $1,000 in the future is: $(\$1,000)(1 + 0.05)^{-1} = \$952.38$
- So, you should be indifferent between accepting $952.38 now versus $1,000 a year from now.
- Now, what if you were to receive several payments over time? For example, suppose you are a landlord and charge a tenant $500 per month for rent at the end of each month. The tenant offers to pay you six months' rent in advance but would like a discount for doing so. You are excited about this prospect since you could put the advance payment into an investment certificate that will yield 6% return per annum. How much of a discount do you offer? This is what is known as the present value of an annuity, the annuity being $500 per month for one year.

  First, it is necessary to determine interest monthly: 0.06/12 = 0.005
  Present value = $500/0.005 \times (1 - 1/(1 + 0.005)^6) = \$2,948.19$

  If you received $2,948.19 in advance, it would accumulate to $(2,948.19)(1.005)^6$ = $3,037.75 by the end of six months in the investment certificate.

Alternatively, if you received \$500 per month for six months, it would accumulate to:

Month	Months to earn interest	Future value at end of 6 months	
1	5	$500 \times (1.005)^5 =$	\$ 512.63
2	4	$500 \times (1.005)^4 =$	510.07
3	3	$500 \times (1.005)^3 =$	507.54
4	2	$500 \times (1.005)^2 =$	505.01
5	1	$500 \times (1.005)^1 =$	502.50
6	0	$500 \times (1.005)^0 =$	500.00
			\$3,037.75

So, the maximum discount you might offer this tenant is:

\$3,000 (6 months' rent) – \$2,948.19 =	\$51.81
\$3,037.75 – 3,000 =	37.75
	\$89.56

The tenant would thus pay you \$3,000 – \$89.56 or \$2,910.44. If you received this amount now, it would accumulate to (\$2,910.44)$(1.005)^6$ = \$2,998.85 (approximately \$3,000 due to rounding). This discount of \$89.57, then, leaves you no worse or better off by offering it. If you took the \$2,910.43 now and invested in the certificate, you would have \$3,000 at the end of six months. Otherwise, you could take \$500 each month and forgo the interest from each month's payment (as per the above table) as a discount and still have \$3,000 at the end of the six months.

- These present value and future value analyses are especially helpful when trying to evaluate potential investment possibilities, as the above example reveals.
- The implication to management is that financial accounting and disclosure are critical.

10.8 "What If" (Effects) Analysis

- Business owners and managers often need to know how financial performance or position would change if one course of action were taken instead of another.
- This is done for historic re-evaluation as well as planning.
- Effects analysis means taking an event, a policy, or an accounting method change, and determining what happens to financial figures if the change is implemented.
- This effects analysis skill builds on your accounting knowledge. Your facility to perform this will increase as your knowledge increases.
- Many of the same users who were identified in earlier chapters have concerns about the potential changes. Now, you will begin to evaluate the policies to make well-informed decisions.
- Remember, no financial decision can be made in a vacuum. There are many pieces of information that must be evaluated.
- Here are some examples of "what if" changes:

(1) Earlier Revenue Recognition

If a revenue recognition policy was changed from recognizing revenues when cash is received to recognizing revenues at the time of sale, this would have the effect of increasing the amount of revenues recognized in a current period. Hence, net income would increase in the current period.

(2) Cash Basis vs. Accrual Accounting

The effect of changing from accrual recognition to cash basis might be that cash basis income is higher than accrual basis income. Hence, net income is higher.

- Remember that "what if" changes have not actually happened. You are simply trying to determine what results would appear if such a policy change were implemented.
- It is usually not necessary to re-prepare entire sets of statements; the effects of a "what if" change usually only affect a few accounts so it is only necessary to examine these accounts.
- As noted in Section 10.2 of this guide, if income is being affected by a "what if" change, then income tax must also be affected.
- Multiplying the before-tax effect on income by (1 – Tax rate) yields the effect of a change on net income.

10.9 Multi-Year "What If" (Effects) Analysis

- Reminders for trying effects analysis:
    - Debits should equal credits for every change.
    - The income statement, the statement of retained earnings, and the cash flow statement will contain the annual effects. The balance sheet will contain the cumulative effects. This can help you to figure out what is going on. If you know what the cumulative effect is on the balance sheet, you can deduce the annual effects and vice versa.
    - Consider the tax effect of any changes.
    - Generally, there is no effect on cash of "what if" changes unless, of course, cash is being spent or received as part of the change. For most policy changes, we are changing receivables, revenues, amortization, etc. and as a result, cash is not affected.
- The chart on page 689 of the text is very useful when doing effects analyses.
- Consider another example (framework shown below):

Suppose Christine Wright Inc. decided to change its revenue recognition policy to increase revenues by $15,000 in the current year and by a total of $13,000 in prior years (accounts receivable are increased correspondingly). As a result, expenses must also be increased in the current year by $9,000 and in prior years by $8,000 (so accounts payable increase as well). The company's income tax rate is 30%.

Christine Wright Inc.

ASSETS	**REVENUE**	**LIABILITIES**
LIABILITIES	**EXPENSES**	
Other than tax	Other than tax	Other than tax
+$121,000	*+ $13,000*	*+$134,000*
Income Tax	Income Tax	Income Tax
($36,300)	*($3,900)*	*($40,200)*
EQUITY	**NET INCOME**	**EQUITY**
Retained Earnings		Retained Earnings
($84,700)	*($9,100)*	*($93,800)*

Christine Wright Inc.

ASSETS	**REVENUE**	**ASSETS**
+$13,000	*+$15,000*	*+$28,000*
LIABILITIES	**EXPENSES**	**LIABILITIES**
Other than tax	Other than tax	Other than tax
+$8,000	*+ $9,000*	*+$17,000*
Income Tax	Income Tax	Income Tax
+$1,500	*+ $1,800*	*+ $3,300*
EQUITY	**NET INCOME**	**EQUITY**
Retained Earnings		Retained Earnings
+$3,500	*$4,200*	*+ $7,700*

EXERCISES

E1. Ratio Interpretation "I've cranked out every possible ratio," muttered a junior stock analyst, "and there is simply no way I can recommend this company to any of my brokers. The numbers are absolutely dismal. I've seen enough!" Is the stock analyst acting prematurely?

E2. Ratio Interpretation Why might TD–Canada Trust have a low inventory turnover?

E3. Ratio Interpretation Is a 2 to 1 current ratio always adequate?

E4. Ratio Interpretation Why would the creditors of a business prefer to see a high proportion of assets being financed by shareholders' equity?

E5. Ratio Interpretation Kevin Klone was reviewing the statements of a company he was interested in acquiring. Although Kevin was a brilliant graphic designer, he could not understand why the ROA was 10% and the return on common shareholders' equity was 15%. How would you explain it to Kevin?

E6. Ratio Calculation If the Scott formula simply uses other ratios such as sales return, asset turnover, and so on, of what value is the formula? Why not just look at the other ratios instead?

E7. Inventory Change Effect Morty Fahler owns and operates MortySports, a supplier of parts for Nissan Datsun 1970–1978 "Z" cars. Since these vehicles were prone to rusting, Morty stocks a variety of body parts. Amongst them are fenders. Because these are bulky and readily sold, Morty uses FIFO in accounting for inventory of these fenders as well as other body parts. The winter months are his busiest as restoration enthusiasts take to their garages. The inventory record for November showed the following:

Date	Purchase Price	Units Purchased	Units Sold	Balance
Nov. 2	$145.00	4		4
Nov. 4			3	1
Nov. 5	155.00	6		7
Nov. 12	165.00	3		10
Nov. 16			2	8
Nov. 18			1	7
Nov. 22	150.00	6		13
Nov. 25	155.00	6		19
Nov. 28			2	17
Nov. 30			2	15

(a) Using FIFO, what is the value of inventory November 30 and what is the cost of goods sold for November?

(b) Using LIFO perpetual, what is the value of inventory November 30 and what is the cost of goods sold for November?

(c) MortySports' income tax rate is 30%. Based on your calculations above, what would be the effect of changing from FIFO to LIFO perpetual on:

(i) the net income for November?
(ii) the balance sheet at the end of November?

E8. Amortization Change Effect Two years ago, Dent-A-Wreck Auto Body acquired a frame straightening machine for $150,000. The machine was expected to have a 12-year life with no salvage value. Over the past two years (2005 and 2006), the company amortized this machine using the straight-line method. However, the company's accountants have been instructed by management to use the double declining balance method for 2006. The income tax rate is 40%.

(a) Calculate the amortization expense Dent-A-Wreck would have recorded in 2005 and 2006. What would the journal entry have been in each year?

(b) Calculate the amortization expense Dent-A-Wreck would have recorded had it used the declining balance method since it acquired the machine (for both 2005 and 2006).

(c) Calculate the effects of changing to the declining balance method on:

(i) the balance sheet, end 2005;
(ii) the income statement, 2006;
(iii) the balance sheet, end 2006.

PROBLEMS

P1. Statement Analysis "I think Great Tree Nurseries is a great investment," your friend Carol says to you over coffee one day. "I bought 100 shares. If I were you, I'd call my broker right away." You reply that, if you were to invest, you would need to see a copy of the annual report at the very least. She hands it to you and says, "What do you want to look at this for? All you need to know is that the company has earnings per share of $8 and the price is $40 per share. If you wait, the price will go up even more." What do you say to Carol?

P2. Ratio Calculations and Interpretation

(a) Refer to Installment 3 of the Continuing Demonstration Case, Mato, Inc., in your text to prepare a ratio analysis for the first six months, as was done for the full year in Installment 10 in your text.

(b) What does this analysis tell you about Mato for its first six months? Looking at the figures from the full year (see Installment 9), what do you think of the business that Mavis and Tomas have begun?

P3. Ratio Interpretation The price-earnings ratio seems to be a departure from traditional accounting practice, since it uses market price, not historical price. Explain this comment.

P4. Change Effects Interpretation You are considering making some changes in the operations and financial structure of your company. The following information is available to you:

- Net income is $12,000.
- Interest expense is $8,000.
- Tax is 32%.
- Revenues are $197,000.
- Total assets are $175,000.
- Total debt is $82,000.

The following changes are contemplated. Consider the effect on ROE of each of the changes *separately* and comment briefly on each.

(i) Renegotiating debts such that interest payments are reduced bringing the after-tax cost of borrowing to 5.39%

(ii) Purchasing an additional $15,000 in assets, using long-term debt

(iii) Increasing selling prices to increase revenues by 5%

(iv) Allowing another investor to purchase a $12,000 share in the company

(v) Moving to another province where the combined federal and provincial tax rate would be 27%

P5. Scott Formula Calculation The following financial statement information is available for Merchandise Shippers, Ltd.:

- Total assets at the end of this year are $495,000.
- Total debt at the end of this year is $305,000.
- Revenues for this year are $602,000.
- Operating expenses for this year are $415,000.
- Interest expense for this year is $92,000.
- Tax rate is 32%.

(a) Comment on the company's performance for the year using the Scott formula to assist you.

(b) Last year's performance showed the following results:
SR = 0.2071 IN = 0.1295
AT = 1.341 D/E = 1.405
ROA = 0.2777

Explain the changes to ROE from last year to this year.

P6. Ratio Change Effect Suppose Microsoft decided to capitalize some research and development expenses. What ratios would be affected by such a change?

P7. Multi-Year Change Effect As a result of an accounting policy change introduced by the accounting department at Feiser Construction, Ltd., accounts receivable at the end of 2003 would fall by $690,000, at the end of 2004 would fall to $8,310,450, and at the end of 2005 would fall to $10,345,250. Associated decreases in the allowance for doubtful accounts at year-end would decrease the 2003 allowance by $17,425, and bring the 2004 allowance to $108,500 and the 2005 allowance to $189,750. The following information shows account balances before the policy change:

	2004	2005
Revenue		$21,435,250
Ending Accounts Receivable	$9,295,450	11,975,850
Bad Debts Expense		124,775
Allowance for Doubtful Accounts at the end of the year	142,350	212,625

(a) Is revenue being recognized sooner or later by the new policy?

(b) What are the income, liability, and cash flow effects of the policy change? (Assume a constant tax rate of 32%.)

P8. Multi-Year Change Effect Pommigran Canoes makes canoes and other fibreglass products such as water storage tanks, corrugated sheets, and hammer shafts. In 2005, accounting policies were changed by management:

- The first change was to expense some previously capitalized costs. Notably, fibreglass injection molds had been repaired in previous years. These repair costs were capitalized under the assumption that they were extraordinary repairs. It was now felt, however, that these were routine repairs considered maintenance expenses.

- The second change was to recognize less amortization on other equipment to bring amortization rates more in line with CCA rates.

The effects of these changes on the expenses concerned are shown below. The company's tax rate is 30% and the changes would affect deferred taxes, not current.

	2004	2005
Maintenance Expense		
Old method	$87,000	$100,000
New method	96,000	108,000
Amortization expense		
Old Method	2,500	3,500
New Method	2,100	2,900

Determine the combined effect of both these changes on the following items for both 2004 and 2005:

(i) net income;
(ii) year-end working capital;
(iii) year-end total assets;
(iv) year-end debt-equity;
(v) year-end return on equity;
(vi) asset turnover.

INTEGRATIVE QUESTIONS

IP1. Loan Assessment "Listen, Bryan, I've been doing personal and business banking here for more than 18 years," said Geoffery, "and I need an extension to our operating loan to carry us through the next two quarters. You know the circumstances—the economy is down, sales are hurting, etc. Look at our balance sheets. We've got reasonable working capital; in fact, it's improved over last year. Our sales are down a little but we know that'll rebound. We haven't borrowed a lot from you recently and I know you guys are worried about getting your interest. After all, I'm sure that you heard our largest competitor is having difficulty meeting its interest payments. What do you say, do we get the extra $200,000 loan or not?" If you were Bryan, would you extend the loan? What else might you request from Geoffery?

Balance Sheets
As at December 31
(in $000s)

		2007		2006
Current Assets				
Cash		22		155
Accounts Receivable		230		110
Inventories		410		360
Total Current Assets		662		625
Fixed Assets				
Land		310		310
Buildings	240		240	
Accum. Amortization	(96)	144	(84)	156
Vehicles	60		60	
Accum. Amortization	(36)	24	(24)	36
Total Fixed Assets		478		502
Total Assets		1,140		1,127
Current Liabilities				
Operating Loan		35		45
Accounts Payable		145		175
Notes Payable		30		55
Total Current Liabilities		210		275
Non-Current Liabilities				
Mortgage		602.5		605
Total Liabilities		812.5		880
Equity				
Share Capital		200		200
Retained Earnings		127.5		47
Total Equity		327.5		247
Total Liabilities and Equity		1,140		1,127

Income Statements
For the Years Ended December 31
(in $000s)

	2007	2006
Sales	900	1,200
Cost of Goods Sold	675	860
Gross Profit	225	340
Operating Expenses	110	145
Operating Income	115	195
Income Taxes	34.5	58.5
Net Income	80.5	136.5

IP2. Statement Analysis Use the information below to prepare whatever financial analyses and recommendations you think are necessary:

Sunn Office Systems, Ltd.
Balance Sheets
As at December 31
(in $000s)

	2005	2004	2003
Current Assets			
Cash	27	55	70
Accounts Receivable	198	159	147
Inventory	310	200	205
Total Current Assets	535	414	422
Fixed Assets			
Land	400	400	350
Buildings	275	230	230
Equipment	290	275	275
	965	905	855
Accumulated Amortization			
Buildings/Equipment	(315)	(260)	(195)
Net Fixed Assets	650	645	660
Total Assets	1,185	1,059	1,082
Current Liabilities			
Demand Loan	250	337	175
Accounts Payable	325	215	400
Tax Payable	95	25	40
Total Current Liabilities	670	577	615
Non-Current Liabilities			
Mortgage Payable	240	220	230
Total Liabilities	910	797	845
Equity			
Share Capital	100	100	100
Retained Earnings	175	162	137
Total Equity	275	262	237
Total Liabilities and Equity	1,185	1,059	1,082

Sunn Office Systems, Ltd.
Income Statements
For the Year Ended December 31
(in $000s)

	2005	2004	2003
Sales	2,700	5,300	2,200
Cost of Goods Sold	1,900	3,600	1,600
Gross Profit	800	1,700	600
Expenses	653	1,581	543
Net Income	147	119	57
Additional Information			
Dividends Paid	134	94	-
Interest Expense	110	85	94
Income Tax	72	55	26

IP3. Change Effect Result on Ratio What effect does lease capitalization have on financial statement analysis (that is, what does it do to ratios)?

IP4. Multi-Year, Multiple Change Effect Norton Bauxite Company is contemplating making the following accounting policy changes:

(i) Earlier revenue recognition, thus increasing 2003 receivables by $70,000 and 2004 receivables by $34,000 from their current figures. Attendant increases in the allowance for doubtful debts would be $5,600 for 2003 and $2,720 for 2004.

(ii) Product development costs of $120,000 in 2003 and $72,000 in 2004 are to be capitalized instead of expensed.

(iii) Patents are to be amortized at twice the current rate due to supercedent technology rendering the patents useful for only half their legal life. The current amortization expense is $1,000 per year.

(a) What effect will the above policy changes have cumulatively on 2003 and 2004 incomes, assuming a 32% tax rate?
(b) What financial ratios are affected by such policy changes?

EXPLORATIVE QUESTIONS

EQ1. Ratio Interpretation Can ratios be used to evaluate management's performance?

EQ2. Value of Ratios "I can't believe it," your friend Anna said. "If we had just bothered to look at the ratios earlier, we could have seen the whole story of the problems with my business, Kooky Kookies." What is your response to Anna?

SOLUTIONS

EXERCISES

E1. Calculating the ratios for a company's statements is not a sufficient basis on which to make an unequivocal decision. A good understanding of the company, the industry within which the company competes, the company's accounting policies, and prior year financial analyses is necessary, among other things. Indiscriminately calculating ratios has no useful purpose. Ratios should be calculated with the user or decision maker in mind.

E2. TD–Canada Trust (or, for that matter, any bank or service industry) might have a low inventory turnover due to the fact that even though it takes in and gives out lots of money, cash is not really an inventory item.

E3. A 2 to 1 current ratio may be perfectly fine or it may be too low, depending on a number of factors such as the type of business, the composition of current assets, inventory turnover rate, and credit terms. If a company has a consistently high current ratio, it may have an unnecessary accumulation of funds, which could mean a sales problem (not being able to turn over inventory) or poor financial management.

E4. Obviously, a creditor will feel more comfortable knowing that the debt that is owed could be covered by the owners' interest in the firm. A ratio greater than 1 means that the owners have financed less of the assets than the creditors have. A ratio less than 1 means that the owners have financed more of the assets than the creditors have. So, the lower the debt-equity ratio, the larger the owners' stake in the company.

E5. ROA is how much net income the company was able to generate given its assets. So, for every dollar of assets, the company he is interested in generated $0.10. More correctly, the assets were used to generate a 10% return on them. This should tell him how efficiently the company is employing its assets.

The ROE is how much net income is generated for the equity of the owners. This should tell him how much return shareholders have earned for their investment in the company. This return is not cash, that's what dividends are for. The ROE should show him whether the company has used invested funds to the shareholders' benefit.

E6. The value of the Scott formula lies in its interpretation, as with any other ratio. The formula shows you where and how a company has earned a return, not just that it earned a return. The operating component shows you how much of a company's return was due to what the company actually does. It tells you whether a company is selling "a little, a lot," or selling "a lot, a little." The leverage component tells you whether a company is using debt to its advantage. Since debt is used primarily to buy assets, the return on those assets should offset the cost of the debt, and, if that is the case, the company would do well to borrow. So, the Scott formula tells you that the return on equity is both a function of what the company does with what it has (operating return) and a function of how it achieves what it has (leverage return).

E7. (a) In each year:

		Dr.	Cr.
Dr.	Amortization Expense	12,500	
Cr.	Accumulated Amortization		12,500

(b) Straight-line rate = $12,500/$150,000 = 8.33%
Double declining balance rate: 8.33% × 2 = 16.66%

		Dr.	Cr.
2001:	Amortization Expense	25,000	
	Accumulated Amortization		25,000
2002:	Amortization Expense	20,825	
	Accumulated Amortization		20,825

($150,000 – $25,000)(16.66%) = $20,825

ASSETS *($12,500)*	**REVENUES**	**ASSETS** *($20,825)*
LIABILITIES Other than tax	**EXPENSES** Other than tax *+ $8,325*	**LIABILITIES** Other than tax
Income Tax *($5,000)*	Income Tax *($3,330)*	Income Tax *($8,330)*
EQUITY Retained Earnings *($7,500)*	**NET INCOME** *($4995)*	**EQUITY** Retained Earnings *($12,495)*

E8. (a) FIFO:

COGS = 4 @ \$145 + 6 @ \$155 = \$1,510
End. inventory = 3 @ \$165 + 6 @ \$150 + 6 @ \$155 = \$2,325

(b) LIFO perpetual:

COGS = 3 @ \$145 +
2 @ \$165 +
1 @ \$165 +
2 @ \$155 +
2 @ \$155 = \$1,550
End. inventory = 1 @ \$145 + 6 @ \$155 +
6 @ \$150 +2 @ \$155 = \$2,285

(c) As immaterial as these numbers may be, COGS increases by \$40, tax expense falls by \$12, and net income falls by \$28. Inventory falls by \$40, tax liability falls by \$12, and retained earnings fall by \$28.

PROBLEMS

P1. You would probably want to know more about the history of the firm, and whether the stock price has gone up or down over time. You would also want to know if the earnings are paid out in the form of dividends or retained within the company for another purpose. Part of the decision you make will depend on what you could use the money for if you didn't purchase the stock—such as for paying your tuition, or buying a car, or whatever you might want or need.

P2. (a) Mato, Inc., ratios for the first six months:
The ratios here are presented just as they are in Installment 10 of the Continuing Demonstration Case in the text. These use the first six months' results calculated in Installment 3 of the case.

Performance ratios:

(1) Return on equity: –\$49,378/\$75,622 = –0.653 (notice that it's negative)
(2) Return on assets: –\$49,378/\$211,238 = –0.234 (negative)
(3) Sales return: –\$49,378/\$42,674 = –1.157 (negative)
(4) Common size financial statements: (see below)
(5) Gross margin: \$14,472/\$42,674 = 0.339. Cost of goods sold is 0.661 of sales revenue, so the average markup is 0.339/0.661 = 51% of cost.
(6) Average interest rate: None at this point.
(7) Cash flow to total assets: –\$87,089/\$211,238 = –0.412
(8) Earnings per share: The number of shares is not known, and EPS is not as meaningful for a private company as for a publicly traded one.

(9) Book value per share: The number of shares is not known, however, the owners' original equity of $125,000 is now down to $75,622, which means the book value of the shares is only 60.5% of the amounts the owners contributed.

(10) Price-earnings ratio: not determinable because the shares of a private company like this are not traded and therefore their price is not known.

(11) Dividend payout ratio: no dividends declared because there was a loss.

Activity (turnover) ratios:

(12) Total asset turnover: $42,674/$211,238 = 0.202

(13) Inventory turnover: $28,202/$73,614 = 0.383

(14) Collection ratio: $18,723/($42,674/365) = 160 days

Financing ratios:

(15) Debt-equity ratio: $135,616/$75,622 = 1.793

(16) Long-term debt/equity ratio: zero (no long-term debt)

(17) Debt to assets ratio: $135,616/$211,238 = 0.642

Liquidity and solvency warning ratios:

(18) Working capital ratio: $96,844/$135,616 = 0.714

(19) Acid-test ratio: ($4,507 + $18,723)/$135,616 = 0.171

(20) Interest coverage ratio: not calculated because with this large a loss there is no coverage.

Common Size Analysis:

Note: (1) rounding errors account for minor discrepancies
(2) see Installment 9 for February 2007 data.

Mato Inc.
Income Statement
Six Months Ended August 31, 2006, and Year Ended February 28, 2007

	August–Mid Year	February–Year-End
Revenues	100%	100%
Cost of Goods Sold	66.0%	60.5%
Salaries	60.0%	29.4%
Travel	20.5%	4.0%
Telephone	6.0%	1.8%
Rent	28.0%	10.5%
Utilities	3.8%	1.5%
Office & General	8.0%	2.5%
Amortization	23.7%	9.2%
Bad Debts	–	1.0%
Inventory Shortage	–	0.2%
Interest	–	2.8%
Total Expenses	216.0%	123.4%

Mato Inc.
Balance Sheet
August 31, 2006, and February 28, 2007

	August - Mid Year	February - Year End
Cash	2.1%	4.0%
Receivables	8.7%	8.8%
Inventory	34.9%	20.9%
Prepaid Expense	–	0.3%
Net Equipment	24.3%	31.1%
Net Leasehold	27.3%	31.8%
Net Software	2.0%	2.4%
Incorporation Costs	0.5%	0.7%
	100.0%	100.0%
Bank Loan	35.5%	29.5%
Payables	21.6%	26.0%
Loan Payable	7.1%	0.0%
Deferred Revenue	–	0.3%
Share Capital	59.2%	77.7%
Deficit	(23.4%)	(33.6%)
	100.0%	100.0%

(b) When you compare the six-month ratios to the one-year ratios (given in your text), a number of comments can be made.

- The company lost the majority of its beginning equity in its first six months (39.5%). The situation was similar for sales return, return on assets, and cash flow to total assets.
- The one-year activity ratios show a considerable improvement over the six-month figures, so you can see that the company made considerable efforts to minimize its losses.
- The one-year financing ratios show that the company reduced its reliance on debt considerably from the middle of the year.
- The one-year working capital ratio, however, worsened from mid-year. The quick ratio improved, but mostly because of reduced current debts.
- The six-month ratios point to a company that was in an extreme squeeze and in a precarious position as a borrower. The company acquired too much debt too quickly without the ability to use that debt wisely to generate returns. Without even preparing a statement of cash flow (as done in Installment 4 in your text), it would have been quite clear that the company would experience cash flow problems. Its 160-day collection ratio and negative cash flow to assets ratio would suggest that the company was in a cash crunch.

Based on the comparisons with one-year ratios, you can see that the company's woes started in the first six months and it spent the next six months trying to undo its errors. The company must concentrate on improving its working capital, and, in particular, improving its cash flow. Investors and creditors should be concerned about the security of their funds tied up in Mato, Inc.

Looking at the common size income statements, you can see that the company had considerable difficulty managing its costs in the first six months, but managed to cut the rate at which costs were being incurred sufficiently to bring them to 123% of sales—which was still a loss, however. Once again, it is apparent that the up-front costs were overburdening for the company.

The common size balance sheet shows that the company was able to improve its cash position slightly, and the statement of cash flow for the year-end supports this, showing that cash flow was better in the second half of the year (albeit still in the red for the whole year). The reason the working capital ratio worsened in the second half must then be because receivables or inventories had not sufficiently decreased. Inventories are the only significant current asset to have changed, but the overall decrease in current assets was not as great as the decrease in current liabilities. The company's overall asset base shrank by year-end due to decreases in current assets, and this made its non-current assets a larger component of its mix of assets. Liabilities have clearly been reduced. Share capital has increased, but this should not be interpreted as a good sign since return on equity is negative.

So, just as the ratios suggested, the company fared far worse in its first six months than in the year overall. The company has clearly taken steps to remedy its six-month performance, but it is far from being in the clear.

P3. Firstly, ratio analyses are not governed by accounting principles such as GAAP and are not considered accounting practice *per se*. Ratio analyses use accounting information and allow interpretation of accounting information, and could therefore be considered an accounting tool as opposed to an accounting convention. Secondly, to address the use of current share prices vs. historical prices, users of financial statements often use current prices in a predictive manner, believing that previous performance is a predictor, to some extent, of future performance. We already know that capital markets do respond to accounting information, particularly earnings, but the strength of the correlation has yet to be shown. A company's stock price reflects the optimism or pessimism that the market has for the company. The justification for using current prices for the PE ratio lies in the predictive ability offered by the current value that the market places on the company's stock; the higher the value, the more optimism the market holds, and the more favourable the interpretation of the ratio.

P4. Note: rounding accounts for minor differences.
Before calculating the effects of the changes, you should calculate the initial ROE:

ATI = ($8,000)(1 – 0.32) = $5,440
SR = ($12,000 + $5,440)/$197,000 = 0.089
AT = $197,000/$175,000 = 1.126
ROA = ($12,000 +$5,440)/$175,000 = 0.10
IN = $5,440/$82,000 = 0.066
D/E = $82,000/($175,000 – $82,000) = 0.882
ROE = $12,000/($175,000 – $82,000) = 0.129

ROE = SR × AT + (ROA – IN)(D/E)

0.129 = (0.089)(1.126) + (0.10 – 0.066)(0.882)
= 0.10 + (0.034)(0.882)
= 0.10 + 0.030
= 0.130

(i) If interest payments are reduced, you must figure out by how much.
IN = 0.0539 = ?/$ 82,000
After-tax interest expense must be $4,419.80. Before-tax interest expense is therefore (?)(1 – 0.32) = $4,419.80(?) = $6,500. So, if interest expense has dropped by $1,500, net income increases by ($1,500)(1 – 0.32) = $1,020.

ATI = (\$6,500)(1 – 0.32) = \$4,419.80
SR = (\$13,020 + \$4,419.80)/\$197,000 = 0.0885
AT = \$197,000/\$175,000 = 1.126
ROA = (\$13,020 + \$4,419.80)/\$175,000 = 0.0997
IN = \$4,419.80/\$82,000 = 0.0539
D/E = \$82,000/(\$175,000 – \$82,000) = 0.882
ROE = \$13,020/(\$175,000 – \$82,000) = 0.14

$$\begin{aligned} 0.14 &= (0.0885)(1.126) + (0.0997 - 0.0539)(0.882) \\ &= 0.0997 + (0.0458)(0.882) \\ &= 0.0997 + 0.0404 \\ &= 0.1401 \end{aligned}$$

Compared to the present, the effect of the refinancing is to increase leverage return (since a lower average interest rate is achieved) and not to affect operating return, since a change was made only to financial structure.

(ii) ATI = (\$8,000)(1 – 0.32) = \$5,440
SR = (\$12,000 + \$5,440)/\$197,000 = 0.0885
AT = \$197,000/\$190,000 = 1.037
ROA = (\$12,000 + \$5,440)/\$190,000 = 0.092
IN = \$5,440/\$97,000 = 0.056
D/E = \$97,000/(\$190,000 – \$97,000) = 1.043
ROE = \$12,000/(\$190,000 – \$97,000) = 0.129

$$\begin{aligned} 0.129 &= (0.0885)(1.037) + (0.092 - 0.056)(1.043) \\ &= 0.0918 + (0.036)(1.043) \\ &= 0.0918 + 0.0375 \\ &= 0.129 \end{aligned}$$

Compared to the present, the effect of additional borrowing to purchase assets is inconsequential. The operating and leverage components of the formula change moderately. Operating return is somewhat reduced but the additional leverage capitalizes on the leverage potential.

(iii) ATI = (\$8,000)(1 – 0.32) = \$5,440
SR = (\$18,698 + \$5,440)/\$206,850 = 0.117
AT = \$206,850/\$175,000 = 1.182
ROA = (\$18,698 + \$5,440)/\$175,000 = 0.138
IN = \$5,440/\$82,000 = 0.066
D/E = \$82,000/(\$175,000 – \$82,000) = 0.882
ROE = \$18,698/(\$175,000 – \$82,000) = 0.2011

$$\begin{aligned} 0.2011 &= (0.117)(1.182) + (0.138 - 0.066)(0.882) \\ &= 0.138 + (0.072)(0.882) \\ &= 0.138 + 0.064 \\ &= 0.202 \end{aligned}$$

The effect of additional sales revenues is to increase both operating leverage and leverage return from the present. Leverage return increases, since leverage potential has increased due to an improved ROA.

(iv) ATI = ($8,000)(1 – 0.32) = $5,440
SR = ($12,000 + $5,440)/$197,000 = 0.089
AT = $197,000/$187,000 = 1.053
ROA = ($12,000 + $5,440)/$187,000 = 0.093
IN = $5,440/$82,000 = 0.066
D/E = $82,000/($187,000 – $82,000) = 0.781
ROE = $12,000/($187,000 – $82,000) = 0.1143

$$\begin{aligned} 0.1143 &= (0.089)(1.053) + (0.093 - 0.066)(0.781) \\ &= 0.094 + (0.027)(0.781) \\ &= 0.094 + 0.021 \\ &= 0.115 \end{aligned}$$

Since equity has increased, the debt-equity ratio has dropped, thus reducing leverage return. Operating return and leverage potential also decreased, since the equity injection was simply to bolster cash.

(v) ATI = ($8,000)(1 – 0.27) = $5,840
SR = ($12,000 + $5,840)/$197,000 = 0.091
AT = $197,000/$175,000 = 1.126
ROA = ($12,000 + $5,840)/$175,000 = 0.102
IN = $5,840/$82,000 = 0.071
D/E = $82,000/($175,000 – $82,000) = 0.882
ROE = $12,000/($175,000 – $82,000) = 0.129

$$\begin{aligned} 0.129 &= (0.091)(1.126) + (0.102 - 0.071)(0.882) \\ &= 0.102 + (0.031)(0.882) \\ &= 0.102 + 0.027 \\ &= 0.129 \end{aligned}$$

The change in tax rates has the effect of increasing operating returns but reducing leverage potential and hence leverage returns. The net change in ROE is nil.

P5. (a) Scott formula analysis:
Net income = $64,600
ATI = ($92,000)(1 – 0.32) = $62,560
SR = ($64,600 + $62,560)/$602,000 = 0.2112
AT = $602,000/$495,000 = 1.2162
ROA = ($64,600 + $62,560)/$495,000 = 0.2569
IN = $62,560/$305,000 = 0.2051
D/E = $305,000/($495,000 – $305,000) = 1.605
ROE = $64,600/($495,000 – $305,000) = 0.34

$$\begin{aligned} 0.34 &= (0.2112)(1.2162) + (0.2569 - 0.2051)(1.605) \\ &= 0.2569 + (0.0518)(1.605) \\ &= 0.2569 + 0.0831 \\ &= 0.34 \end{aligned}$$

The company is generating an extremely good return on equity, the majority of which is due to a very good operating return.

(b) Last year's ROE

$$\begin{aligned} \text{Last year's ROE} &= (0.2071)(1.341) + (0.2777 - 0.1295)(1.405) \\ &= 0.2777 + (0.1482)(1.405) \\ &= 0.2777 + 0.2083 \\ &= 0.4860 \end{aligned}$$

ROE dropped dramatically from last year. Sales returns increased marginally and asset turnover worsened, combining to reduce operating return from 27.77% to 25.69%. So, it appears that the company's operations deteriorated to make less use of its assets in generating only marginally better return on sales.

The cost of borrowing rose dramatically while the return on assets declined. Thus, the leverage potential dropped considerably. The company increased its borrowing, thus softening the blow to leverage return, but this was insufficient to compensate for the decreased leverage potential. Only a severely high debt-equity ratio would make up for the loss in leverage return.

So, the majority of the drastic drop in ROE was due to reduced leverage return, while the company has done little to change its operations.

P6. Capitalization of R&D expenses would result in reduced expenses, increased net income, increased tax liability (whether deferred or current), increased assets, and increased retained earnings. As a result, the following ratios would be affected: ROE; ROA; sales return; cash flow to total assets; EPS; PE; book value per share; asset turnover; debt-equity; debt to assets; and working capital ratio (if tax effect is current).

P7. (a) Revenue is being recognized later by the new policy, given that receivables (and, therefore, revenues) are decreased.

(b) 2003: Accounts Receivable decreases $690,000.
Allowance for Doubtful Accounts decreases $17,425.
2004: Accounts Receivable decreases $985,000.
Allowance for Doubtful Accounts decreases $33,850.
2005: Accounts Receivable decreases $1,630,000.
Allowance for Doubtful Accounts decreases $22,875.

2004 revenues: down by $985,000 but up by $690,000 from 2003 for a net decrease of $295,000.

2004 bad debts expense: down by $33,850 but up by $17,425 from 2003 for a net decrease of $16,425.

2004 net income = (–$295,000 + $16,425)(1 – 0.32)
= (–$278,575)(1 – 0.32)
= –$189,431

2004 tax liability = (–$278,575)(0.32) = –$89,144

2005 revenues: down by $1,630,000 but up by $985,000 from 2004 for a net decrease of $645,600.

2005 bad debts expense: down by $22,875 but up by $33,850 from 2004 for a net increase of $10,975.

2005 net income = (–$645,600 – $10,975)(1 – 0.32)
= (–$656,575)(1 – 0.32)
= –$446,471

2005 tax liability = (–$656,575)(0.32) = –$210,104

There would be no effect on cash or cash flow, but the reduction in tax liability would save the company cash when taxes were eventually paid as opposed to if the company had not changed to this revenue recognition policy.

P8. (a)

	2004		2005	
Maintenance expense	up	$9,000	up	$8,000
Amortization expense	down	400	down	600
Net expense change	up	8,600	up	7,400
Tax	down	2,580	down	2,220
Net income change	down	$6,020	down	$5,180

(b) Year-end working capital: no effect since tax liability is non-current.

(c) Year-end total assets: down $8,600 down $7,400

(d) Year-end debt/equity:

Tax liability	down	$2,580	down	$2,220
Retained earnings	down	$6,020	down	$5,180

Hence, the ratio could be improved or worsened depending on percent change in numerator and denominator values from original values.

(e) Year-end return on equity:

Net income	down $6,020	down $5,180
Retained earnings	down $6,020	down $5,180

Ratio likely worsened due to numerator.

(f) Year-end return on assets:

Revenues	no change	no change
Total assets	down $8,600	down $7,400

Hence, improved ratio in both years.

INTEGRATIVE PROBLEMS

IP1. (a) Working capital did improve from 2.27 in 2006 to 3.15 in 2007. However, cash decreased by $133,000 or 86%. Receivables went up by 109% and inventories increased by 14%, meaning that cash is being tied up. The mortgage decreased by only 0.41%, indicating that the majority of payments are likely going toward interest and the interest expense seems to be buried in the operating expense figure (should be shown separately).

(b) A few ratios highlight some issues:

(1) 2006: Debt/equity = 3.56
2007: Debt/equity = 2.48
Plowing back income helped reduce the ratio although little debt was actually repaid. Total debt decreased by only 7.7% from $880,000 to $812,500.

(2) 2006: Receivables collection = 33.45 days
2007: Receivables collection = 93.27 days
The collection period considerably worsened and Geoffery should be worried about his credit policies.

(3) 2006: Inventory turnover (using ending inventory) = 2.38
2007: Inventory turnover (using ending inventory) = 1.57
Turnover has decreased, indicating a piling up of inventories possibly due to purchasing policies not having been adjusted for decreasing sales.

(4) 2006: Sales return = 11.38%
2007: Sales return = 8.9%
Sales return could be expected to decline as the economy worsens.

(5) 2006: Gross margin = 28.3%
2007: Gross margin = 25%
This means that prices are not being maintained while sales are dropping. Markups fell somewhat from 39.5% (0.283/(1 – 0.283)) in 2006 to 33.3% (0.25/(1 – 0.25)) in 2007.

(c) Borrowing another $200,000 would increase the debt-equity ratio to 3.09 which seems high. Now, that may not be the case depending on the industry in question, but, given few fixed assets, this seems rather high.

(d) Overall, Geoffery's company has had a poor year. The only real shining spot is that the company reduced its debt-equity ratio but did so without paying back much of its debt. The banker should question where all the cash has gone. It appears to have gone to finance receivables and inventories and to pay back debt. He should be concerned about how Geoffery intends to repay the loan since cash flow has fallen.

The banker may want to prepare a cash flow statement for 2007 ($000s):

Net Income		80.5
Amortization		24
Working Capital		
Receivables	(120)	
Inventories	(50)	
Bank Loan	(10)	
Accounts Payable	(30)	
Notes Payable	(25)	(235)
Cash from Operations		(130.5)
Investing		0
Financing		
Mortgage Repayment		(2.5)
Net Change in Cash		(133.5)

Other information that the banker might request:

(1) an explanation of why markups cannot be maintained;
(2) an explanation of why, in Geoffery's opinion, sales have declined (i.e., what operating reasons);
(3) a business plan to work the company through the next two quarters at minimum;
(4) audited statements if they are not already so;
(5) reasons for wanting an additional $200,000—to pay down other debts or to pay operating expenses, etc;
(6) a repayment schedule.

IP2. Your analysis might start with cash flow statements:

Sunn Office Systems, Ltd.
Cash Flow Statement
For the Year Ended December 31
(in $000s)

	2005	2004
Net Income	147	119
Non-Cash Items		
Amortization	55	65
Working Capital Changes		
Receivables	(39)	(12)
Inventories	(110)	5
Accounts Payable	110	185
Tax Payable	70	(15)
Cash From Operations	233	(23)
Dividends	(134)	(94)
Investing		
Land Purchase	–	(50)
Buildings Purchase	(45)	–
Equipment Purchase	(15)	–
Net Investing	(60)	(50)
Financing		
Additional Mortgage	20	-
Mortgage Repayment	–	(10)
Net Financing	20	(10)
Net Change in CCE	59	(177)
CCE, beginning		
(55 – 337)	(282)	
(70 – 175)		(105)
CCE, ending		
(27 – 250)	(223)	
(55 – 337)		(282)
Net Change in CCE	59	(177)

The cash flow statement highlights a number of issues:

(a) While 2005 saw an improvement in CCE, CCE in both years are still negative meaning that other current assets would have to be liquidated if the demand loans were called.

(b)

	2005	2004
Sales change	(49%)	140.9%
Receivables	24.5%	8.16%

In 2005, receivables increased while sales decreased, indicating a worsening collections policy. The collection ratio proves this:

2005: $198/($2,700/365) = 27 days
2004: $159/($5,300/365) = 11 days

While 27 days is still quite good, it represents a considerable fall for the company that can lead to additional cash flow problems.

(c)

	2005	2004	2003
Gross profit ratio	29.6%	32.1%	27.7%
Inventory change	55%	(2.4%)	
Inventory turnover	7.45	17.78	

Although sales dropped dramatically in 2005, the company was somewhat able to maintain its prices as given by the gross profit ratio (a 42% markup in 2005, a 47% markup in 2004, and a 38% markup in 2003, calculated as: Gross profit ratio/(1 – Gross profit ratio).

Inventory turnover decreased dramatically, thus leading to stockpiling inventory and taking up cash.

(d) The increased receivables in 2005, the payment of dividends, and the purchase of fixed assets have been financed from cash and from additional long-term financing. The demand loans have been absolutely necessary because the company would have no cash at all without them and would not, in fact, be able to meet its cash expenses, buy assets, or pay dividends.

It is odd that the company would, in fact, pay a dividend with borrowed money. It may have done so to attract investors by improving the dividend payout ratio. The company may be after an inflow of equity, since this would be what it needs to remove some of its short-term debt from the balance sheet.

In 2004, the company also relied heavily on operating loans and used them to buy assets and pay down long-term debt. It is possible that the operating loans cost less and such a move was made to reduce interest charges.

(e)

	2005	2004	2003
Debt-equity ratio	3.31	3.04	3.57

Debt-equity is rather high and an equity infusion may be the only way to reduce it at this point, since the company has no cash of its own to pay down debt.

(f)

	2005	2004	2003
Working capital ($)	(135)	(163)	(193)
Current ratio	0.799	0.712	0.686

Clearly, the company is in a weak current position. It is surprising that the company was able to secure operating loans in 2004 and 2005, given that the current ratio had been so weak.

Scott formula analysis: (note: rounding accounts for minor differences)

	2005	2004	2003
Tax Rate			
$72/(147 + 72)	32.9%		
55/(119 + 55)		31.6%	
26/(57 + 26)			31.3%
Interest After Tax ($)	73.81	58.14	64.55
SR	0.0818	0.0334	0.0552
AT	2.279	5.005	2.033
ROA	0.1863	0.1673	0.1123
IN	0.0811	0.0729	0.0764
D/E	3.309	3.042	3.565
ROE (NI/Equity)	0.534	0.4542	0.2405

2005

$$\begin{aligned} 0.534 &= (0.1863) + (0.1863 - 0.0811)(3.309) \\ &= (0.1863) + (0.1052)(3.309) \\ &= 0.1863 + 0.3481 \\ &= 0.5344 \end{aligned}$$

2004

$$\begin{aligned} 0.4542 &= (0.1673) + (0.1673 - 0.0729)(3.042) \\ &= (0.1673) + (0.0944)(3.042) \\ &= 0.1673 + 0.2872 \\ &= 0.4545 \end{aligned}$$

2003

$$\begin{aligned} 0.2405 &= (0.1123) + (0.1123 - 0.0764)(3.565) \\ &= (0.1123) + (0.0359)(3.565) \\ &= 0.1123 + 0.1280 \\ &= 0.2403 \end{aligned}$$

- Operating returns are fairly high and overall returns are bolstered considerably by leverage.
- ROE has increased primarily because of the increased use of leverage.
- SR fell in 2004 and rebounded in 2005 and since markups actually fell in 2005, this means that expenses were more tightly controlled, excluding interest and taxes.
- Leverage potential has been increasing and it would seem wise to capitalize on this. However, there is already significant debt in the company's structure.
- So, overall, the Scott formula analysis says that the company is working hard to earn a return and is doing well despite rocky sales. It does, however, have cash flow and working capital problems and seems overburdened with debt, particularly short-term debt (although it is using debt wisely to earn a return). The shortcoming of the Scott formula is that it overlooks problems identified earlier with an increasing collection period, inventory build-up, and negative CCE (i.e., it overlooks liquidity, solvency, and cash flow issues). Given that so much of the company's debt is current, liquidity and solvency should be prime concerns despite its strong earnings performance.

Recommendations:

(1) Improve receivables collection efforts to increase cash.
(2) Increase share capital or long-term financing to get short-term borrowing down.
(3) Allow inventory reductions (curtail inventory purchases).

IP3. Lease capitalization increases assets and liabilities on the balance sheet and affects expenses on the income statement. How expenses are affected depends on what amount the original rent expense was and what amount the lease amortization and interest charges are.

The ratios that are affected are, thus, the following:

- Return on equity
- Return on assets
- Sales return
- Average interest rate
- Cash flow to total assets
- Earnings per share
- Price-earnings
- Interest coverage
- Dividend payout
- Total asset turnover
- Debt-equity
- Long-term debt-equity
- Debt to assets
- Working capital
- Acid test

IP4. (a) Earlier revenue recognition will have the following effects:

- **2003 net income increases by ($70,000 – $5,600)(1 – 0.32) = $43,792.00**
- 2003 income tax liability increases by ($70,000 – $5,600)(0.32) = $20,608
- 2004 revenue increases by $34,000 but $70,000 of 2002's revenue is moved into 2003 (since it was realized earlier) for a net revenue decrease of $36,000.
- 2004 bad debts expense is reduced by $5,600 (moved into 2001) and increased by $2,720 for a net decrease of $2,880.
- **2004 net income decreases by ($36,000 – $2,880)(1 – 0.32) = $22,521.60**
- 2004 income tax liability decreases by ($36,000 – $2,880)(0.32) = $10,598.40

Capitalization of product development costs will have the following effects:

- If the product development costs are capitalized, they must be amortized. We will assume a 10% amortization rate.
- **2004 net income will increase by ($120,000 – $12,000)(1 – 0.32) = $73,440.00**
- 2004 income tax liability will increase by ($120,000 – $12,000)(0.32) = $34,560
- **2004 net income will increase by ($72,000 – $7,200)(1 – 0.32) = $44,064.00**
- 2004 income tax liability will increase by ($72,000 – $7,200)(0.32) = $20,736

Increased amortization of the patents will have the following effects:

- **2003 and 2004 incomes will decrease by ($1,000)(1 – 0.32) = $680.00**
- 2003 and 2004 income tax liabilities will decrease by ($1,000)(0.32) = $320

The cumulative effect, then, on 2003 income is to increase it by $116,552, and on 2004 income, to increase it by $65,905.60.

(b) A variety of ratios are affected by all of the policy changes taken together. Some of these include:

• Return on equity	Return on assets
• Total asset turnover	Price-earnings
• Sales return	Debt-equity
• Cash flow to total assets	Debt to assets
• Earnings per share	Working capital (assuming income tax liability is a current liability)

EXPLORATIVE QUESTIONS

EQ1. Yes, ratios can be used to evaluate management's performance, but, no, they should not be the sole measures of their performance. Managers are responsible for making a number of decisions that affect the composition of assets and the incurrence of revenues and expenses. A number of the performance ratios, liquidity ratios, and financing ratios are affected by such management decisions. However, some things are beyond management's control and affect some of these same ratios. Things such as the interest rate, the market price of the company's stock, and income tax rates all affect various ratios. To some extent, management cannot control bad debts or even the cost of goods sold. So, ratios do not adequately measure total management performance.

In addition, any evaluation of management should consider important qualitative performance measures such as creativity, initiative, or leadership ability. These are out of the realm of accounting but are an important assessment nonetheless.

Lastly (at least for the purposes of this discussion), in evaluating management performance, you should keep in mind what their objectives are with respect to the firm's performance. It would be unfair to prematurely take action on short-run managerial performance results when there are long-run performance objectives in place, unless, of course, the short-run results were clearly out of line and not expected.

EQ2. Whatever problems Anna is referring to may not have been entirely foreseeable by simply looking at ratios earlier. It is true that examining ratios periodically will indeed help flag trouble areas in a company—such as a receivables problem, or stockpiling inventory, or poor returns on assets. So, in this regard, earlier ratio analyses would indeed have been beneficial to Anna. But Anna may be experiencing difficulties that ratios would not have flagged. She might be experiencing extreme cash flow problems because a formerly reliable credit customer lost a lawsuit and went bankrupt. Or she may be experiencing low returns on equity because she had been highly leveraged and the interest rate suddenly turned sharply upward in response to economic policies.

Ratios do help, to some extent, in identifying trouble areas or potential trouble areas. But ratios do not tell fortunes. Their predictive ability is limited. A number of management decisions could turn a company for the worse. These decisions could be made independently of a company's past and could affect the balance sheet, income statement, and/or the cash flow statement.

Anna has to be keenly aware of how significant management decisions affect her business, as much as possible, *before* she makes those decisions. Waiting to see what the ratios say is poor management.